New Casebooks

POETRY

WILLIAM BLAKE Edited by David Punter
CHAUCER Edited by Valerie Allen and Aries Axiotis
COLERIDGE, KEATS AND SHELLEY Edited by Peter J. Kitson
JOHN DONNE Edited by Andrew Mousley
SEAMUS HEANEY Edited by Michael Allen
PHILIP LARKIN Edited by Stephen Regan
DYLAN THOMAS Edited by John Goodby and Chris Wigginton
VICTORIAN WOMEN POETS Edited by Joseph Bristow
WORDSWORTH Edited by John Williams
PARADISE LOST Edited by William Zunder

NOVELS AND PROSE

AUSTEN: *Emma* Edited by David Monaghan
AUSTEN: *Mansfield Park* and *Persuasion* Edited by Judy Simons
AUSTEN: *Sense and Sensibility* and *Pride and Prejudice* Edited by Robert Clark
CHARLOTTE BRONTË: *Jane Eyre* Edited by Heather Glen
CHARLOTTE BRONTË: *Villette* Edited by Pauline Nestor
EMILY BRONTË: *Wuthering Heights* Edited by Patsy Stoneman
ANGELA CARTER Edited by Alison Easton
WILKIE COLLINS Edited by Lyn Pykett
JOSEPH CONRAD Edited by Elaine Jordan
DICKENS: *Bleak House* Edited by Jeremy Tambling
DICKENS: *David Copperfield* and *Hard Times* Edited by John Peck
DICKENS: *Great Expectations* Edited by Roger Sell
ELIOT: *The Mill on the Floss* and *Silas Marner* Edited by Nahem Yousaf and Andrew Maunder
ELIOT: *Middlemarch* Edited by John Peck
E.M. FORSTER Edited by Jeremy Tambling
HARDY: *Jude the Obscure* Edited by Penny Boumelha
HARDY: *The Mayor of Casterbridge* Edited by Julian Wolfreys
HARDY: *Tess of the D'Urbervilles* Edited by Peter Widdowson
JAMES: *Turn of the Screw* and *What Maisie Knew* Edited by Neil Cornwell and Maggie Malone
JOYCE: *Ulysses* Edited by Rainer Emig
LAWRENCE: *The Rainbow* and *Women in Love* Edited by Gary Day and Libby Di Niro
LAWRENCE: *Sons and Lovers* Edited by Rick Rylance
TONI MORRISON Edited by Linden Peach
GEORGE ORWELL Edited by Bryan Loughrey
SHELLEY: *Frankenstein* Edited by Fred Botting
STOKER: *Dracula* Edited by Glennis Byron
WOOLF: *Mrs Dalloway* and *To the Lighthouse* Edited by Su Reid

(continued overleaf)

D1321688

DRAMA

BECKETT: *Waiting for Godot* and *Endgame* Edited by Steven Connor
APHRA BEHN Edited by Janet Todd
MARLOWE Edited by Avraham Oz
REVENGE TRAGEDY Edited by Stevie Simkin
SHAKESPEARE: *Antony and Cleopatra* Edited by John Drakakis
SHAKESPEARE: *Hamlet* Edited by Martin Coyle
SHAKESPEARE: *Julius Caesar* Edited by Richard Wilson
SHAKESPEARE: *King Lear* Edited by Kiernan Ryan
SHAKESPEARE: *Macbeth* Edited by Alan Sinfield
SHAKESPEARE: *The Merchant of Venice* Edited by Martin Coyle
SHAKESPEARE: *A Midsummer Night's Dream* Edited by Richard Dutton
SHAKESPEARE: *Much Ado About Nothing* and *The Taming of the Shrew*
   Edited by Marion Wynne-Davies
SHAKESPEARE: *Othello* Edited by Lena Cowen Orlin
SHAKESPEARE: *Romeo and Juliet* Edited by R. S. White
SHAKESPEARE: *The Tempest* Edited by R. S. White
SHAKESPEARE: *Twelfth Night* Edited by R. S. White
SHAKESPEARE ON FILM Edited by Robert Shaughnessy
SHAKESPEARE IN PERFORMANCE Edited by Robert Shaughnessy
SHAKESPEARE'S HISTORY PLAYS Edited by Graham Holderness
SHAKESPEARE'S PROBLEM PLAYS Edited by Simon Barker
SHAKESPEARE'S ROMANCES Edited by Alison Thorne
SHAKESPEARE'S TRAGEDIES Edited by Susan Zimmerman
JOHN WEBSTER: *The Duchess of Malfi* Edited by Dympna Callaghan

GENERAL THEMES

FEMINIST THEATRE AND THEORY Edited by Helene Keyssar
POSTCOLONIAL LITERATURES Edited by Michael Parker and
   Roger Starkey

New Casebooks Series
Series Standing Order
ISBN 0–333–71702–3 hardcover
ISBN 0–333–69345–0 paperback
(*outside North America only*)

You can receive future titles in this series as they are published by placing a standing order. Please contact your bookseller or, in case of difficulty, write to us at the address below with your name and address, the title of the series and the ISBN quoted above.

Customer Services Department, Macmillan Distribution Ltd,
Houndmills, Basingstoke, Hampshire RG21 6XS, England

New Casebooks

SHAKESPEARE'S PROBLEM PLAYS

ALL'S WELL THAT ENDS WELL, MEASURE FOR MEASURE, TROILUS AND CRESSIDA

WILLIAM SHAKESPEARE

EDITED BY SIMON BARKER

First published in 2005 by
PALGRAVE MACMILLAN
Houndmills, Basingstoke, Hampshire RG21 6XS and
175 Fifth Avenue, New York, N.Y. 10010
Companies and representatives throughout the world.

PALGRAVE MACMILLAN is the global academic imprint of the Palgrave
Macmillan division of St. Martin's Press, LLC and of Palgrave Macmillan Ltd.
Macmillan® is a registered trademark in the United States, United Kingdom
and other countries. Palgrave is a registered trademark in the European
Union and other countries.

ISBN-13: 978 0 333 65427 9 hardback
ISBN-10: 0–333–65427–7 hardback
ISBN-13: 978 0 333 65428 6 paperback
ISBN-10: 0–333–65428–5 paperback

This book is printed on paper suitable for recycling and made from fully
managed and sustained forest sources.

A catalogue record for this book is available from the British Library.

A catalog record for this book is available from the Library of Congress.

10 9 8 7 6 5 4 3 2 1
14 13 12 11 10 09 08 07 06 05

Printed in China.

Contents

v

Acknowledgements

The editor would like to acknowledge the support of a research leave grant from the Arts and Humanities Research Board in the preparation of this volume and the assistance given by library staff at the University of Gloucestershire and University College, Winchester.

The editor and publishers wish to thank the following for permission to use copyright material:

Carolyn Asp, for 'Subjectivity, Desire and Female Friendship in *All's Well That Ends Well*', Rhode Island: *Literature and Psychology*, 32 (1986), 48–61; Jonathan Dollimore, for 'Transgression and Surveillance in *Measure for Measure*', from Jonathan Dollimore and Alan Sinfield (eds), *Political Shakespeare*, Manchester University Press (1985), pp. 73–87, by permission of Manchester University Press, Manchester, UK; Peter Erickson, for 'The Political Effects of Gender and Class in *All's Well That Ends Well*' from *Rewriting Shakespeare, Rewriting Ourselves*, University of California Press (1991), pp. 57–73, © University of California Press, 1991, by permission of the Regents of the University of California and the University of California Press; Matthew Greenfield, for 'Fragments of Nationalism in *Troilus and Cressida*', *Shakespeare Quarterly*, 51 (2) (Winter, 2000), 181–200, by permission of the Johns Hopkins University Press; Richard Hillman, for 'Love's Tyranny Inside–out in the Problem Plays: Yours, Mine and Counter-mine' from *Shakespearean Subversions*, Routledge (1992), pp. 150–79, by permission of Routledge; Heather James, for ' "Tricks We Play on the Dead": Making History in *Troilus and Cressida*' from *Shakespeare's Troy: Drama, Politics and the Translation of Empire*, Cambridge University Press (1997), pp. 106–18, © Cambridge University Press, 1997, by permission of Cambridge University Press; Leah Marcus, for 'London in *Measure for Measure*' from *Puzzling*

Shakespeare: Local Reading and its Discontents, University of California Press (1988), pp. 171–82, by permission of the author; Leah Scragg, for '*All's Well That Ends Well* and the Tale of the Chivalric Quest' from *Shakespeare's Alternative Tales*, Longman (1996), pp. 106–30, © Longman, 1996, by permission of Pearson Education, Ltd; Vivian Thomas, for 'Shakespeare's Problem Plays: Concepts and Perspectives' from *The Moral Universe of Shakespeare's Problem Plays*, Routledge (1987), pp. 14–21, by permission of Routledge; Valerie Traub, for 'Invading Bodies/Bawdy Exchanges: Disease, Desire, and Representation' from *Desire and Anxiety: Circulations of Sexuality in Shakespearean Drama*, Routledge (1992), pp. 71–87, by permission of Routledge.

Every effort has been made to trace the copyright holders but if any have been inadvertently overlooked the publishers will be pleased to make the necessary arrangement at the first opportunity.

General Editors' Preface

The purpose of this series of New Casebooks is to reveal some of the ways in which contemporary criticism has changed our understanding of commonly studied texts and writers and, indeed, of the nature of criticism itself. Central to the series is a concern with modern critical theory and its effect on current approaches to the study of literature. Each New Casebook editor has been asked to select a sequence of essays which will introduce the reader to the new critical approaches to the text or texts being discussed in the volume and also illuminate the rich interchange between critical theory and critical practice that characterises so much current writing about literature.

In this focus on modern critical thinking and practice New Casebooks aim not only to inform but also to stimulate, with volumes seeking to reflect both the controversy and the excitement of current criticism. Because much of this criticism is difficult and often employs an unfamiliar critical language, editors have been asked to give the reader as much help as they feel is appropriate, but without simplifying the essays or the issues they raise. Again, editors have been asked to supply a list of further reading which will enable readers to follow up issues raised by the essays in the volume.

The project of New Casebooks, then, is to bring together in an illuminating way those critics who best illustrate the ways in which contemporary criticism has established new methods of analysing texts and who have reinvigorated the important debate about how we 'read' literature. The hope is, of course, that New Casebooks will not only open up this debate to a wider audience, but will also encourage students to extend their own ideas, and think afresh about their responses to the texts they are studying.

John Peck and Martin Coyle
University of Wales, Cardiff

Introduction

SIMON BARKER

I

This collection of essays is aimed at students who are working on the three texts that have customarily been grouped together as Shakespeare's 'problem plays'. At first sight these plays appear to have only a little in common. *All's Well That Ends Well*, written around 1602–4, was based on a section of the fourteenth-century Florentine writer Giovanni Boccaccio's stories in the collected *Decameron*, and in terms of form is clearly a comedy. The action moves between a number of European cities, with all the intricacies and confusions of plot that the reader might associate with such plays as Shakespeare's early comedy success, *A Midsummer Night's Dream* (1595–6), or the popular *Twelfth Night*, which was written slightly before *All's Well That Ends Well*.

The second play, *Measure for Measure* (1604–5), was based on George Whetstone's *Promos and Cassandra* (1578), which was itself drawn from an older collection of stories.[1] Whetstone's play is of great interest in its own right, since despite its rather odd structure and difficult style, its representation of women and sexuality is so intriguing that modern readers of *Measure for Measure* might valuably go back to Whetstone's work. Critics have sometimes described *Measure for Measure* as a 'tragi-comedy' in that, although there is a formal 'happy ending', the Vienna of Shakespeare's imagination is a society beset with the kind of moral dilemmas and dangers that seem familiar from the tragic plays of the period such as *Hamlet*.

In a number of significant ways, *Troilus and Cressida* (1601–2) contrasts completely with the other two plays in the 'problem play' group. Drawing on sixteenth-century histories of the classical world, Shakespeare sets his love story in a rather claustrophobic society dominated by military and masculine values.[2] Little positive seems to emerge from its retelling of the betrayal of Troilus by Cressida. James Ruoff has remarked that a major critical problem with *Troilus and*

Cressida 'has been to establish the unity of a play so evenly divided between the argument of Mars and the theme of Venus', and this appears right: the play seems to set violence and love against each other in a bitter, non-comic action.³

The labelling of Shakespeare's plays as, say, 'tragedies', 'comedies', 'Roman plays', 'histories', or, indeed, 'problem plays' provides a somewhat unsatisfactory shorthand, especially if such terms are taken at face value. Particularly in performance, it is hard to ignore the comedy that is woven into, say, Shakespeare's great tragedy *Hamlet*, a play that at moments can stir audiences to uncontrollable laughter. The same is even more true of *Richard III*, the demonic anti-hero of which draws audience and action together like a kind of early stand-up comic, making the broad classification of the play as either a 'history', and/or a 'tragedy' and/or a 'variation on a medieval morality play', rather limited. The play seems capable of being read as any or all of these at once, so throwing such categories into doubt.

Given the uncertainties and pitfalls of classification with regard to Shakespeare's plays, or any other work of literature for that matter, an introduction to a set of critical essays on these particular three plays needs, first then, to address the history and impact of the term 'problem play' itself. It is also important to establish a context for this collection of essays in terms of significant developments in contemporary criticism. It is hoped that the volume will appeal to readers who are seeking to read Shakespeare not in terms of a simple enquiry into character or plot (although these aspects of the play can never be entirely dismissed) but in terms of the priorities that have been set by recent theoretical approaches.

One shared assumption made by all the critics writing here, however, is that Shakespeare wrote in a period of probably unprecedented change within the institutions that shaped early modern society in the overlapping realms of politics, religion, the family, the law, and economics – as well as in the creative representation of how these institutions conditioned the very experience of what it meant to be human. Although it was common in Shakespeare's time to emphasise, at least officially, the harmony and order of society, much of the writing of the day, and especially that produced for the stage, exposed the intense fragility of this vision. These signs of contradiction and discontinuity in the social order of Shakespeare's time are to the fore in these three plays. Indeed, so unsettled are the plays that they have produced the unique shorthand term 'problem play' to distinguish them from the relatively straightforward categories that serve the main body of Shakespeare's work.

II

Several underlying factors have contributed to the categorisation of the three texts as 'problem plays'. For many years they were variously described as 'dark comedies' or 'problem comedies' because they did not share a notion of hopefulness and resolution with the more traditional comedies in the Shakespeare canon.[4] Contrasted with earlier plays such as *A Midsummer Night's Dream*, with its fantasy world of spirits and its final reconciliation of lover with lover, or the promises of marriage and contentment that close *Twelfth Night* or *As You Like it*, the 'problem comedies' were considered problematic because they featured strong elements of tragedy, an abrasive sense of realism, and often privileged sexual love (as against romantic love) in a way that set them apart from the more mainstream form of comedy. This may have been an oversimplification and sentimentalising of the earlier comedies since it is clear that, for example, the sheer cruelty of the baiting of Malvolio towards the end of *Twelfth Night*, the sinister nature of the forest in *As You Like It*, or even the threat that hangs over Egeus throughout *A Midsummer Night's Dream* show that potential tragedy haunts these comedies just as surely as humour threads through the tragedies. But no one has seriously suggested that *Twelfth Night* is a tragicomedy or that *Hamlet* is a comic tragedy: the plays do mix or conflate genres in that way. There is, however, clearly a quality in *All's Well That Ends Well*, *Measure for Measure* and *Troilus and Cressida* that critics over the years have found hard to define.

In his celebrated book *Shakespeare's Problem Plays* the mid-twentieth-century critic E. M. W. Tillyard, although admitting that it was highly unsatisfactory, argued for the term 'problem play' because there were clearly some Shakespearean plays that did not conform to the recognisable norms of those that could be more easily categorised. However, he also insisted that the term should embrace *Hamlet* as well. In this broadening of the range of plays that might be labelled thus, Tillyard was influenced by the work of F. S. Boas who had also included *Hamlet* and had borrowed the idea of the 'problem play' from a term that was being used at the time for the work of George Bernard Shaw and Henrik Ibsen.[5]

Tillyard noted in 1950 that *All's Well That Ends Well* and *Measure for Measure* were like one kind of 'problem child whom no efforts will ever bring back to normality', and that *Hamlet* and *Troilus and Cressida* were like a 'second kind of problem child, full of interest and complexity'. He concluded that '*Hamlet* and *Troilus and Cressida* are problem plays because they deal with and display interesting problems: *All's Well* and *Measure for Measure* because they *are* problems'.[6] To this extent he expanded the term but also tried to draw differences between the plays.

Tillyard's notion of the problem play as 'problem child' may seem outlandish to a modern reader, yet his more detailed analysis of what the plays had in common (in order to form a separate category) remains interesting. Although he acknowledged the spirit of gloom, disillusionment and morbidity in the plays (characteristics that earlier critics had suggested were due to some personal crisis in Shakespeare's life), Tillyard's more immediate concerns were with three elements or preoccupations in the four plays that he (and other critics) had grouped together. First, he noted a common concern with 'religious dogma' and abstract speculation revolving around the experiences of a young man who 'gets a shock' and has to develop quickly: Hamlet, Claudio in *Measure for Measure*, Bertram in *All's Well That Ends Well* and Troilus. Secondly, Tillyard observed that this rapid progress towards maturity was transacted at night when 'thought and the dark go together'. Thirdly, he placed great emphasis on the fact that all the plays were based upon a sense of the relationship and contrast between generations. It was not that these elements were unique to the plays he singled out as 'problem plays', but that there was a *concentration* of these elements in four plays that had been written within a few years of each other.

The idea of including *Hamlet* in the problem play grouping was controversial before Tillyard's book and is now considered somewhat eccentric.[7] In his introductory chapter to *The Moral Universe of Shakespeare's Problem Plays*, an extract from which is included in the present volume, Vivian Thomas (essay 1) perceptively notes that not only is *Hamlet* 'a tragedy, but it is a particular kind of tragedy – the most popular kind of tragedy to occupy the stages of Elizabethan and Jacobean England – a revenge tragedy', and that the point of the three problem plays proper, so to speak, is that they 'evade any such adequate classification'.[8] This seems right, and yet Tillyard's highlighting of certain features in *Hamlet* and the other plays is not without its point. And although other critics have seen *The Merchant of*

Venice as a problem play but excluded *All's Well That Ends Well* from the group (regarding is as a 'late romance' along with plays such as *The Tempest* and *The Winter's Tale*), and although Peter Ure, writing in 1961, proposed the addition of *Timon of Athens* to the group, the three plays examined in this book were generally thought of as 'the problem plays' by the 1960s and the label has been fairly stable and widely used ever since.[9]

The work of a few major critics dominated the study of the problem plays in the 1960s and 1970s. An interesting and fairly typical example is A. P. Rossiter's acclaimed book *Angel with Horns*, which dealt with the plays' preoccupation with matters of paradox, inversion, and the discovery of unpleasant realities beneath superficial codes of nobility and human worth. Rossiter suggested that, above all, the plays demonstrate a lack of resolution that leaves the reader and the audience unsettled. While freely using the term 'problem play', Rossiter finally opts for the notion of 'tragi-comedy' to best serve this sense of the three plays' open-ended nature, both with respect to the lack of resolution at the end of each and the clear sense of uncertainty generated during the course of the action. Profound questions over morality, appearance and reality, and the power of language to deceive are raised in all three of the plays. Although no effect in the theatre is ever guaranteed, these questions, for Rossiter, potentially invite a reader or an audience to share what seems to be a broad sense of cynicism, which, even if overcome by the good actions of certain characters, none the less seems to prevail in the dramatic atmosphere that has been created as each play reaches a conclusion:

> They are all about 'Xs' that do not work out. *Troilus and Cressida* gives us a 'tragedy-of-love' pattern that is not tragic (nor love?); *All's Well* a 'happy ending' that makes us neither happy nor comfortable; *Measure for Measure* a 'final solution' that simply does not answer the questions raised.[10]

To a large extent the pattern that emerged in criticism of the problem plays over the course of the 1960s and 1970s was one of refusal and displacement. Each new critic would refute an earlier rationale for the problem plays as a distinct group (even if the membership of the group was now fairly established) and replace it with a new set of criteria. There were exceptions, however, which showed that even at a relatively recent point in the history of criticism of these somewhat troublesome plays, the grouping itself was open to question. Ernest Schanzer, for example, was at pains to undermine the arguments of

Boas, Tillyard and others, but he did so in a manner that was fairly orthodox in post-war criticism. His emphasis was, as was fairly typical of the period, on problems of *morality* in Shakespeare's plays – and, in a sentence that is often remarked upon by modern critics of the plays, he states that a problem play is:

> A play in which we find a concern with a moral problem which is central to it, presented in such a manner that we are unsure of our moral bearings, so that uncertain and divided responses to it in the minds of the audience are possible or even probable.[11]

Schanzer goes on to dismantle the by now commonly acceptable problem play grouping and proposes in their place *Julius Caesar*, *Antony and Cleopatra* and *Measure for Measure*. What is interesting about his rather caustic attack on earlier critics (and the dismissal of their grouping of plays) is that his audacity, which Schanzer perhaps intended for effect, is overwritten by the pronounced conservatism of his viewpoint. Far from being a radical overthrow of perceived notions both of the rationale for the idea of 'problem', and thus the constitution of the group, the approach is one that comes close to patronising the plays' readers and audiences. Schanzer's comment begs a number of questions. Who are the 'we' spoken of with such confidence? Is this an obvious and homogeneous group? And what of 'our' morality – is it the same for 'us' as it was for an early-Stuart audience watching these plays in a public theatre in London? And was the morality of this popular audience the same as the morality of a courtly one, or of the increasingly confident political dissidents in parliament who took such a strong stand against the theatre itself on the basis of moral values?

Schanzer, then, in common with many earlier critics, assumes a sort of trans-historical audience for Shakespeare which shares a common perspective. The kind of criticism attached to the problem plays during the years from, say, 1950–70, leading up to what some observers have seen as a revolution in the business of cultural criticism – the emergence of modern literary theory – might be summarised along the following lines. First, there was the argument over which plays belong to the group. The 'problem play' label proved flexible and controversial and, possibly, in the end, rather unhelpful to the modern scholar except in as far as it signals disquiet in the history of criticism of certain kinds of play. What is more interesting however, in looking back at this criticism, and turning to the plays in the light of the more recent critical approaches (exemplified by the essays in this book), is the reasoning behind the disquiet of these traditional critics.

Indeed, the second major element of their work was their obvious unease over what was perceived as a discontinuity in some of Shakespeare's plays in terms of a coherent moral outcome. For these critics this flaw was inevitably bound up with a sense of generic non-conformity: where there is moral ambivalence there is also stylistic or compositional deviation. The established labels ('comedy', 'tragedy', 'history'), with their comforting provenance derived from the First Folio, classical authorities, and a long tradition of critical scholarship, seemed insufficient faced with what appears to have been judged a departure in Shakespeare's work from a steady course of moral certainty. In short, the 'problem' with the problem plays was their sheer pessimism of tone, which disrupts and challenges an orthodox view of Shakespeare's 'vision' of humanity. As will be seen below, it is this very unsteadiness and discontinuity that excites modern critics – and to the same degree that it perplexed earlier ones.

It is worth noting that the many hesitations or uncertainties over the 'problem' of these plays inevitably led to a third current in much of the post-war traditional criticism of the twentieth century. Troubled by the difficult moral tone or generic eccentricity of the plays, some critics concluded that the plays were aesthetically inferior, although it is possible to sense here a slight embarrassment in their writing when they reached this conclusion.[12] W. W. Lawrence, writing in 1930, had concluded that the plays 'are, of course, greatly inferior to the better known drama written by Shakespeare in the opening years of the new century'. This opinion, although perhaps not quite always so boldly stated, suffused much of the criticism of the middle years of the last century, albeit sometimes with an apologetic air to it.[13]

The fortunes of the Shakespeare canon overall, however, have rarely been absolutely steady. For a long time the tragedies were given precedence over the comedies for their more serious tone and philosophical weight. The histories were occasionally written off as Tudor propaganda or too narrowly nationalist in their outlook. In the late seventeenth and early eighteenth centuries the whole of Shakespeare's drama was open to question to the extent that many of the plays were rewritten in order to fit the rationale of the times and the aesthetics of new audiences. Since the early 1980s, however, while scholarship and technology were denying or endorsing the authenticity of Shakespeare's texts, and new 'replica' theatres were constructed in which to perform them, the whole realm of

Shakespeare criticism (and literary criticism in general) was subjected to a kind of revolution in method, objective and rationale.[14]

This was the fundamental shake up in critical thinking heralded by structuralism in the 1970s that arrested traditional criticism and was to set the scene for a long battle over not only what constituted the canon of English Literature, but also what the practice of criticism should entail, and what contribution a new body of critical theory could make to the understanding of literature and criticism. A tiny corner of this battlefield was inevitably, and fruitfully, devoted to Shakespeare's problem plays, and while none of the contributors to this book would necessarily endorse the totality of this revolution (their essays can speak for themselves in this respect), none was immune from the significant changes in the critical agenda that have emerged in the last twenty years of criticism. Their contributions have been chosen, in part, for their application of aspects of 'theory' in their critical readings of the plays, but also, given the stylistic difficulty that has characterised much modern critical writing, for their lucid approach to challenging critical questions.

III

The theory that has recast criticism of Shakespeare's plays since the 1970s is a striking but complex phenomenon that cannot fully be explained in an introduction such as this. An examination of some of its key components, however, will help to provide a context for the essays that follow. Three general points can be made about the kind of approach that has overturned many of the assumptions found in the earlier criticism of the problem plays described above. The first is to do with the established literary canon, the body of 'accepted' great works that privileged certain writers above others. This has been viewed for the last twenty-five years or so as an ascendancy of male, western authors that necessarily led to the exclusion or neglect of writers whose works did not fit an exacting but nonetheless partial, or even prejudiced, set of criteria. Thus, in the realm of Renaissance drama, Shakespeare ruled supreme, to the detriment of the dozens of writers classified as his 'contemporaries'. If Shakespeare could be said, rightly or wrongly, to have occupied the upper levels of such a hierarchy in terms of his value, achievement and appeal, then a book of essays about three of Shakespeare's plays might be viewed as reinforcing that structure. After all, many of the themes and issues that the problem plays address are present in the plays of Shakespeare's contemporaries, including the work of such 'rediscovered' women dramatists of the period as Elizabeth Cary.[15]

Value judgements, however, have always been applied across the range of Shakespeare's work (as has been demonstrated above), leaving the problem plays marginalised as 'problem children'. Consequently the very fact that these three plays have been treated to the kind of critical approach characterised by the essays in this volume is evidence of a new way of approaching Shakespeare's plays overall. Plays traditionally seen as a 'problem' in their own right might yield new and exciting conclusions about their own status, and they might, under close examination, encourage readers to reflect upon the rest of Shakespeare's work in a new light. It is also the case that some of the readings found here are themselves a product of critics productively exploring a juxtaposition between Shakespeare and his traditionally less-favoured contemporaries.

A second major theme of modern theory has been the sense of its own politics, and the politics of its predecessors. Traditional criticism, modern theorists would claim, was based on a covert sense of the apparent innocence of its assumptions and practices. Where it was seemingly harmless, in, say, claiming an educational and even moral purpose in 'close reading', or learning extracts of Shakespeare by heart, or in recognising 'timeless values' in the literature of the past, there was none the less, theorists argue, a political significance in the assumptions made about what constituted those timeless values and their role in reinforcement of the accepted social order. Thus, if a great work like *Hamlet* was read in order to show the timelessly tragic nature of the 'human condition' and the 'flaw' at the heart of even the noblest of men, then this tended to 'fix' human nature as unchanging and unchangeable. Accordingly, modern readers and theatre audiences enjoy the play not for its sense of historical *distance* from their own experiences, but in terms of identification with an historical continuum: history means nothing because nothing has really changed in the core of human experience since the period when Shakespeare was alive. Implied in this kind of traditional approach, if never clearly announced, was that the desire for societal change found at the heart of radical political criticism, such as Marxism or feminism, was pointless, but was simultaneously (and paradoxically) a danger to the status quo.

Equating critical practice with politics in the first place may seem to some absurd. Yet modern theory has been thoroughly committed to exploring the 'ideological' nature of this traditional vision of the relationship between humanity and culture, exposing the politics of the old criticism by contrast with its own, explicitly stated, agenda for change. One objective of this book is to include a variety of approaches to Shakespeare's problem plays, but none of the essays can be read in isolation from the critical upheavals of recent years, and some are extremely explicit in their politicising of criticism. Much modern criticism has been linked to political movements at work beyond academic circles and this is recognisable in the terms that have been used to describe various subsections or varieties of modern critical thought, including feminism, postcolonialism, and Marxism. And although Marxist criticism is rarely to the fore in the realm of the most recent criticism, its influence was an important factor in the re-examination of the theory and practice of criticism in the 1980s. This was partly due to its insistence upon the decentring of the individual as an agent in the creation and transformation of social formations and its emphasis upon structures (classes, groups, and economic systems) and the collective 'consciousness' of people subject to those systems.

Thirdly, and most challenging, has been the influence upon modern criticism of various schools of critical theory. These have often repudiated the strictures and simplicity of Marxism. Yet they often shared with it (explicitly or otherwise) a strong sense that human beings are products of systems of language, culture, and identity, which actually *generated* the concept of the 'individual', promoting it as the source rather than the effect of those systems. The radicalism of the many strands of theory that have influenced critical approaches in the last quarter of a century has been in their understanding that meaning is not fixed or stable, but plural and contingent. Texts as diverse as a Shakespeare play, a political speech or even the signs that direct us from place to place in our everyday lives, render not a set of transparent truths, but a range of sites where there are contests for meaning.[16] We may not be unduly troubled by what might simply be seen as ambiguities in signage in public places, such as arrows apparently directing us the wrong way. But it becomes clear that, for example, the meanings of phrases such as 'a just war' or the idea 'love and marriage' are altogether more problematic and unstable when seen in terms of twenty-first-century international relations and gender politics, just as they can said to have been in Shakespeare's problem plays.

IV

The theoretical approaches that have informed approaches to Shakespeare's plays over the last quarter of a century are, then, diverse and complex. The terms that have emerged, such as 'structuralism', 'poststructuralism' and 'psychoanalysis', are perhaps better understood by readers when they are applied in practice to literary texts, although Marxism and feminism are more easily apprehended because of their clear political provenance. However, there is common ground in the different areas of theory that is particularly significant in terms of Shakespeare's plays.

The philosophical and linguistic approaches that draw to a large degree on the work of the French structuralist Roland Barthes and the poststructuralist Jacques Derrida (who modified the earlier 'structuralism', of the Swiss linguist Ferdinand de Saussure) have been particularly influential with respect to texts written for theatrical performance. In proposing that meaning is not fixed, either by the intentions of the author, or by the text itself, Bathes and Derrida unsettled the emphasis that more traditional criticism had placed on the author. An author produces a text, but cannot control the meanings that flow from it into the communal systems and cross-currents of language; and meanings are not his or her private realm, but operate in a *public* way – in what might collectively be termed 'culture'. In many respects this idea is especially true of the dramatic text – written perhaps by a single hand, but manifestly opened up in terms of the plurality of its meanings by the collaborative nature of production. Were this not the case, the impulse individuals have to see many different 'interpretations' of the same play would become meaningless. The theatre might be said to be a complex system for the production of meaning that inherently reinforces the idea of 'plurality' of meaning that theorists have ascribed to any kind of written text. The theatre is a system of signification in which meaning circulates through a range of agents, such as actors, directors, stage managers, and by means of its own mechanics – set, scenery, lighting and costume. Faced with this proliferation of devices for the production of meaning, audiences are invited to experience systems that reveal the way that meaning is 'produced' in a very practical way. The objective may be to create an illusion of reality, but the mechanics of that illusion are very apparent, and the raw material of any production, the text, is necessarily but one component in the overall process.

The process through which meaning is produced seems especially 'open' in the plays of Shakespeare and his contemporaries where there is an extremely close correspondence between the texts and the theatre environments for which they were written in terms of an awareness of the conditions of production. Although this openness also has much to do with contemporary attitudes towards language and meaning in a world before literacy was common and before the widespread use of the printing press, the dramatists of the late sixteenth and early seventeenth centuries seemed particularly aware of the instability and plurality of meaning. The plays are full of double-meanings, slips of the tongue and puns. In a period that valued rhetoric as an expression of scholarship, the plays constantly reflect upon the power of speech itself and its potential for deception as well as truth: language seems less a transparent medium for 'truth' and more a complex of variations and uncertainties of meaning. When this phenomenon is considered in the context of the way that the plays were staged, the self-reflexivity of Renaissance drama is even more apparent. The stage was itself a system of signs, simple in its construction but complex in terms of its signification. If, as it is widely thought, the canopy in public theatres such as the Globe represented Heaven, and a trapdoor in the stage could mean Hell, then the meanings of those terms could be unfixed by being used in other pieces of stage business, or simply by being seen as part of the theatre. Meanwhile, the stage could be a platform or a forest, a castle or a field, but certainly a space where meaning could be played with and played out.

Such a complex system of signification might be said to reinforce and, indeed, amplify ideas about language and meaning that have underpinned recent critical approaches to Shakespeare's problem plays. Instead of searching for universal truths and timeless continuities such as 'human nature' or the 'human condition', the emphasis of recent critical thinking has shifted to the way that the theatre represents a *contest* between competing sets of ideas. Far from providing a smooth hierarchy of meaning, with the 'truth' of any dramatic situation as inevitable and easily accessed, the theatre tends towards inviting its audience to ponder a range of contrasting positions and viewpoints over which it has to make a judgement.

Recalling the theoretical work of Emile Benveniste, Catherine Belsey has described the plays of the Renaissance as 'interrogative', distinguishing them from the 'declarative' texts of classic realism.[17]

The Renaissance play, or 'interrogative' text, she argues,

> invites an answer or answers to the questions it poses. Further, if the interrogative text is illusionist it also tends to employ devices to undermine the illusion, to draw attention to its own textuality. The reader is distanced, at least from time to time, rather than wholly interpolated into a fictional world. Above all, the interrogative text differs from the class realism text in the absence of a single privileged discourse which contains and places all the others.[18]

The scholars whose work has been reproduced in this volume do not necessarily subscribe in full to the implications of the theoretical debate that has informed critical approaches to Shakespeare's problem plays in recent years. Indeed, they have been selected for the diversity of their approaches and concerns. Yet the originality of their positions indicates a departure from the orthodoxy that informed the earlier work that struggled to classify these extraordinary plays in terms that were often negative or grudging. However complex its source, the term 'problem play' retained a sense of negativity. Whatever their relations to the theoretic developments that have characterised literary criticism of late, the critics who have contributed to this volume have clearly reversed this negativity. They demonstrate that this small portion of the Shakespeare canon is not only worth engaging with in its own terms, but may well raise important questions for our understanding of Shakespeare's canon in its entirety.

V

In 'Shakespeare's Problem Plays: Concepts and Perspectives' (essay 1) Vivian Thomas approaches the question of what distinguishes the 'problem play' from the rest of the Shakespearean canon by looking at a list of features, themes and concepts. The essay is particularly useful and important because Thomas implies a settling, in his mind at least, of the debate over which plays should be included in the 'problem play' classification. The list of distinguishing features is firm, authoritative and shows a keen grasp of the kind of issues that are to come under closer scrutiny in the succeeding essays in this volume. Thomas is also sensitive to the fact, sometimes overlooked by literary critics, that what makes these plays challenging (and difficult to pigeonhole) is their effect, notably a sense of 'incongruity', upon an audience in the theatre rather than simply the reader of a text. The book from which the essay for this volume is extracted shows Thomas exploring in detail the kinds of concerns he raises here and is thus recommended as further reading. As an essay in itself, it can be seen as a preface to the varied work on the three plays that this volume includes. It is worth noting that Thomas seems to predict many of the central issues dealt with by later critics, and this gives his own piece a special resonance in terms of critical approaches to the plays over the last twenty years.

Leah Scragg's 'All's Well That Ends Well and the Tale of the Chivalric Quest' (essay 2) is the first of three very compelling but contrasting essays on the play. Scragg invites her reader to re-examine the sources of All's Well That Ends Well in considerable detail and her conclusions are the result of painstaking and original research. Starting with a quotation from an early seventeenth-century story of the chivalric quest by George Wilkins, Scragg reminds us that this kind of story had a long and widespread pedigree in Western European literature. Making links between the Wilkins story, Shakespeare's source in Boccaccio's Decameron, and a range of other examples from the tradition, she explains the unique appeal of All's Well as both belonging to and modifying this tradition. Of particular interest in this essay is Scragg's analysis of the way that women are given an unusually prominent voice. This is a play that includes many reversals of 'gender expectations' and invites us to consider quite fundamental issues of gender and identity which were of concern to its audiences at the time of first production and clearly have a resonance for twenty-first-century readers and theatregoers. Above all, Scragg demonstrates that Shakespeare's play, however original it might have been in its framing of a traditional story, none the less had a relationship with its sources and contemporary narratives, a knowledge of which enriches our reading of Shakespeare's version.

Peter Erickson's 'The Political Effects of Gender and Class in All's Well That Ends Well' (essay 3), as its title implies, is a distinctly political reading of the play. The essay is of value both for its originality and as a good example of the kind of criticism characteristic of the last decade of the twentieth century. Erickson examines the layers of authority in the play and unpicks the rhetoric that promotes certain values associated with hierarchical relationships. A surprisingly involved and textured linguistic system is revealed that supports but sometimes undermines concepts of masculinity, kingship, love and social class. Erickson concludes by comparing All's Well with Hamlet because of their mutual sense of 'restiveness' – a good word for the

atmosphere that concludes both plays. While Erickson is not returning to the old school of critics that would have included *Hamlet* as a
fourth 'problem play', his thesis reminds us that one of the more
thought-provoking approaches to the three plays examined is that
their 'restiveness' illuminates the unsettled nature of much of the
whole Shakespearean canon, even those plays more easily pinned
down by the seemingly straightforward generic groupings such as
'comedy' and 'tragedy'. It is almost as if the three problem plays are
a kind of laboratory for the other plays, testing and teasing their
audiences with new ideas and a distinctive lack of philosophical
certainty.

In 'Subjectivity, Desire and Female Friendship in *All's Well That
Ends Well*' (essay 4) Caroline Asp begins with her interpretation of
what has given the play the 'problem' label but renews the term by
offering a psychoanalytical reading. Some criticism of this kind can
be difficult for the new reader, depending as it does on knowledge of
the kind of psychoanalytical theory derived from the work of Jacques
Lacan, whom Asp acknowledges in her essay. Asp's essay, however,
has the virtue of explaining many of its terms as it goes along, and
while it is a thorough and demanding piece, there is also a com-
mendable lucidity and sense of engagement with the reader. Asp is
concerned that the play can be read in the context of Renaissance
theories of male superiority and the gender relations that result from
the policing, or otherwise, of sexual desire. She makes a case for the
singularity of *All's Well That Ends Well* in these terms, but in her
conclusion invites her readers to look again at the representation of
female figures in other Shakespeare plays. Like other essays in this
volume, Asp gives a detailed analysis of the play itself and argues for
its importance as a distinctive work, but also asserts that a 'problem
play' is also of value for the comparisons and contrasts that can be
made with other plays in the canon.

VI

The three essays in this volume on *Measure for Measure* have been
chosen for their individual merit as original and compelling pieces
of interpretation. They are all representative of the kind of critical
energy that has been applied to the play in recent years and will
hopefully inspire readers to look at the longer works from which

they come, at the other works of criticism to which they refer, and at Shakespeare's play with new insight.

Jonathan Dollimore's 'Transgression and Surveillance in *Measure for Measure*' (essay 5) with Peter Erickson's essay, is another overtly political reading of the Shakespeare derived not only from historical research and the application of critical theory, but from the context in which the essay itself was written. Dollimore is at pains both to open up a text from history to the available relationships that can be forged between the text and historical circumstances that conditioned its production, and also to suggest its absolute relevance to modern readers. His reading of *Measure for Measure* is thus informed by his reading of his own times – in this case the political dissensus of the mid-1980s which found many of the issues addressed in Shakespeare's play very much to the fore in the modern world that was forged from developments in the early-modern world of the English Renaissance. It is certainly not outlandish to suppose that Dollimore wrote with one eye on the extreme political context of Shakespeare's England and another on the unfolding narrative of Margaret Thatcher's Britain. If Shakespeare's world was a dangerous one for dissenters and the marginalised, then it may have reminded Dollimore of the contests that were taking place in a divided Britain in terms of political power and human rights. Whatever the case, Dollimore's essay has a sense of urgency and authority that remains fresh and compelling, perhaps suggesting that the issues raised in this essay and in *Political Shakespeare* in general, the book (co-produced with Alan Sinfield in 1985) from which it comes, have not gone away.

In 'London in *Measure for Measure*' (essay 6), Leah Marcus takes us on a tour of the legal systems that operated in Shakespeare's London and are addressed in the imagined Vienna of *Measure for Measure*. The approach is historical and necessarily 'political' in that to the fore in this essay are concerns with the way that the law regulated (or attempted to regulate) sexual behaviour and the institutions of marriage and the family. What emerges from Marcus's analysis, apart from the admirable breadth of her knowledge of early-modern legal systems, is a compelling argument that determines the 'problem' of *Measure for Measure* as a virtue – for what it reveals about the relationship between power and law in the emerging Jacobean state.

Richard Hillman's 'Love's Tyranny Inside-out in the Problem Plays: Yours, Mine, and Counter-mine' (essay 7) concludes the section on *Measure for Measure* with a memorable argument about the subversive possibilities of Shakespeare's plays. We usefully return to the theme of the problem plays in general, but are specifically invited to consider the instability of the idea of the 'state' in *Measure for Measure* and its implications for our understanding of the political context in which it was written. Much of Hillman's work (see the further reading section for his book on the problem plays in general) is underpinned by his understanding of the work of Mikhail Bakhtin who explored the political potential of carnival, trickery, and the inversion of order in his own analysis of Rabelais.[19] Hillman's work on the problem plays is well known and influential; this essay is a good example of his approach to *Measure for Measure*, but usefully concludes with an analysis of *Troilus and Cressida*, the subject of the final three essays in this volume.

VII

In ' "Tricks We Play on the Dead": Making History in *Troilus and Cressida*' (essay 8) Heather James shows how Shakespeare's inter- pretation of the legend of Troy intersects with a more general inscrip- tion of classical legend in the official ideologies of the Tudor and early-Stuart governments. Classical images shaped an ideal of the nation and its leaders through a variety of media – including fine art, costume and architecture – and legends from the past were appropri- ated as models of national identity, heroism and military masculinity. However, as James shows, the use of the classical legend was neither stable nor seamless – and in the special environment of the public theatre the relationship between classical legend and contemporary politics was revealed to audiences in an open and interrogative way, which contrasted with the imperatives of government myth-making. A fascinating aspect of the essay is the way that James shows that classical figures and events were available to a wide range of people through a variety of non-official and popular media, such as ballads. She argues that early-modern English culture was seemingly satu- rated with classical images made to work in different ways for a variety of ideological causes. A 'problem play', such as *Troilus and Cressida*, with its complex treatment of the classics, invites a reading that suggests its audiences might discover discontinuities in the treatment of classical legend, and therein a critique of the purposes to which legend was put in the world beyond the theatre.

Valerie Traub's 'Invading Bodies/Bawdy Exchanges: Disease, Desire, and Representation' (essay 9) begins with a reminder to its reader that sexually transmitted disease has throughout history been blamed on a scapegoat in the shape of certain minorities or races. She cites the example of AIDS, but traces the formulation back to the period that produced *Troilus and Cressida*. This essay is disturbing because of its relevance, once again showing that broadly historicist readings of Shakespeare can show how the early-modern era gave rise to the values, institutions and prejudices of the modern. Traub notes that 'diseases' is the final word of a play that uses images of disease to address a range of issues and relationships, including a central one in Traub's thesis, the relationship between disease, desire and warfare. The essay concludes with an appeal to the reader to see how studying *Troilus and Cressida* can, at the very least, defamiliarise our own concepts of sexuality and disease.

The last essay in the volume, Matthew Greenfield's 'Fragments of Nationalism in *Troilus and Cressida*' (essay 10), reflects on *Troilus and Cressida* in relation to the ideas it presents about nation and community. Given the importance of classical legend in the presentation of early-modern notions of 'nation', Greenfield argues that, whilst Shakespeare's history plays, often with some difficulty, seek to promote continuity in terms of nation or the genealogies of royal leaders, *Troilus and Cressida*, from the outset, does the opposite. Greenfield reminds us of the fragmented nature of nation in the play and the attacks it contains on the notions of genealogy. For an audience as sensitive to the use of classical legend as Heather James (in essay 8) claims it would have been, these aspects of *Triolus and Cressida* make it a potentially subversive play, and Greenfield's essay is a learned and readable account of these issues.

As the most recent essay in this collection Greenfield's contribution also shows how a 'problem play' is provoking original criticism for a new and inquisitive readership. The essays in this collection together show that despite the troubled response among earlier critics to *All's Well That Ends Well*, *Measure for Measure*, *Troilus and Cressida* and indeed other plays gathered into the problem play grouping, these are plays that have excited and inspired recent critics. For some of the earlier generations of critics, the problem plays seemed somehow unfinished or crude – in short, somehow *un-Shakespearean*. It is hoped that the essays in this volume show that Shakespeare may be at his most provocative when he is being least predictable, or at least at his most difficult to categorise.

Notes

1. George Whetstone based his two-part play on Giambattista Giraldi Cinthio's *Hecatomithi* (1565) and his posthumous drama *Epithia* (1583).

2. Shakespeare's main sources for *Troilus and Cressida* were William Caxton's *Recuyell of the Histories of Troy* (1475), John Lydgate's *The Troy Book* (c. 1412–20) and Robert Henryson's *Testament of Cressid* (1532), although he would have known Chaucer's *Troilus and Criseyde* and Homer's *Illiad*.

3. James E. Ruoff, *Handbook of Elizabethan and Stuart Literature* (London and Basingstoke, 1975), p. 435.

4. It is generally accepted that the critic Edward Dowden originated the 'problem' label for the plays in his *Shakspere: A Critical Study of his Mind and Art*, 3rd edn (London, 1877).

5. See F. S. Boas, *Shakespeare and his Predecessors* (London, 1896). Interestingly, George Bernard Shaw saw in the three plays examined in this volume evidence of Shakespeare's modernity, 'ready and willing to start at the twentieth century if only the seventeenth century would let him'. See *Plays Pleasant and Unpleasant*, revised edn (London, 1906), vol. 1, p. xxi.

6. E. M. W. Tillyard, *Shakespeare's Problem Plays* (London, 1950), p. 2.

7. Perhaps the clearest rebuttal of Boas's inclusion of *Hamlet* is in W. W. Lawrence's *Shakespeare's Problem Comedies* (New York, 1931).

8. Vivian Thomas, *The Moral Universe of Shakespeare's Problem Plays* (London and New York, 1991), p. 4.

9. Peter Ure, *Shakespeare: The Problem Plays: 'Troilus and Cressida', 'All's Well That Ends Well', 'Measure for Measure', 'Timon of Athens'* (London, 1961).

10. A. P. Rossiter, *Angel with Horns* (London, 1961), pp. 126–8.

11. Ernest Schanzer, *The Problem Plays of Shakespeare: A Study of 'Julius Caesar', 'Measure for Measure', 'Antony and Cleopatra'* (London, 1963), pp. 1–3.

12. I was reminded here of William Makepeace Thackeray's embarrassed verdict on Shakespeare's *Coriolanus*. He returned from a performance attended with friends and wrote in his diary that 'we all found the play a bore; [...] it is almost a blasphemy to say that a play of Shakespeare's is bad, but I can't help it if I think so.' See Thackerary's *Letters*, Vol. II (Oxford, 1945), p. 292.

13. W. W. Lawrence, *Shakespeare's Problem Comedies*, 3rd edn (Harmondsworth, 1970). On the theme of the aesthetic status of the

problem plays, see also: Northrop Frye, *The Myth of Deliverance: Reflections on Shakespeare's Problem Plays* (Brighton, 1983), Arnold Kettle (ed.), *Shakespeare in a Changing World* (London, 1964); Ernest Schanzer, *The Problem Plays of Shakespeare* (London, 1963); Peter Ure, *Shakespeare: the Problem Plays* (London, 1961); Richard Wheeler, *Shakespeare's Development and the Problem Comedies* (Berkeley and Los Angeles, 1981).

14. The restored Globe Theatre at Southwark, in London, provoked fierce and occasionally humorous debates over whether or not its productions were 'authentic', with purist critics and theatre historians lined up against its sponsors, developers and practitioners.

15. See Elizabeth Cary, *The Tragedy of Mariam, The Fair Queen of Jewry* (1604) in Simon Barker and Hilary Hinds (eds), *The Routledge Anthology of Renaissance Drama* (London and New York, 2003), pp. 191–230.

16. For a clear and engaging account of these aspects of meaning see Terry Eagleton, *An Introduction to Literary Theory*, 2nd edn (Oxford, 1996).

17. See Emile Benveniste, *Problems in General Linguistics* (Miami, 1971), p. 110.

18. Catherine Belsey, *Critical Practice* (London and New York, 1980), p. 92.

19. See Mikhail Bakhtin, *Rabelais and His World*, trs. Helene Iswolsky (Indiana, 1984).

1

Shakespeare's Problem Plays: Concepts and Perspectives

VIVIAN THOMAS

[A] number of strong connecting links have been discerned between *Troilus and Cressida, All's Well and Measure for Measure* and it is worth specifying their precise nature in an attempt to evaluate the argument for grouping together these three plays as opposed to other possible combinations.

The first significant unifying feature of these plays is that we are left pondering the questions raised by the action rather than contemplating the sense of loss characteristic of tragedy or of feeling the release or joy inherent in Shakespeare's romantic comedies. Whatever affinities these plays may share with *Hamlet* or *Timon of Athens* the feelings engendered by those plays are different and belong distinctly to the world of tragedy. Thus we are caught up with the problems which form the stuff of these plays and feel at a loss to categorise them. They are truly problem plays. The matter of genre is not merely one of wanting to pigeonhole plays out of an excessive sense of order. Rather, the nature of the contemplation provoked by these plays is such that we ponder both the social realities encompassed by them and the dramatic form in which they are embodied. Incongruity is perhaps the word that most effectively conveys the feeling of the audience: it does not really believe in the happy end and is more engaged by the concerns of character, relationships and institutions, both inside and outside the drama. As for *Troilus and*

Cressida, bewilderment appears to have been historically the most characteristic response, and in recent times there has been a temptation to tilt the play towards tragedy in order to diminish the ambivalence of the audience which this play usually engenders.

Second, each of the three plays possesses a crucial debate scene which focuses sharply on the central themes. Moreover, the scene occurs in almost an identical position in each play. In *Troilus and Cressida* (II.ii) the issue is one of value, worth and honour; in *All's Well* (II.iii) the critical question relates to human valuation in terms of intrinsic and extrinsic considerations; the debate in *Measure for Measure* (II.ii) centres on law and justice.

Third, all the plays interrogate the relationship between human behaviour and institutions. Each play is concerned with authority, hierarchy, decision-making and the consequence of these decisions for the society as a whole and for particular individuals. Who are the decision-makers (in the Trojan war)? What are the foundations for these decisions? What are the consequences? What is the nature of obligation and privilege (in the French court)? How far can the law go in controlling human behaviour (in Vienna)? What is the nature of the obligation placed on a ruler? These are merely a few of the most central questions relating to human behaviour and social institutions in the plays.

Fourth, these plays are particularly concerned with contrasts between appearance and reality. Continually an attractive exterior gives way to an unattractive interior. The great hero Achilles resorts to murder when he is incapable of defeating his enemy by fair means; Bertram has fine breeding and upbringing but behaves despicably. Parolles has an extravagant manner which covers a coward's heart. Angelo is a most precise and unrelenting judge but descends to the lowest depths of depravity. Occasionally this aspect is emblematic: the soldier in sumptuous armour killed by Hector turns out to be diseased.

Fifth, all the plays provoke a considerable degree of detachment. This feature is most marked in *Troilus and Cressida*, where Pandarus and Thersites are key figures in ensuring that the audience is not afforded the luxury of identifying too closely with any of the characters. But this feature is also present in the other two plays: despite the passionate intensity created through the collision of characters, the action is placed in such a way that the issues remain clear and constantly on the surface. Irony, paradox and deflation are essential elements in maintaining the detachment of the audience. There are exemplary characters but they form part of the structure that underlines the questioning of characters like Isabella and Bertram. Moreover, scurrilous individuals like Thersites, Parolles and Lucio have an attractive side and represent features of life that make for human vitality: Thersites precludes sentimentality by constantly reminding the audience of stark realities; Parolles' dishonesty is charmingly innocuous compared with Bertram's vicious lying; Lucio's scandalous tongue and disreputable behaviour must be checked, but his refusal to be put down represents a defence against the authoritarianism of Angelo – it is he, after all, who presses Isabella to persist with and reinforce her plea on Claudio's behalf.

Sixth, Thersites, Parolles and Lucio share another characteristic which links the plays: they are not clowns or fools but denigrators. Thersites exposes the boils on the body politic with his savage insights; Lucio delights in scandalous lies and abuses his associates – particularly the woman who has borne his child; Parolles lacks the sharpness and bite of Thersites and Lucio but seeks to deceive through presenting a false appearance to the world. Interestingly, they all play a major role in the action but remain outsiders. Thersites is tolerated with amusement or contempt by his associates but his status remains the same throughout the course of the play and his presence makes the audience continually aware of the bleakest interpretation of the action. Like Thersites, both Parolles and Lucio have tongues which run away with them but ultimately it lands them in trouble which changes their status. But if Lucio is a liar and a scoundrel he presents a healthy counter-weight to Angelo's interpretation of justice in sexual matters and he uses his energy to drive Isabella to greater exertions in an attempt to save Claudio. Moreover, while his interruptions in the last scene are irritating he represents a type which cannot be bludgeoned into subservience – a valuable antidote in any society threatened with totalitarianism. Parolles is the most innocuous of the three: he neither exposes nor commits a significant crime, unless his willingness to surrender secrets to the enemy is taken seriously. However, he does attempt to perpetuate fraud by pretending to be what he is not and it is he who experiences the greatest change of circumstances by the end of the play: he is given a new and humbler role. Parolles' vices do not go deep, they are effectively beyond his own control and he is easily exposed for what he is. Contemplation of his character and actions inevitably produces a more severe critique of Bertram's character and actions. Thus it is evident that there are significant differences between these characters in terms of behaviour and dramatic function, but as Northrop Frye recognises, each of them provides 'a focus for slander and railing'.[1]

Seventh, a major theme in these plays is honour. The plays all invite a probing of this concept and insist on separating its various strands. Bertram inherits honour, but surprisingly the King, among others, expresses the hope that Bertram will prove worthy of his inheritance: honour derived from ancestry has to be reaffirmed by the behaviour of the recipient. Moreover, honour can be attained in different ways, but different kinds of honour are not necessarily interchangeable. The Countess insists that Bertram cannot recover the honour lost in his treatment of Helena by means of his exploits on the battlefield. Angelo has behaved in a totally dishonourable way in his treatment of Mariana, but seems oblivious of the fact when we first encounter him. His conscious abandonment of honour is rapid after his initial meeting with Isabella. Hector asserts the primacy of honour over life but simplifies the equation by failing to recognise the dependence of others on his life. Moreover, for his chief antagonist honour can be put on and off like a suit of armour depending on the circumstances. Throughout these plays honour is a central concept and theme which, however significant in other Shakespeare plays, is so intimately linked to the major themes that it binds them together.

Eighth, these plays are all peculiarly concerned with sex. At the centre of the Trojan war are two faithless women who are fought over, enjoyed and denigrated. (Of the four outstanding cases of jealousy in Shakespeare three of the women are incapable of infidelity. Only in *Troilus and Cressida* do we find a mad outburst of jealousy which is justified.) Diomedes provides an annihilating evaluation of Helen while Troilus has to endure the agony of watching Cressida's betrayal. But women are both sex objects and symbols. Troilus is prepared to risk his arm to regain a tarnished love token, while the very existence of Troy is gambled through the retention of Helen. Angelo will treat a novice like a whore for sexual gratification and yet will execute a man for consummating his unofficial marriage with the woman he loves and by whom he is loved. Meanwhile sex as a commodity and a means of livelihood displays a vitality and ubiquity which is beyond the reach of the most restrictive legal system. Bertram is prepared to seduce and dishonour a woman without a blush or a moment's remorse and then denounce her in public as a prostitute. Yet he is loved by a woman remarkable for her virtue, perception and energy. Love and lechery feature powerfully in all three plays and provoke serious questions about sexual attraction, sexual desire and repression and the extent to which institutions ought to impinge on these fundamental human drives.

Ninth, disillusionment is close to the centre of these plays and is intimately connected with love and lechery. By the end of the play Troilus is disillusioned with both love and war – as indeed are most of the major characters long before the end. The Countess and the King are bitterly disillusioned by the failure of Bertram to measure up to his father, while several of the young men are disillusioned by the incongruity between Bertram's performance on and off the battlefield. Angelo is disillusioned about his moral rectitude: he is shocked and distressed when he discovers his vulnerability. In the latter two plays disillusionment may be dispelled by the rapid adjustment which takes place at the conclusion of the action – even so the audience may feel disillusioned that characters as worthy as Helena and Mariana can be so deeply attached to such dubious characters as Bertram and Angelo. In *Troilus* the sense of disillusionment is pervasive: the Greeks scent victory but they have long since relinquished their ideals. The audience is deprived of any illusions about the ability of human beings to conduct their most vital affairs in a rational manner.

Tenth, the other side of the disillusionment which the three plays exhibit, is a passionate desire to believe in total integrity: a wholeness and beauty in life which cannot be tarnished. Hector is emphatic in placing honour before life itself, and believes that the code to which he adheres is universal. His dying words express disbelief that this code can be discarded by Achilles. Helen thinks of Bertram as god-like ('my idolatrous fancy/Must sanctify his relics' (I.i.95–6) but has to adjust to a reality that is very different. However, she moves from image to reality without any apparent sense of disillusionment except for one poignant moment (when Bertram refuses to kiss her farewell). It is as if her integrity will be enough for both of them. The confidence of several other characters in the play, however, suffers more severely and the King is evidently disillusioned with life before he is healed by Helena – a disillusionment which is made abundantly clear by his references to the hopes, beliefs and expectations he had held when younger and surrounded by such men as Bertram's father. Isabella yearns for the nunnery, and an austere regime, presumably to live in a world that is pure. Her encounter with Angelo forces upon her a recognition that the world outside the nunnery is far worse than she imagined. But what is the consequence for her after this initial disillusionment? She shows herself capable of an astonishing capacity for forgiveness and perhaps has developed the ability to live in an impure world. She seems as impervious to the destructive consequences of disillusionment as Helena. Arguably idealism triumphs over disillusionment in two of these plays, but that interpretation may be limited to the characters in the drama. The audience may experience a severe sense of disillusionment in all three plays while recognising the force of the aspiration for wholeness or purity in a flawed universe.

Another explicit concern of these plays is with the matter of identity and kinship. Virtually every character in *Troilus and Cressida* is identified in terms of kinship and several implications are suggested. Even the illegitimate Margarelon and Thersites emphasise the kinship network, and the one man who relinquishes his place in this pattern, Calchas, virtually loses his identity. Although the pattern is not as ubiquitous or persistent in the other two plays it still plays a remarkable role. *All's Well* opens with comments on two dead fathers and these live on vividly in the minds of others. Helena is the adoptive child of the Countess who would gladly receive her as a daughter-in-law. Lafew promises that the King will be a second father to Bertram, and later agrees that his own daughter be allowed to marry the prodigal son. Diana is accompanied by her mother and is advised by her. In *Measure for Measure*, Isabella and Julietta play at being cousins; Isabella has temporarily to leave her chosen vocation to fight for the life of her brother; Mariana initially loses Angelo because her brother is lost at sea; Lucio denies his paternity in order to avoid marriage to a whore. Angelo demands Claudio's head but he can be satisfied with a substitute because death creates a kinship through disguising identity; Claudio's fear of death with all its implications leads Isabella to doubt the fidelity of her mother. Mistress Overdone has run through more husbands than stockings. Thus once more a pattern that is discernible in several plays is greatly accentuated in the problem plays.

A number of critics appear to feel that there is something peculiar about the societies portrayed in these plays. It was Boas who suggested that they are 'highly artificial societies' and that an 'atmosphere of obscurity surrounds them'.[2] What decidedly seems the case is that in each instance we enter a society which is introspective and manifests a sense of having a major problem. The Greeks and Trojans have punched themselves to a standstill and no longer seem to possess the capacity to change direction: they lack the energy and imagination to transform their situation. The disasters of the past have not illuminated their difficulties in any way but press down upon them like a dead weight. Vienna seethes with a licentiousness that is a matter of concern to the Duke but which is hardly a serious social threat in comparison with the unfeeling harshness of one of the out-standing deputies in the state. However, the feeling remains that if Angelo has been transformed there is little likelihood of transforming Vienna. *All's Well* also conveys a feeling of social strain: it is an ageing society: one in which a gap has opened up between the generations and there are too few talented young people mature enough to take the place of those who have died or are about to relinquish their positions. In varying degrees the leaders in these societies recognise that they are confronted by a social problem. In the case of *Troilus and Cressida* the failure of both societies is manifest, but in *All's Well* and *Measure for Measure* the audience is left with a dim awareness that these societies have not resolved their problems. Nowhere else in Shakespeare is the feeling articulated in this way. *The Tempest* leaves the audience doubting the ability of any state to remain invulnerable to the manoeuvres of the politically ambitious, but that remains, as it were, one of the ongoing contests or tensions intrinsic to the political process. In the problem plays something less tangible and therefore more intractable is alluded to. Paradoxically, *Troilus and Cressida* is less problematical in this sense: the failure of the society is apparent and this directs attention to the parallels between the world of the Trojan War and the world inhabited by the audience. This is one of the reasons why *Troilus and Cressida* now appears so fresh and so meaningful to a modern audience. We share the problems of the Trojans and Greeks – the possession of an advanced civilisation under severe threat, slipping inexorably beyond rational control – and are fascinated by it; we don't quite understand the full extent and nature of the problems of Vienna and the French court because they are only partially articulated. They remain obscure.

The final unifying characteristic is the toughness of the language. Although the language of each play is very distinctive (only *Troilus and Cressida* is rich in imagery) these plays contain many speeches which are not merely ambiguous but have a construction which is positively awkward: the verse occasionally exhibits a strain and tension which reflect the stress of conflicting emotions within the characters who voice them. [...]

The foregoing summary has provided an indication of the way in which the concept of the problem play has been perceived by some distinguished critics during the course of the past century. Definitions have varied, the plays encompassed by the term have changed and perceptions of the essential elements which go to make up the plays have differed. Nevertheless, there have been common points of reference and these have been delineated and developed during the preceding discussion. Moreover, additional parallels and comparisons have been made in order to suggest the relevance of the term problem plays when attached to *Troilus and Cressida, All's Well* and *Measure for Measure*. The most significant of these connections will be underlined in the concluding chapter [of *The Moral Universe*].

What is essential, however, before proceeding to detailed discussion, is to have a clear definition of the term problem play which will provide a useful framework for the ensuing analysis. The term problem play is here used to encompass three plays which defy absorption into the traditional categories of romantic comedies, histories, tragedies and romances, but share striking affinities in terms of themes, atmosphere, tone and style. In particular, they explore fundamental problems relating to personal and social values within a framework which makes the audience acutely aware of the problems without providing amelioration through the provision of adequate answers or a dramatic mode which facilitates a satisfactory release of emotions.

From Vivian Thomas, *The Moral Universe of Shakespeare's Problem Plays* (London, 1987), pp. 14–21.

Notes

[This extract is from Vivian Thomas's full-length study *The Moral Universe of Shakespeare's Problem Plays*, which was first published in 1987 but republished for a new readership in 1991. In a bold and incisive introduction Thomas sets out the unifying features of the three plays and raises critical issues that he explores more thoroughly in the book as a whole. The section reproduced here lists ten key features that distinguish the plays, as a group, from those 'contained' by the easier categories of 'comedy' or 'tragedy'. Thomas thus looks back at the old debate about what constitutes a 'problem play', but forward, thematically, and in many ways ahead of his time, to the complexities of interpretation represented by the nine other essays reproduced in this volume. References are to the New Arden editions of Shakespeare's plays. Ed.]

1. Northrop Frye, *The Myth of Deliverance: Reflections on Shakespeare's Problem Comedies* (Brighton, 1983), p. 65.

2. F. S. Boas, *Shakspere and his Predecessors* (London, 1896), p. 384.

2

All's Well That Ends Well and the Tale of the Chivalric Quest

LEAH SCRAGG

His joyful mariners ... spread forth their comely sails, and with their brazen keels cut an easy passage on the green meadows of the floods. At last, Fortune having brought him here where she might make him the fittest tennis ball for her sport. ... the heavens began to thunder, and the skies shone with flashes of fire; day now had no other show but only name, for darkness was on the whole face of the waters ... And partly through that dismal darkness, which unfortunately was come upon them, they were all drowned, [the prince] only excepted, till (as it were Fortune being tired with this mishap) by the help of a plank, which in this distress he got hold on, he was with much labour and more fear driven on the shore. ... Certain fishermen, who had also suffered in the former tempest, and had been witness of his untimely shipwreck, the day being cleared again, were come out of their homely cottages to dry and repair their nets. ... The chief of these fishermen was moved with compassion toward him, and lifting him up from the ground himself, with the help of his men led him to his house. ... Being somewhat repaired in heart by their relief, he demanded of the country on which he was driven, of the name of the king. ... and then how far his court was distant from that place, wherein he was resolved some half a day's journey, and from point to point also informed that the king had a princely daughter ... in whom was beauty so joined with virtue that it was as yet unresolved which of them deserved the greater comparison, and in memory of whose birthday her father yearly celebrated feasts and triumphs, in the honour of which many princes and knights from far and remote countries came, partly to prove their chivalry, but especially (being her father's only child) in hope to gain her love ... [The prince], sighing to himself ... broke out thus, 'Were but my fortunes answerable to my desires, some should feel that I would be one there.' When, as if all the gods had given a plaudite to his words, the fishermen who before were sent out by their master to drag out the other nets, having found somewhat in the bottom too ponderous for their strength to pull up, they began to ... halloo to their master for more help ... [but] before help came, up came the fish expected, but proved indeed to be a rusty armour ... The armour is by [the prince] viewed, and known to be a defence which his father at his last will gave him in charge to keep, that it might prove to be a defender of the son, which he had known to be a preserver of the father. So, accounting all his other losses nothing ... and thanking Fortune that after all her crosses she had yet given him somewhat to repair his fortunes, begging this armour of the fishermen [he told them] that with it he would show the virtue he had learned in arms, and try his chivalry for their princess ... Which they applauding, and one furnishing him with an old gown to make caparisons for his horse ... and other furnishing him with the long sideskirts of their cassocks to make him bases,[1] his armour rusted and thus disgracefully habilited, [the prince] ... came to the court. In this manner also, five several princes, their horses richly caparisoned, but themselves more richly armed, their pages before them bearing their devices on their shields, entered then the tilting place ... The sixth and last was [the prince] who, having neither page to deliver his shield, nor shield to deliver, making his device according to his fortunes, which was a withered branch being only green at the top, which proved the abating of his body decayed not the nobleness of his mind, his word,[2] *In hac spe vivo*. ... The peers attending on the king forbore not to scoff, both at his presence and the present he bought ... which the king mildly reproving them for, he told them that as virtue was not to be proved by words, but by actions, so the outward habit was the least table of the inward mind ... They went forward to the triumph, in which noble exercise they came almost all as short of [the prince] ... as a body dying of a life flourishing. To be short, both of court and commons, the praises of none were spoken of but of the mean knight's ... The triumphs being ended, [the prince] as chief (for in this day's honour he was the champion) with all the other princes were ... conducted into the presence ... at whose entrance the lady, first saluting [him] gave him a wreath of chivalry, welcomed him as her knight and guest, and crowned him king of that day's noble enterprise ... Both king and daughter, at one instant were so struck in love with the nobleness of his worth, that they could not spare so much time to satisfy themselves with the delicacy of their viands for talking of his praises ... At last, the father, being no longer able to subdue that which he desired as much as she ... clapped them hand in hand, while they as lovingly

joined lip to lip, and with tears trickling from his aged eyes, adopted
him his happy son, and bad them live together as man and wife.
(George Wilkins, *The Painful Adventures of
Pericles Prince of Tyre*, 1608)[3]

The story of the chivalric quest, exemplified by George Wilkins' tale
of the shipwrecked prince, combines a number of very ancient folk
tale motifs. At the heart of the story lies the concept of life as a journey,[4] with storm representing the vicissitudes to which all human
beings are subject. The motif is a common one throughout western
European literature, and is found in the vernacular English tradition
as early as the Anglo-Saxon period in such poems as *The Seafarer*. At
the same time the story also has its roots in the fertility myths, common to many cultures, in which the health of a society is seen as
dependent upon the virility of its ruler. In Wilkins' story the ageing
king has no son to succeed him, and the ritual combats between
those seeking to achieve his daughter's hand ensure that the heir to
the kingdom will marry a husband capable of maintaining the health
of the state. Once again, the story enjoyed wide currency during the
Middle Ages, flourishing both in the form of a heroic deed on behalf
of a lady (looking back to such classical myths as that of Perseus and
Andromeda), and as a quest to rejuvenate a waste land ruled over by
a stricken king (cf. the legend of the holy grail).

A common feature of many of the items making up this complex
of tales is the prowess or supreme virtue of a person of seemingly low
rank. Just as Wilkins' destitute prince is scorned by his fellow com-
batants for his mean appearance, but proves his valour and wins the
princess's love, so Sir Gareth (ultimately one of the most celebrated
of the knights of the round table) begins his career as a kitchen boy
despised by Sir Kay, but exhibits his knightly virtue in the performance of a quest, marries the lady of Lyoness and is revealed to be
the son of a king.[5] As in Wilkins' tale, moreover, the fulfilment of the
hero's destiny is frequently accomplished, both in romance and classical fable, by means of an object of particular value inherited from a
father, or provided by supernatural powers. Hercules, for example,
a son of Zeus, receives arms and armour from the gods, while
Sir Galahad, who comes to Arthur's court without weapons, is mag-
ically provided with a sword and shield.

The density of meaning afforded by the overlap between strands
within this nexus of stories is exhibited by Spenser's *The Faerie
Queene* (1590 and 1596). Like Wilkins' narrative, the poem draws
together a number of familiar elements, firmly locating the work in a

literary tradition. The central figures of Book I, a knight and a lady, are first encountered in the course of a journey; the knight is of mean appearance (in that his armour is battered and old), while the lady is in need of help. The knight's identity is uncertain, and he discovers his destiny in the course of his mission to slay a dragon, restore the stricken land of his companion's parents and thus win the lady herself as his bride. While the elements of the story clearly correspond to those of Wilkins' narrative, however, the significance of the poem is much more profound. Spenser's work is an allegory, marrying folk tale and chivalric romance to Christian teaching, and thus endowing the strands of the inherited fable with a new richness. The Redcross Knight is not simply mankind engaged upon the eventful journey through life, or the embodiment of a life-force dispelling winter and bringing new growth, he is a Christian everyman seeking to overcome evil and perfect himself, emulating the conduct of Christ in reversing the fall. His battered armour is not merely a physical inheritance derived from an earthly father, but the gift of God in the form of his word (cf. St Paul's injunction to the Ephesians to 'take unto you the whole armour of God'), while the wasteland awaiting its saviour is not only a land gripped by winter but the post-lapsarian world. The reader of the poem thus engages with the knight's adventures on a number of levels, each incident carrying a range of resonances by virtue of the fusion effected between different traditions.

At first sight, *All's Well That Ends Well* has little in common with the type of story exemplified by Wilkins' tale. The plot of the play is derived from Boccaccio's *Decameron* (Day 3, Story 9) mediated, in all probability, through William Painter's sixteenth-century anthology, *The Palace of Pleasure* (Story 38).[6] Rather than concerning the deeds of a knight or the winning of a lady, Boccaccio's story is centred upon the career of a physician's daughter (Gilette of Narbonne) and her pursuit of the young Count of Roussillon, son of her father's former patron. Being of lower rank than the man she loves, Gilette has no hope of being his bride, until on hearing that the King is suffering from an illness, she attends the court and effects his cure, asking for the hand of the Count (a ward of the King) as her reward. The King reluctantly complies with her request, and Gilette returns home to manage her husband's estates, but the Count refuses to consummate the marriage, requiring his virgin bride to bear his child and to produce a ring he values from his finger before he will accept her as his wife. Faced with such seemingly impossible conditions, and fearing her presence at Rousillon is barring the Count from returning home, Gilette undertakes a pilgrimage to Florence, only to learn upon her arrival that her husband is engaged there upon the seduction of another woman. Seeing an opportunity to fulfil his conditions, Gilette persuades the other lady to demand the Count's ring as the price of her compliance, and to allow her to take her place in her husband's bedchamber. Having become pregnant with twins after a number of encounters, Gilette presents herself before the Count with the ring and not one but two children and is gladly received by him as his wife.

Though heavily reliant upon folk tale, Boccaccio's story clearly derives from a different tradition from that to which Wilkins' narrative belongs. Gilette's experience looks back to the fable of the long-suffering wife (cf. Chaucer's *The Clerk's Tale* and Renaissance plays such as John Phillip's *Patient and Meek Grissil*, 1558–61), while the conditions imposed by her husband belong to 'the tale of impossibilities', and the achievement of a seemingly unattainable goal.[7] In taking up Painter's version of Boccaccio's story, however, Shakespeare fuses the borrowed material with elements from a different literary stock (cf. Spenser's treatment of the chivalric quest in *The Faerie Queene*), interrogating the assumptions underlying his inherited stories through the interaction that he sets up between them.

Though broadly comparable with the situation of Boccaccio's heroine, Helena's position at the opening of *All's Well That Ends Well* differs from that of her romance progenitor in a number of respects. Gilette, like Painter's Giletta, conceives a passion for the young Count at a very early age, and there is a hint of impropriety in the degree of her infatuation with him. Boccaccio describes her as 'more passionately attached to him than was strictly proper in a girl of so tender an age',[8] while Painter notes that she 'fervently fell in love with Beltramo, more than was meet for a maiden'.[9] Shakespeare's heroine, by contrast, is noted for her virtue from the outset, the lines in which she is introduced to the audience placing particular emphasis upon her purity of mind:

Laf[ew]   Was this gentlewoman the daughter of Gerard de Narbon?
Count[ess]   His sole child, my lord, and bequeathed to my overlook-
             ing. I have those hopes of her good that her education
             promises her dispositions she inherits – which makes fair
             gifts fairer; for where an unclean mind carries virtuous
             qualities, there commendations go with pity; they are
             virtues and traitors too. In her they are the better for their

> simpleness: she derives her honesty and achieves her goodness.
>
> (I.i.33–42)

The heroine's social position has also undergone a notable change between prose works and play. Gilette is the daughter of a very wealthy man, and the latter's kinsmen are concerned to ensure that his daughter should make an appropriate marriage after his death. Boccaccio emphasises that Gilette 'had inherited the whole of her father's fortune', that she was 'kept under constant surveillance' and that 'after reaching marriageable age' because of her love of the young Count she 'rejected numerous suitors whom her kinsfolk had urged her to marry' (p. 305). Similarly Painter's Giletta was 'diligently looked unto by her kinsfolk (because she was rich and fatherless) ... and refused many husbands with whom her kinsfolk would have matched her' (pp. 389–90). Helena by contrast is a 'poor physician's daughter' (II.iii.123), friendless but for her patroness, the Countess,[10] and thus at a far greater social distance from the man she hopes to attain than the figures from whom she derives. Where both Gilette and Giletta have independent means, Helena is a dependent of the Count's household, her position heightening the improbability of her achieving her goal. At the same time, the circumstances surrounding the relationship between the heroine's father and the former Count of Rousillon (Shakespeare's Rossillion) [have] also been significantly adapted between source and play. Boccaccio's old Count is described as 'something of an invalid' (p. 305) requiring the constant attendance of a physician, while Painter's nobleman is more emphatically 'sickly and diseased', obliged to keep a doctor 'always in his house' (p. 389). Shakespeare's Count, by contrast, was an outstanding individual in both physical and mental terms, his exceptional gifts vividly evoked for the audience through the words of the King:

> I would I had that corporal soundness now,
> As when thy father [i.e. the young Count's] and myself in friendship
> First tried our soldiership. He did look far
> Into the service of the time, and was
> Discipled of the bravest. He lasted long,
> But on us both did haggish age steal on,
> And wore us out of act. It much repairs me
> To talk of your good father; in his youth
> He had the wit which I can well observe
> Today in our young lords; but they may jest

Till their own scorn return to them unnoted
Ere they can hide their levity in honour.
So like a courtier, contempt nor bitterness
Were in his pride or sharpness; if they were,
His equal had awak'd them, and his honour,
Clock to itself, knew the true minute when
Exception bid him speak, and at this time
His tongue obey'd his hand. Who were below him
He us'd as creatures of another place,
And bow'd his eminent top to their low ranks,
Making them proud of his humility
In their poor praise he humbled. Such a man
Might be a copy to these younger times;
Which, followed well, would demonstrate them now
But goers backward.

(I.ii.24–48)

The King's eulogy of the former Count, while establishing the exemplary nature of the dead man, also serves to associate his virtues with those of an old order. His nobility of mind and vigour of body are linked with the condition of the state in that he and the King were bound together in 'friendship', enjoyed a similar 'corporal soundness', and 'tried [their] soldiership' together. The eminent physician associated with the Count's family is thus not a necessary prop to a decayed household, but a further instance of the excellence of an earlier age when both the military and social arts flourished. The demise of the old Count, together with the King's illness and the death of Helena's father consequently suggest the decay of an entire society, a point emphasised by the King's comparison between the limited capacities of the younger members of his court and the qualities of his former friend.

The King's response to the reward that the heroine asks in return for the cure that she effects is also indicative of the different shape that Shakespeare imposes on his inherited narrative. Boccaccio's King, having agreed to permit Gilette to marry the man of her choice, is disturbed when she asks for the Count of Roussillon for 'it was no laughing matter to [him] that he should be obliged to give her Bertrand' (p. 307). Similarly, Painter's sick ruler agrees to Giletta's conditions, but when appraised of her choice of husband is 'very loath to grant him unto her' (p. 391). The hesitation on the part of both monarchs contributes to the sense of impropriety surrounding the early stages of the heroine's career, while providing implicit justification for the Count's refusal to accept his low-born wife.

Shakespeare's King by contrast has no hesitation in granting Helena's request, rebuking the reluctant Bertram for the false values that he exhibits in repudiating the match:

> 'Tis only title thou disdain'st in her, the which
> I can build up. Strange is it that our bloods,
> Of colour, weight, and heat, pour'd all together,
> Would quite confound distinction, yet stands off
> In differences so mighty. If she be
> All that is virtuous, save what thou dislik'st –
> A poor physician's daughter – thou dislik'st
> Of virtue for the name. But do not so.
> From lowest place when virtuous things proceed,
> The place is dignified by th'doer's deed.
> Where great additions swell's and virtue none,
> It is a dropsied honour. Good alone
> Is good, without a name; vileness is so:
> The property by what it is should go,
> Not by the title. She is young, wise, fair;
> In these to nature she's immediate heir,
> And these breed honour; that is honour's scorn
> Which challenges itself as honour's born
> And is not like the sire. Honours thrive
> When rather from our acts we them derive
> Than our forgoers. The mere word's a slave,
> Debosh'd on every tomb, on every grave
> A lying trophy, and as oft is dumb,
> Where dust and damn'd oblivion is the tomb
> Of honour'd bones indeed. What should be said?
> If thou canste like this creature as a maid,
> I can create the rest. virtue and she
> Is her own dower; honour and wealth from me.
> (II.iii.117–44)

The King's stance contributes to the contrast established by the dramatist between the true nobility of an old order and the corruption of a new age, and this contrast is heightened by Shakespeare's introduction of an old courtier, Lafew, who endorses the King's position. While Bertram exclaims that he 'cannot love her nor will strive to do't' (II.ii.145), Lafew regrets that he cannot be among those from whom Helena is to make her choice (II.iii.78–9), and is horrified by the attitude of the younger lords towards her:

> Do all they deny her? And they were sons of mine I'd have them whipp'd, or I would send them to th'Turk to make eunuchs of.
> (II.iii.86–8)

While heightening the contrast between the former condition of society and the decayed nature of the world in which the miraculous cure is to be effected, Shakespeare also draws much greater attention than the sources on which he draws to the difficulties of the journey that his central figure undergoes. Boccaccio's Gilette, a wealthy woman, simply learns of the King's illness, prepares 'certain herbs' and 'rode off to Paris' (pp. 305–6), while Painter's Giletta 'made a powder of certain herbs which she thought meet for that disease, and rode to [the capital]' (p. 390). Helena, by contrast, initially conceives of winning Bertram through curing the King at the close of the first scene, but fails to act upon her plan until after the young Count's arrival at court (scene ii). Rather than being free to act as she pleases, she is dependent upon her patroness, the Countess, and the difficulties that her project poses are emphasised by the stress laid by the latter upon the improbability of her gaining the King's ear, and on the means that the older woman provides to enable her to undertake the journey:

Count. But think you, Helen,
  If you should tender your supposed aid,
  He would receive it? He and his physicians
  Are of a mind; he, that they cannot help him;
  They, that they cannot help. How shall they credit
  A poor unlearned virgin, when the schools,
  Embowel'd of their doctrine, have left off
  The danger to itself?
Hel.   There's something in't
  More than my father's skill, which was the great'st
  Of his profession, that his good receipt
  Shall for my legacy be sanctified
  By th'luckiest stars in heaven; and would your honour
  But give me leave to try success, I'd venture
  The well-lost life of mine on his grace's cure
  By such a day, an hour.
  ...
Count. Why, Helen, thou shalt have my leave and love,
  Means and attendants, and my loving greetings
  To those of mine at court. I'll stay at home
  And pray God's blessing into thy attempt.
  Be gone tomorrow; and be sure of this,
  What I can help thee to, thou shalt not miss.
                                        (I.iii.230–51)

The adaptations made by Shakespeare to his source material clearly serve to move his story away from one designed to exhibit the way in which individuals may 'by dint of their own efforts [achieve] an object they greatly desired' (*Decameron*, p. 231) towards a very different literary tradition. The drama welds the tale of the enterprising woman to that group of stories concerned with the exemplary worth of a person of humble origins, who journeys to regenerate a stricken kingdom through an inheritance of mysterious potency, and is rewarded with marriage to one of higher rank. That Shakespeare was consciously imposing the pattern of the chivalric quest upon his inherited material is indicated, moreover, by an exchange between the Countess and her Steward in Act I scene iii. Having overheard Helena confess her love for Bertram, the Steward conveys the news to his mistress, the terminology in which he does so serving to locate the heroine's conduct in a very different arena from that evoked by the source:

> Stew. Madam, I was very late more near her than I think she wish'd me; alone she was and did communicate to herself her own words to her own ears ... Her matter was, she loved your son. Fortune, she said, was no goddess, that had put such difference betwixt their two estates; Love no god, that would not extend his might only where qualities were level; [Diana no] queen of virgins, that would suffer her poor knight surpris'd without rescue in the first assault or ransom afterward.
>
> (I.iii.102–12)

While the fusion with a different tradition expands the resonance of Boccaccio's story, the transference of the tale of the heroic quest into the formula supplied by the *Decameron* affords an alternative version or mirror image of the chivalric story. The traditional tale is concerned with the exhibition of masculine virtue, and takes place within the male arena. As in Wilkins' narrative, the central figure is a prince or knight, who proves his virtue in physical combat and wins a passive and admiring bride. By adapting Boccaccio's story into conformity with this pattern, Shakespeare reverses the terms of the inherited tale. His central figure is not a youthful knight attempting to prove his worth and win a bride, but a young woman in pursuit of a husband, while those that support her endeavours are not the conventional embodiments of the chivalric ideal (e.g. the members of King Arthur's court), but female figures traditionally hostile to virtue (a mother-in-law and a widow).[11] Rather than being written from the perspective of a male protagonist, the play thus encourages audience alignment with the female point of view, the implication of impropriety in Boccaccio's narrative functioning as a springboard for an exploration of the assumptions governing gender behaviour encoded within the traditional story.

Where Wilkins' tale centres firmly upon the travels and experience of a prince, Shakespeare's alternative version of the chivalric story begins in the domestic, and thus implicitly female, sphere. The opening lines of the play are unique in the Shakespearian canon in that they are spoken by a woman,[12] while the absence of male authority at Rossillion is indicated by the fact that the speaker is in mourning for her husband and is in process of yielding up her son to the guardianship of the King. The opening conversation, moreover, rather than centring upon the character of the young Count, swiftly shifts to Helena's outstanding virtue. While Bertram is largely a spectator to the conversation between Lafew and his mother, and thus plays a traditionally female role, the Countess's gentlewoman is quickly foregrounded by a reference to her parentage, and it is her situation which is then revealed, through soliloquy, when the other characters leave the stage. Though she is then joined by Parolles, the remainder of the scene is concerned, not with the expectations of the men leaving for Paris, but with male attitudes to women and Helena's state of mind, concluding with a soliloquy that reveals a mental cast wholly at odds with the marginalised role in which the young Count seeks to cast her (cf. 'Be comfortable to my mother, your mistress, and make much of her', I.i.73–4):

> Hel. Our remedies oft in ourselves do lie,
> Which we ascribe to heaven; the fated sky
> Gives us free scope; only doth backward pull
> Our slow designs when we ourselves are dull.
> What power is it which mounts my love so high,
> That makes me see, and cannot feed mine eye?
> The mightiest space in fortune nature brings
> To join like likes, and kiss like native things.
> Impossible be strange attempts to those
> That weigh their pains in sense, and do suppose
> What hath been cannot be. Who ever strove
> To show her merit that did miss her love?
> The king's disease – my project may deceive me,
> But my intents are fix'd, and will not leave me.
>   (I.i.212–25)

While this speech would be unexceptionable in the mouth of a man, indicating nobility of mind and steadfastness of purpose, it is not one that fits comfortably with Renaissance assumptions about the nature of women and their social role. As recent criticism has demonstrated,[13] female figures on the Elizabethan-Jacobean stage tend to fall into three classes – virgin, whore and witch – and though Helena clearly belongs in physical terms to the first category, she betrays none of the retiring character generally associated with that figure. While Bertram plays a passive, and hence stereoptypically female, part, in that he is removed from the custody of his mother into the guardianship of the King, who assigns him a marital partner and forbids him to go to the wars, Helena actively pursues the husband of her choice, and plans to leave the shelter of the Countess's protection in order to seek her fortunes in the larger world. Though she clearly corresponds to Boccaccio's Gillete, moreover, in 'being more passionately attached' to Bertram than conventionally 'proper' for a girl of her age, it is clear from the opening exchanges that in the world of *All's Well That Ends Well* female tenacity of purpose is in no way an index of moral failure. Placed in the context of a mind which 'derives [its] honesty and achieves [its] goodness' (I.i.42), the heterodox attitudes that Helena exhibits serve to redefine feminine virtue, setting up a tension between the stances adopted by the characters and the expectations generated by the inherited pattern to which the action of the drama conforms.

The reversal of gender expectations effected in Act I, scene i is sustained in the remainder of the act. Though the second scene is set in the court and is dominated by the King it occupies only seventy-five lines (largely devoted to evoking the decayed nature of the play world), and Bertram's role (consisting of only seven lines) is again a minor one. Rather than establishing the youthful Count's heroic resolution, the scene reinforces his dependency, closing with him being 'comfortable' to the King in lending him his arm (I.ii.73), and thus playing the role he assigned to Helena. Scene iii, by contrast, which returns to Rossillion, is the longest of the act, and focuses almost exclusively on female figures. The scene is dominated by the Countess and her opening line, 'I will now hear. What say you of this gentlewoman?' (I.iii.1) serves both to establish her authority and confirm the interest in female concerns. The firmness of tone with which she addresses those about her (cf. 'What does this knave here?' [I.iii.7]; 'Get you gone, sir; I'll talk with you more anon' [I.iii.62]) is in sharp contrast to the elegiac style adopted by the King (cf. 'Since I nor wax nor honey can bring home, / [I wish] I ... were dissolved from my hive / To give some labourers room' [I.ii.65–7]), while the deference exhibited towards her by her male servants confirms her ability to govern (cf. 'May it please you, madam' [I.iii.63]). The Clown's comment, 'that man should be at woman's command, and yet no hurt done' (I.iii.89–90) draws the attention of the audience towards the play's reversal of roles, while confirming the positive nature of the transgressive stances that the female characters adopt.

The second half of the scene widens the discrepancy between the expectations generated by the play's pattern and the positions that the dramatis personae assume. The Steward reveals to the Countess that her protégé is in love with, and dreams of marrying, her son, and the older woman responds by commanding the younger to be brought before her. A host of literary conventions invites the audience to expect a violent confrontation to ensue between the two women. The Countess's role in relation to Helena is analogous to that of a stepmother, and indeed she refers to herself in these terms (cf. 'You ne'er oppress'd me with a mother's groan / Yet I express to you a mother's care' [I.iii.142–3]), encouraging the audience to equate her with the malign step-dames of folk tale inveterately hostile to those in their charge (cf. *Snow White*).[14] At the same time, the exclusivity of the Countess's relationship with Bertram, as a widow with an only son, invites the assumption of maternal possessiveness (cf. the stereotype of the embittered mother-in-law), while the stress upon the discrepancy between Helena's station and that of the man she presumes to love touches upon tales of maternal pride. The initial exchange between the two women, moreover, appears to confirm audience expectation. In seeking to evade a definition of her relationship with the Countess that would make her Bertram's sister, Helena betrays the cause of her grief at the Count's departure, producing a seemingly hostile response from her mistress:

> Hel.   You are my mother, madam; would you were –
> So that my lord your son were not my brother –
> Indeed my mother! or were you both our mothers
> I care no more for than I do for heaven,
> So I were not his sister. Can't no other
> But, I your daughter, he must be my brother?
>
> Count. Yes, Helen, you might be my daughter-in-law.
> God shield you mean it not! daughter and mother
> So strive upon your pulse. What! pale again?
> My fear hath catch'd your fondness; now I see
> The myst'ry of your loneliness, and find
> Your salt tears' head. Now to all sense 'tis gross:
> You love my son. Invention is asham'd

> Against the proclamation of thy passion
> To say thou dost not. Therefore tell me true;
> But tell me then, 'tis so; for, look, thy cheeks
> Confess it t'one to th'other, and thine eyes
> See it so grossly shown in thy behaviours
> That in their kind they speak it; only sin
> And hellish obstinacy tie thy tongue,
> That truth should be suspected. Speak, is't so?
> If it be so, you have wound a goodly clew;
> If it be not, forswear't; howe'er, I charge thee,
> As heaven shall work in me for thine avail,
> To tell me truly.

Hel.   Good madam, pardon me.
Count.   Do you love my son?
Hel.   Your pardon, noble mistress.
Count.   Love you my son?
Hel.   Do not you love him, madam?
Count.   Go not about; my love hath in't a bond
> Whereof the world takes note. Come, come, disclose
> The state of your affection, for your passions
> Have to the full appeach'd.
Hel.   Then I confess,
> Here on my knee, before high heaven and you,
> That before you, and next unto high heaven,
> I love your son.

                                (I.iii.156–89)

In the event, however, the conduct of the Countess is at the opposite extreme from that of the conventional 'hag'. Having forced a
confession of love from the younger woman, she facilitates rather
than opposes the socially unequal marriage between her 'gentlewoman' and her son, enabling Helena to travel to Paris, and thus to
prosecute her plans. Rather than being blinded by affection for
Bertram, she is keenly aware of her protégé's worth, becoming
increasingly convinced as the action progresses not that her son is too
good for Helena, but that the Count's conduct shows him to be
wholly 'unworthy' of such a wife (III.iv.26).

While the sympathetic presentation of the assertive women of Act I
serves to subvert gender stereotypes, the events of Act II call in question the assumptions governing the roles that women are conventionally assigned. In a reversal of the traditional pattern of the
chivalric story, the inexperienced virgin (cf. the untried squire)
emerges from her obscure condition and travels to the Court, winning the approbation of the King in curing his illness. Where the

young knight of the conventional tale wins a bride (cf. Wilkins' princess) as a reward for his valour, Helena asks for a husband as the prize for her attempt, and is promised the reward that she seeks. The scene that follows traditionally constitutes the climactic moment of the inherited story representing the turning point in a cycle of decay and renewal, and thus an occasion of joy. The young knight is united in marriage with the bride whom he has won, symbolising both the sanctity and fertility of the new order. Shakespeare's alternative version of this culminatory moment is productive, however, of a very different effect. Rather than generating a sense of happiness and propriety, the scene sends out contradictory signals, undermining the acquiescence of the spectator in the events that are taking place.

Whereas in Wilkins' narrative the principal participants in the betrothment ritual are in emotional accord with one another, in the Shakespearian version of the story a marked tension exists between the attitudes of those caught up in the play's events. Unlike Boccaccio's newly healed monarch, who finds Gilette's choice of husband 'no laughing matter' and acquaints the young man in private with the marriage he must make, the King exhibits no sign of disquiet at the prospect of keeping his promise, requiring his young lords to be brought before him, and ceremonially inviting his benefactress to make her choice among his wards:

> **King.** Go, call before me all the lords in court.
>
> *[Exit Attendant.]*
>
> > Sit, my preserver, by thy patient's side,
> > And with this healthful hand, whose banish'd sense
> > Thou hast repeal'd, a second time receive
> > The confirmation of my promis'd gift,
> > Which but attends thy naming.
> > > *Enter three or four lords.*
> > Fair maid, send forth thine eye. This youthful parcel
> > Of noble bachelors stand at my bestowing,
> > O'er whom both sovereign power and father's voice
> > I have to use. Thy frank election make;
> > Thou hast power to choose, and they none to forsake.
> > …
> > > Peruse them well.
> > Not one of those but had a noble father.
> > > (II.iii.46–62)

The King's stance enforces the propriety of the situation, and its rightness is confirmed on one level by the sense of recognition that the stage spectacle itself evokes. The scene set up by the dramatist is not only a familiar one in chivalric literature, it was acted out until modern times on every dance floor, with a member of a privileged social group making a choice of partner among a gathering of the opposite sex. Where the scene differs from both social and literary norms, however, and thus challenges audience acceptance, is in its reversal of traditional roles. Whereas men are conventionally the active agents in the mating process and women the passive objects of their election, here it is a female character who is in a position to exercise freedom of choice and the male members of society who are obliged to defer to her will. While the King, moreover, is entirely at ease with the situation, the elderly Lafew assumes that his subjects resent their imposed parts (II.iii.86–8), while Helena herself betrays an embarrassment that invites the spectator to assess her conduct against cultural norms:

> Hel. I am a simple maid, and therein wealthiest
> That I protest I simply am a maid.
> Please it your majesty, I have done already.
> The blushes in my cheeks thus whisper me:
> 'We blush that thou should'st choose; but, be refused,
> Let the white death sit on thy cheek for ever,
> We'll ne'er come there again'.
> (II.iii.66–72)

It is Bertram's response to the situation, however, which is most plainly at odds with the joyous harmony evoked by the scene's romance antecedents, crystallising the growing uncase of those outside the play world. Rather than consenting to be given in marriage like his female counterparts in the inherited story, the young Count furiously repudiates the process in which he has been obliged to participate, vigorously maintaining his right to choose his partner in marriage for himself:

> Hel. [*To Bertram*] I dare not say I take you, but I give
> Me and my service, ever whilst I live,
> Into your guiding power. This is the man.
> King. Why, then, young Bertram, take her; she's thy wife.
> Ber. My wife, my liege! I shall beseech your highness,
> In such a business give me leave to use
> The help of mine own eyes.
> King.   Know'st thou not, Bertram,
> What she has done for me?
> Ber.   Yes, my good lord,

> But never hope to know why I should marry her.
>
> **King.** Thou know'st she has rais'd me from my sickly bed.
>
> **Ber.** But follows it, my lord, to bring me down
> Must answer for your raising? I know her well:
> She had her breeding at my father's charge –
> A poor physician's daughter my wife! Disdain
> Rather corrupt me ever!
>
> (II.iii.102–16)

On one level, Bertram's response to his situation clearly invites audience condemnation. As the King's ward and feudal subject he owes him absolute obedience and the tone in which he addresses him is plainly deficient in respect (cf. 'But follows it, my lord, to bring me down / Must answer for your raising?'). His objection to Helena is founded not upon any inadequacies of character or person, but upon the lowliness of her rank, betraying an unthinking snobbery that contrasts unfavourably with his parents' magnanimity (cf. I.ii.41–5 and I.iii.246–51). At the same time, however, the position that he adopts, for all the unfortunate tone in which it is couched, is not entirely devoid of appeal. The situation in which he finds himself is a demeaning one in terms of the conventional relations between the sexes, while his contention that he has a right to be consulted on a subject upon which his future happiness depends is a sympathetic one, carrying weight in the context of a drama in which the principal characters are motivated by love (cf. Helena and the Countess) rather than pragmatic considerations.

It is not solely the divergent responses of the dramatis personae and consequent division of audience sympathy, however, that serves to problematise the interpretation of this scene. The play's evocation of the events of chivalric romance sets up a species of dialogue between the on-stage action and the procedures of the traditional story, encouraging the spectator to ponder the workings of the one in the light of the other. The inherited tale, as noted above, is male-authored in that it is narrated from the hero's point of view, and the bride achieved in the course of his endeavours is assumed to be complicit in his goals. Shakespeare's alternative version of the tale of the chivalric quest interrogates the gender expectations implicit in this assumption. By reversing the terms of the traditional story and making the man the object of choice, he defamiliarises the conventional situation, obliging the members of the audience to view a customary process with new eyes. The terms in which Bertram speaks are only marginally gender specific (in that he refers to a 'wife', and to a prospective partner as 'she') and it is useful to consider the implications that his lines would have held for a reader had they been spoken by the 'prize' of the conventional tale:

> Ber.   I shall beseech your highness,
> In such a business give me leave to use
> The help of mine own eyes.
> King.   Know'st thou not ...
> What she has done for me?
> Ber.   Yes, my good lord,
> But never hope to knor why I should marry her.
> ...
> I cannot love her nor will strive to do't.
>   (II.iii.106–45)

In the mouth of a female character, the repudiation of patriarchal authority and resistance to a proposed marriage would define the speaker as a 'shrew' or 'scold', and thus as a disruptive force within the play world. By reversing the conventional tale, however, and making the man the object of choice, the dramatist turns the traditionally compliant reward for virtuous endeavour into a site of resistance to social norms, while evading the gender stereotyping that might otherwise ensue. In conceding the force of Bertram's objection to being given without consultation in marriage, the spectator is responding to a cry for human dignity that implicitly calls in question the role conventionally assigned to women, and thus encourages consideration of the female point of view. Where the damsel won by the valiant knight has no voice in the traditional tale, Helena's choice feels empowered by virtue of his sex to question the position in which he finds himself placed, unconsciously problematising the very assumptions to which he appeals.

While Bertram's protest offers an insight into a conventionally female predicament, the uneasiness experienced by the spectator at the Count's situation (deriving in large measure from the fact that he is a man) invites a comparison between the capabilities of the sexes. The assumed inferiority that would warrant the conventional subjugation of women and justify the spectator's discomfort at Bertram's predicament is not borne out in the course of the action, which consistently elevates the female characters and exposes the limitations of the masculine world. The King's male physicians, for all their presumed skill (cf. I.iii.232–7), are unable to effect his cure; Bertram is disobedient, easily swayed and mendacious (cf. II.iii.261ff.; II.iii.274–82;

V.iii.80ff.); while Parolles is a garrulous coward, ready to betray his comrades to save his own life (cf. IV.iii.113ff.). The Countess, by contrast, is wise and generous (cf. her conduct towards Helena and her son); Helena is courageous and capable of self-sacrifice (cf. her plan to win the King, and readiness to abjure the world for her husband's sake [III.iv.4–17]), while Diana and the Widow who aid Helena in Florence, are quick to come to another's aid (cf. IV.vii, *passim*). The 'masculine' virtues, in short, are here exhibited not by the male characters, but by the women whom Bertram attempts to position within their traditional roles, while it is the men who display the physical and mental deficiencies conventionally associated with the female sex. The uneasiness aroused in Act II scene iii by the seemingly demeaning position in which the hero is placed is thus set in a wider context that serves to authenticate the Clown's recognition that a 'man [can] be at woman's command, and yet no hurt done' (I.iii.89–90).

Whereas the marriage between the knight and the damsel constitutes the climax of the conventional tale and the moment of joyful renewal in a cycle of death and rebirth, in Shakespeare's antithetical version of the story the heroine's election of her husband initiates a period of sterility and decay. While Boccaccio's Count merely 'sought the King's permission to depart [after his marriage] saying that he wished to return to his own estates and consummate his marriage there', [but instead] 'came to Tuscany, where he learned that the Florentines were waging war' (p. 308), Shakespeare's reluctant husband repeatedly stresses his refusal to share a bed with his bride (cf. 'I will not bed her', 'I'll to the Tuscan wars and never bed her' [II.iii.266 and 269]), and declines in an enactment of the non-consummation of their union to understand her request for a kiss:

> Hel. I am not worthy of the wealth I owe,
> Nor dare I say 'tis mine – and yet it is;
> But, like a timorous thief, most fain would steal
> What law does vouch mine own.
> Ber.   What would you have?
> Hel. Something, and scarce so much; nothing indeed.
> I would not tell you what I would, my lord.
> Faith, yes:
> Strangers and foes do sunder and not kiss.
> Ber. I pray you, stay not, but in haste to horse.
>   (II.v.79–87)

Rather than acceding to Helena's and the King's wishes, he resolves while still in Paris to throw himself into a conflict of no relevance to his own land, preferring the dangers of battle to his wife's bed (cf. 'I'll send her straight away. Tomorrow / I'll to the wars, she to her single sorrow' [II.iii.291–2]).

Helena's career subsequent to her repudiation by Bertram also bears witness to the sterility proceeding from the Count's decision. Just as the youthful husband leaves his native land for the Italian wars, where he turns to lust rather than sanctified love, so Helena leaves France on a pilgrimage, abjuring the world and thus all hope of fruition:

> I am Saint Jaques' pilgrim, thither gone.
> Ambitious love hath so in me offended
> That barefoot plod I the cold ground upon,
> With sainted vow my faults to have amended.
> ...
> Bless him [Bertram] at home in peace, whilst I from far
> His name with zealous fervour sanctify.
> His taken labours bid him me forgive;
> I, his despiteful Juno, sent him forth
> From courtly friends, with camping foes to live
> Where death and danger dogs the heels of worth.
> He is too good and fair for death and me;
> Whom I myself embrace to set him free.
>
> (III.iv.4–17)

Though Helena's quest is finally achieved at the end of the play, and a process of renewal is implied in that she is pregnant by her husband, it is notable that the closing moments of the action again hold up a mirror to the ending of the conventional story through a significant reshaping of Boccaccio's tale. Whereas in the *Decameron*, Gilette prostrates herself before her husband, having fulfilled his conditions for winning his acceptance, and is raised by the Count who smothers her 'with kisses and embraces' (p. 314), Helena retains her ascendancy over Bertram throughout the closing scene, fulfilling her desires and holding out the promise of a new order in both claiming and reclaiming the husband she has won. Bertram's misconduct is at once recapitulated and augmented, in that he denies his discreditable behaviour towards Diana, and it is Helena who comes to his rescue, exculpating him of incontinency and suspected murder. Rather than magnanimously accepting his wife, Bertram is driven to recognise his own faults, and embraces the opportunity for social rehabilitation that his marriage offers in a spirit not of joy but of relief. Once again, it is the women, rather than the men, who function as the force of renewal in the world of the play, and the reiteration of the gnomic title in the King's closing lines ('All yet seems well, and if it end so meet' [V.iii.327]) serves, like the Clown's comment, to justify the propriety of the denouement.

While *All's Well That Ends Well* may be regarded as a radical reworking of that group of stories represented by Wilkins' tale of the shipwrecked prince, Wilkins' narrative itself is indebted to another Shakespearian play. *Pericles*, probably written some three or four years after the composition of *All's Well*, is based upon Book 8 of John Gower's *Confessio Amantis* (1393) and Laurence Twine's *The Patterne of Painefull Adventures* (c.1594), and it is from the Shakespearian play, augmented with material derived from Twine, that Wilkins' story, in turn, is constructed. Unlike *All's Well That Ends Well*, *Pericles* is firmly located from the outset within the framework of romance, the action distanced from the audience by a mediaeval narrator who is at pains to assert the antiquity of the tale he has come to present:

> To sing a song that old was sung,
> From ashes ancient Gower is come,
> Assuming man's infirmities,
> To glad your ear, and please your eyes.
> It hath been sung at festivals,
> On ember-eves and holy-ales;
> And lords and ladies in their lives
> Have read it for restoratives:
> The purchase is to make men glorious,
> *Et bonum quo antiquius eo melius.*
> (1 Chorus, 1–10)

The action follows the career of the title figure, who sets off to win a bride by solving a riddle but discovers a dangerous secret and is obliged to flee his land, losing his possessions, and falling victim to the elements, but finally achieving a wife, a daughter and the approbation of the gods through the exhibition of manly virtue. While the plot confirms the dramatist's indebtedness to the chivalric romance, however, and itself contributes through Wilkins' redaction, to the evolution of the tradition, the action simultaneously reveals Shakespeare's awareness of his own earlier work in the process of composition. Having been shipwrecked and succoured by fishermen, Pericles presents himself at the court of Simonides, taking part in a tournament, and winning the admiration through his gentility and prowess of the princess, Thaisa. Aware of his daughter's feelings, Simonides confronts his impoverished guest, seeking to force him to disclose his love of the youthful princess:

Sim.	Let me ask you one thing:
	What do you think of my daughter, sir?
Per.	A most virtuous princess.
Sim.	And she is fair too, is she not?
Per.	As a fair day in summer, wondrous fair.
Sim.	Sir, my daughter thinks very well of you;
	Ay, so well, that you must be her master,
	And she will be your scholar: therefore look to it.
Per.	I am unworthy for her schoolmaster.
Sim.	She thinks not so; peruse this writing else.
	...
Per.	[*Kneels.*] O, seek not to entrap me, gracious lord,
	A stranger and distressed gentleman,
	That never aim'd so high to love your daughter,
	But bent all offices to honour her.
	...
Sim.	Here comes my daughter, she can witness it.
	Enter Thaisa.
Per.	Then, as you are as virtuous as fair,
	Resolve your angry father, if my tongue
	Did e'er solicit, or my hand subscribe
	To any syllable that made love to you.
Thai.	Why, sir, say if you had, who takes offence
	At that would make me glad?
Sim.	Yea, mistress, are you so peremptory?
	Aside. I am glad on't with all my heart. –
	I'll tame you, I'll bring you in subjection.
	...
	Therefore hear you, mistress: either frame
	Your will to mine; and you, sir, hear you:
	Either be rul'd by me, or I'll make you –
	Man and wife.
	(II.v.32–83)

This scene clearly has much in common with the encounter between Helena and the Countess in *All's Well That Ends Well*, Act I scene iii, and it is hard to believe that the dramatist was not conscious of the earlier play while composing the later scene. In both instances a seemingly possessive parent challenges a person of low condition with having fallen in love with their only child, inviting the members of the audience to anticipate an angry confrontation and the frustration of a suit. In the event, however, both parents violate audience expectation through the magnanimity of their behaviour, recognising the virtue of the superficially unworthy lover and actively promoting the match. The similarity between the two scenes helps to confirm the dramatist's conception of *All's Well That Ends Well* as a version of the chivalric quest, while exhibiting the process of reversal at work in the construction of the play. In *Pericles* the angry parent is a father, the conventional head of the family group, while the superficially unworthy lover is in fact of noble blood, his true rank obscured by a series of misfortunes. The object of their debate is a virtuous princess, who has been quick to recognise her lowly suitor's worth, and whose wishes therefore coincide with those of her father. In *All's Well That Ends Well*, by contrast, the seemingly hostile parent is a maternal figure, while the unworthy suitor is a female dependent, whose only dowry is her inherent worth. The object of their debate, the Countess's son, is of dubious virtue, while his desires run counter to those of his mother in that he is reluctant to embrace her choice. Where *Pericles* looks backwards through its narrator to a legendary antiquity in which gender stereotypes hold good, *All's Well That Ends Well* presents a less self-consciously fictive world, inverting romance conventions and thus subjecting the ideology encoded within them to fresh inspection.

It is this process of defamiliarisation exemplified in the relationship between these two scenes that makes *All's Well That Ends Well* a key text for contemporary gender studies. At the heart of the twentieth-century feminist project is the exposure of the constructed nature of social institutions, and *All's Well That Ends Well* with its inversion of sexual norms is readily appropriated to this agenda. Where the 'purchase' of Gower's tale is 'to make *men* glorious' (1 Chorus, 9), the drive of *All's Well That Ends Well* is towards the achievement of a female 'project' (cf. 'My project may deceive me, / But my intents are fix'd, and will not leave me' [I.i.224–5], giving the play a striking modernity. While *Pericles* and its narrative offshoot endorse the proposition that '*Et bonum quo antiquius eo melius*'[15] (1 Chorus, 10), *All's Well That Ends Well* challenges the assumption that all old things are necessarily good.

From Leah Scragg, *Shakespeare's Alternative Tales* (London and New York, 1996), pp. 106–30.

Notes

[Leah Scragg's essay thoughtfully explores the sources and analogues of *All's Well That Ends Well*. She argues for the play as a version of the chivalric quest, a form of narrative that was clearly popular in Shakespeare's time, although open occasionally to high parody, such as in Francis Beaumont's *The Knight of the Burning Pestle* (1607). Scragg points to a 'process of reversal' in Shakespeare's treatment of the chivalric theme, especially at work in the relations between parents and children and between sets of lovers, which gives the play a special importance to readers interested in gender studies and the construction of social identity. The historical scholarship at work here is impressive, as Scragg throws new light on the sheer complexity of Shakespeare's reading of sources. At the same time the essay shows how her work helped open up new issues concerning gender, which became a key focus for Shakespearean criticism in the 1990s, and remains so to the present. This extract is characteristic of the book as a whole, which ranges across Shakespeare's plays and their sources, shedding new light on the way that Renaissance audiences were invited to interrogate the assumptions made, particularly about gender, in the tales that circulated around and within the Shakespearean canon. References are to the New Arden editions of Shakespeare's plays. Ed.]

1. A cloth shirt, usually of rich material, attached to the doublet and extending from waist to knee.

2. i.e. motto.

3. Based upon the text in Kenneth Muir (ed.), *The Painfull Adventures of Pericles Prince of Tyre* (Liverpool, 1967) but with modernised spelling and punctuation. The extracts quoted are from ch. 4 but for the closing sentence which is drawn from ch. 6.

4. Sometimes referred to as the *peregrinatio* (Latin, 'travel') motif.

5. Compare the story of Sir Perceval who also emerges from humble origins to become one of the foremost of Arthur's knights.

6. First published in 1566 and expanded in 1567 and 1575.

7. For a fuller discussion of the folk tale motifs brought together in *All's Well That Ends Well*, see Geoffrey Bullough, *Narrative and Dramatic Sources of Shakespeare*, vol. 2 (London, 1957–75), pp. 375ff; W. W. Lawrence, *Shakespeare's Problem Comedies*, Penguin Shakespeare Library edition (London, 1969), pp. 48ff; and Leah Scragg, *Shakespeare's Mouldy Tales* (London and New York, 1992), pp. 100ff.

8. Quoted from G. H. McWilliam (ed.), *The Decameron*, Penguin Classics (Harmondsworth, 1972), p. 305. All subsequent references to Boccacio's work are to this edition.

9. Quoted from the 1575 edition in Bullough, *Narrative and Dramatic Sources of Shakespeare*, vol. 2, p. 389, but with modernised spelling and punctuation. All subsequent references to Painter's story are to this edition.

10. Her 'poor, but honest' friends (I.iii.190) are referred to in the past tense.

11. For a fuller discussion of the first of these figures, see below. Whereas both the Countess and the Widow who comes to Helena's aid in the close of Act III are known for their virtue, widows are generally noted for their lack of sexual restraint on the Renaissance stage (cf. John Marston's *The Insatiate Countess*, c.1610–13).

12. The first lines of *Macbeth* are spoken by the Witches, but as bearded creatures who 'look not like th'inhabitants o'th'earth' (I.iii.41) their sexual nature is ambiguous.

13. See, for example, Jeanne Addison French, *The Shakespearean Wild: Geography, Genus, Gender* (Nebraska, 1991), *passim*.

14. See also the vicious Queen in Shakespeare's *Cymbeline* for a typical example of this figure.

15. 'And the older a good thing is, the better it is.'

3

The Political Effects of Gender and Class in *All's Well That Ends Well*

PETER ERICKSON

One of the most striking features of *All's Well That Ends Well* is its full rendering of specifically male frustration in the person of Bertram, a besieged and recalcitrant Adonis writ large.[1] But the problem of Bertram cannot be adequately discussed at the level of individual character, as though our response hinged exclusively on the question of his personal defects and of his capacity to overcome them in the end. The analysis must rather be extended to the larger cultural forces operating on, and embodied in, Bertram. This latter approach can be opened up by noting the cultural overlap between Bertram's situation and that of the Essex-Southampton group: in both cases an emphatically military definition of masculinity is placed under intense pressure and ultimately frustrated. Yet the equation of Bertram with Southampton in G. P. V. Akrigg's reading of *All's Well That Ends Well* constitutes a methodological obstacle to this interpretation.[2] Treated as literal topical allusions, such connections are impossible to prove and are readily dismissed by a stringently factual account such as Samuel Schoenbaum's: 'Shakespeare did not again dedicate one of his writings to a noble lord. Southampton now departs from the biographical record.'[3] However, by responding at the same level as the critics he rejects, Schoenbaum remains within the framework of a limited historical mode now challenged by new historicists, among others.

For a cultural analysis of *All's Well That Ends Well*, Mervyn James's essay 'At a Crossroads of the Political Culture: The Essex Revolt, 1601' provides a more promising and substantial starting point than Akrigg's narrowly conceived work.[4] Two elements in James's study of the cultural formation of the Essex-Southampton group have a strong resonance with Bertram's predicament. First, this historically specific male identity had its source in a military subculture, creating a concept of manhood that was potentially volatile, destabilising, and anachronistic.

> But what gave the Essex connection its special tone, and many of its cultural characteristics, was its strongly military orientation. ... Moreover, the military relationship had been given a special aura, of a traditionalist and chivalric kind, by the lavish way in which Essex, in spite of the queen's protests, had used his military prerogative to confer the honour of knighthood on those who distinguished themselves under him on the field. ... To those who received it [as Southampton did], knighthood implied a special relationship with Essex himself.
>
> (pp. 427–8)

As the clause 'in spite of the queen's protests' suggests, this male bonding and solidarity is defensive – a defiant assertion of threatened male privilege:

> Yet the sense of ancestry, in the Essexian context, strikes a special note: often self-confidently arrogant, but marked by a nostalgia for past glories, and a sense of being, as it were, under siege. ... The sense of political frustration, of being unjustly slighted and so their honour defaced, was an experience shared with the leader by many courtier Essexians also, including such peers as ... the earl of Southampton.
>
> (pp. 433–4)

Second, the gendered quality of this thwarted masculinity was accentuated by the mutually suspicious relationship between the cult of male military honour and the cult of Elizabeth. The latter appeared to place men in a double bind because the queen both stimulated chivalric heroism and curbed it – a bind which made graphically clear the queen's female rule and against which Essex bridled in sexual terms:

> Yet his relationship to the queen nevertheless became progressively charged with a tension which contained the seeds of violence. The tension, rooted in political failure and exclusion, was related to his view of their respective sexual roles. ... Essex never wavered in the

conviction that, when important decisions had to be made, the weaknesses of the queen's femininity must be overwhelmed by a rough masculine initiative. ... The so-called 'great Quarrel' of July 1598, the point of no return in relations between Essex and the queen, generated so much bitterness precisely because of the earl's assessment of their respective sexual roles in terms of honour. For by striking him in the course of a Council meeting at which he had rudely turned his back on her, the queen had shown an unnatural male aggressiveness, and had thus submitted Essex to the unbearable dishonour which a publicly administered woman's blow involved. ... He himself replied with a violent gesture, clapping his hand to his sword, and equally violent words, till the other councillors separated them.

(pp. 443–5)

Even before Helena's action has transformed the king into a vehicle for her power, Bertram has already figured the obstruction of his military drive as female:

> I shall stay here the forehorse to a smock,
> Creaking my shoes on the plain masonry,
> Till honour be brought up, and no sword worn
> But to dance with.

(2.1.30–3)

The contrast with *Henry V* is instructive. The military aspirations of Hal as Henry V are given wide scope. The new king's qualms of conscience may create residual complications, but there are no external impediments to stop the forward movement of his nationalist enterprise.[5] Bertram's heroic ambition is sharply circumscribed, his military adventure accorded only abbreviated and truncated dramatisation. Military achievement is discounted and devalued in advance by being presented as a delaying action, an escapist diversion from the central issue – Helena's strongly registered claim: 'his sword can never win / The honour that he loses' (III.ii.93–4); 'The great dignity that his valour hath here acquired for him shall at home be encount'red with a shame as ample' (IV.iii.65–7).

Like Essex, Bertram uses military service as a cultural escape route that enables him to establish a field of male action in a remote location whose distance from the female-dominated central court temporarily affords a measure of protection. But Helena invades this space, thus intensifying the conflict between male prerogative and female rule. While Helena may not match the queen's 'unnatural male aggressiveness' as experienced by Essex, her determined pursuit of Bertram is nevertheless sufficiently forceful and relentless to constitute aggression.[6] *All's Well That Ends Well* thus hits a sensitive cultural nerve, and the open question announced in the title is less one of aesthetics than of sexual politics: can all end well if female power undercuts male heroism?

Mervyn James, citing the Chorus that begins Act V of *Henry V* (V.Cho.29–35), attributes to Shakespeare a strictly orthodox attitude supporting the queen's position with regard to Essex: 'So Shakespeare had seen. ... It was as "the general of our gracious empress" that the earl's heroic image as the embodiment of lineage, arms and honour acquired validity' (p. 452).[7] However, in the larger context of *Henry V*, the effect of this circumspect, correct statement of Essex's subordination to Elizabeth is complicated and counteracted by the appeal of Henry V's male prowess, which runs roughshod over Queen Isabel and Princess Kate in the final scene. In order to make the parallel with Elizabeth-Essex work, Henry V has to occupy both positions: he is both chivalric warrior and monarch, and his dual role displaces Elizabeth as a specifically female ruler. This effect is confirmed by the way subsequent dramatic events assert male domination in Henry V's high-handed appropriation of Katherine: Henry V in the most decisive manner reverses Essex's subordinate position. The uneasy coexistence of two quite different models of male–female relations – the Choric acknowledgement of female authorisation of male chivalry and the dramatisation of male self-authorisation – creates an impression of ambivalence.[8]

This ambivalent response to female authority is pronounced in *All's Well That Ends Well*, where female bonds are strengthened as male bonds are correspondingly weakened: the Countess displays 'a more rooted love' (IV.v.12) toward Helena than is possible for Queen Isabel toward her daughter in *Henry V*, while the chivalric ties glorified in *Henry V* (IV.vii) are denied outright by the satiric exposure of the Parolles–Bertram relationship in *All's Well That Ends Well* (IV.iii.79–311).[9] The Countess's extraordinary readiness to renounce her son Bertram provides a reminder of Queen Elizabeth's ability to sever relations with her male courtiers.

I

One way of minimising Helena's effect is to deny the full impact of her power by portraying it as narrowly and exclusively channelled against Bertram as an individual rather than against the social structure as a whole. This version presents Bertram as an isolated target by stressing Helena's alliance with the older generation. But Helena's interactions with the King of France cannot be characterised as cooperation or service. Rather, her rescue of the king calls attention to his ongoing weakness as nominal head of government while dramatising, by contrast, her own achievement of power to be used for her own ends. The image of male order is vulnerable not simply because Bertram is a weak link in an otherwise solid chain but also because there is no convincing, living embodiment of the ancestral 'first father' (III.vii.25) elsewhere in the play as the king himself conspicuously demonstrates.

The opening lines of the play focus attention on the King of France as the centre of a patriarchal social system, raising high expectations about his capacity to repair breaks in the family network. According to the extended family metaphor developed by Lafew, the king will restore the loss of Bertram's father by offering himself as a paternal equivalent. Thus Bertram is encouraged to see the king as 'a father' (I.i.6–7). The first encounter between the king and Bertram in Act I, scene ii, reinforces this logic. The king begins the meeting by recognising the link between Bertram and his dead father: 'Youth, thou bear'st thy father's face' (I.ii.19).[10] He ends the session by confirming his ability to serve as a paternal substitute and by this mediation to preserve the potential for the continuity of male heritage: 'Welcome, count; / My son's no dearer' (ll.75–6). Yet the smooth functioning of this father–son framework is jeopardised by the irritation aroused in the king by the prospect of his replacement by the younger generation. The king's nostalgic identification with Bertram's father leads to a heightened contrast between older and younger generations at the latter's expense that threatens to forestall the larger momentum of generational continuity: 'Such a man / Might be a copy to these younger times; / Which, followed well, would demonstrate them now / But goes backward' (I.ii.45–8).[11] Pursuing this invidious comparison between the noble past 'when thy father and myself in friendship / First tried our soldiership' (ll.25–6) and the unsatisfactory present of the new generation, the king rehearses a set of highly charged emotions: rage over his ageing and demise ('But on us both did haggish age steal on, / And wore us out of act' [ll.29–30]), resistance to yielding control, defensive antagonism toward his eventual successors, desire for reassurance and appreciation.

The feelings released in the king by Bertram's presence are by no means unprecedented. From the perspective of the *Henriad*, the unstable mood created by the king's critique of male youth can be seen as a standard feature of the generational tension fathers and sons must negotiate. Like the King of France in *All's Well That Ends Well*, Henry IV is a sick king who initiates contact with his youthful counterpart by lashing out against him:

> See, sons, what things you are,
> How quickly nature falls into revolt
> When gold becomes her object!
> For this the foolish over-careful fathers
> Have broke their sleep with thoughts,
> Their brains with care, their bones with industry;
> For this they have engrossed and pil'd up
> The canker'd heaps of strange-achieved gold;
> For this they have been thoughtful to invest
> Their sons with arts and martial exercises;
> When, like the bee, tolling from every flower
> The virtuous sweets,
> Our thighs pack'd with wax, our mouths with honey,
> We bring it to the hive; and like the bees
> Are murder'd for our pains. This bitter taste
> Yields his engrossments to the ending father.
> (2HIV, IV.V. 64–79)

Henry IV's accusation registers the combined explosive pressure of self-pity and anger to which the King of France gives vent. In particular, citing the 'good melancholy' (I.ii.56) of Bertram's father, he employs the same despairing image of the beehive:

> 'Let me not live,' quoth he,
> 'After my flame lacks oil, to be the snuff
> Of younger spirits, whose apprehensive senses
> All but new things disdain; whose judgments are
> Mere fathers of their garments; whose constancies
> Expire before their fashions.' This he wish'd.
> I, after him, do after him wish too,
> Since I nor wax nor honey can bring home,
> I quickly were dissolved from my hive
> To give some labourers room.
> (ll.58–67)

The sarcastic play on the term *father* – 'mere fathers of their garments' – is reminiscent of Henry IV's challenge to Hal's apparent contempt: 'Thy wish was father, Harry, to that thought' (*2HIV*, IV.v.92).

But there is a striking difference in the operation of the bee metaphor that the two kings share. In Henry IV's case, the image conveys richness and abundance: 'Our thighs pack'd with wax, our mouths with honey' (*2HIV*, IV.v.76). The language suggests, even during his momentary despair, a conviction about Henry IV's power and desire to give the crown. The King of France, however, confesses utter depletion and inadequacy, as though he were completely lacking in resources: 'Since I nor wax nor honey can bring home' (I.ii.65). The contrast between fullness and emptiness is emblematic of larger differences in the two situations.

Henry IV's angry outburst is quickly followed by reconciliation, the transmission of royal authority, and the commitment to military action. Henry IV and Hal manage their conflict by themselves without outside interference. The erotic force suggested by the image of Henry IV's 'full thighs' is fulfilled in the intimate emotional exchange between two powerful men. The political resonance of the honey image is later realised in *Henry V* in the 'sweet and honey'd sentences' (I.i.50) which the Archbishop of Canterbury attributes to the new king and in Canterbury's own elaboration of the male state as a beehive (I.ii.187–204).

In *All's Well That Ends Well* decisive action comes from outside male relations. Helena's intervention is what interrupts the sense of drift. She provides the energy and direction needed to overcome the impasse created by the king's listlessness. In the transaction between the king and Bertram, Helena is 'this good gift' (II.iii.151), the object of exchange parallel to the crown which Henry IV gives to Hal. But Helena herself determines the terms of this gift giving. Not only does Bertram receive for his inheritance something he does not want but also the king gives him something which he did not plan and to which he has been forced to agree by the bargain that revived him. The king tries to transform his test of wills with Bertram into an exclusively man-to-man confrontation, but Helena's prior organisational role is too strong. The occasion will not compose into the standard pattern of male traffic in women who serve as incidental tokens by which men determine their relations of power to one another.

Helena's role as a woman who disrupts the normal procedures of patriarchal power can be registered only by a thorough examination of the extent of the king's – and hence the system's – weakness, for this weakness creates a political vacuum that helps to make Helena's control possible. From the outset, the King of France exudes an overall spirit of lassitude and exhaustion consistent with the specific emptiness communicated by his use of the honey motif in his first appearance. Lafew's idealised encomium invoking the king's 'abundance' (I.i.10) is no sooner pronounced than it is undercut by the Countess's abrupt leading question about the king's health (I.i.11), which shifts the emphasis to his incapacity. The king toward whom Lafew directs reparative hopes is himself an empty centre in need of restoration. Moreover, his debilitated condition is not merely a physical problem, but is symbolic of a more general malaise.

Even before Bertram's arrival at court, the king's handling of the business of the Florentine-Sienese war raises doubts about his leadership. His decision to avoid committing the state seems less a matter of sound judgement than of abdication because the policy of noninvolvement is compromised by his further decision to endorse private actions whose effect is random and in principle self-cancelling since individuals are free to fight on either side. The contradictory nature of the king's policy is underlined by the strained language of his subsequent farewell to the two separate – and opposed – groups of young French nobles: 'Share the advice betwixt you; if both gain all, / The gift doth stretch itself as 'tis receiv'd, / And is enough for both' (II.i.3–5). What is being stretched here is the king's logic: the phrase 'both gain all' tries unsuccessfully to deny the division that he himself has introduced.

The cynical aspect of this approach is brought out by the attendant lord's observation: 'It well may serve / A nursery to our gentry, who are sick / For breathing and exploit' (I.ii.15–17). The allusion to sickness generalises the king's personal ill health, suggesting wider cultural malfunction. The patent inability in a subsequent commentary to explain the king's rationale retroactively exposes the hollowness of the king's decision making:

> The reasons of our state I cannot yield,
> But like a common and an outward man
> That the great figure of council frames
> By self-unable motion; therefore dare not
> Say what I think of it, since I have found
> Myself in my incertain grounds to fail
> As often as I guess'd.
> (III.i.10–16)

The king appears to sponsor an ideal of heroic honour, but this honour is vitiated in advance. Through the lack of coherent and principled policy, the king contributes to the conditions for the youthful drift which he goes on to complain about in his initial meeting with Bertram: the king is thus responsible for what he criticises.

Moreover, the king's attitude toward women exhibits the callousness for which he will later so vigorously prosecute Bertram. Like Polonius's tolerance of his son's 'wanton, wild and usual slips' (*Hamlet*, II.i.22), the king's gratuitous final bit of advice to the departing French nobles gives permission for sexual adventure after military service, if not before:

> Those girls of Italy, take heed of them;
> They say our French lack language to deny
> If they demand; beware of being captives
> Before you serve.
>   (II.i.19–22)

Bertram's engagement with Diana conforms to this set of priorities, and his later excuse that he 'boarded her i' th' wanton way of youth' (V.iii.210) fits with the winking spirit of the king's initial formulation. Furthermore, the king's sly generalisation about 'Those girls of Italy' licenses the contemptuous attitude which Bertram exhibits – she 'was a common gamester of the camp' (V.iii.187) – and to which the king himself momentarily succumbs – 'I think thee now some common customer' (l.280).

What convinces the king to undergo Helena's treatment is her willingness so emphatically to differentiate herself from the dangerously seductive foreign women the king has warned against (II.i. 169–73). But this distinction becomes insecure, blurred by the sexual overtones of the power by which Helena performs the king's rejuvenation. Helena's success confirms her control: she gains the initiative and the king loses it. In designating Bertram as her choice, Helena tries to mitigate her power by moderating her language: 'I dare not say I take you, but I give / Me and my service, ever whilst I live, / Into your guiding power. This is the man' (II.iii.102–4). But the 'guiding power' is all too clearly neither Bertram's nor the king's. Helena's negotiation with the king has already unmistakably established her primacy through the decisive phrase 'I will command': 'Then shalt thou give me with thy kingly hand / What husband in thy power I will command' (II.i.192–3). By his consent to this proposition, the king shows that he too 'lacks language to deny / If they [women] demand' (ll.20–1).

Despite the king's cure, he remains exceedingly vulnerable, truculent and ineffectual for the rest of the play. In between his two meetings with Bertram the king's confidence has been recovered through Helena's agency. His earlier despair gives way to renewed conviction in his 'sovereign power and father's voice' (II.iii.54). But the second encounter with Bertram in Act II, scene iii, demonstrates the king's continuing weakness because circumstances draw the king into an overreaction that reveals his insecurity, making the restored self seem defensive and unstable. Forced to 'produce my power' (l.150), the king resorts to a harsher version of his earlier tendency to blame the younger generation for all problems when he threatens Bertram: 'Or I will throw thee from my care forever / Into the staggers and careless lapse / Of youth and ignorance' (ll.162–4). This outburst dramatises the king's own flaws as much as Bertram's, for the king's need to apply pressure so heavy-handedly to Bertram stems from the pressure of the king's prior submission to Helena's intervention. Bertram's resistance calls attention to the king's own ongoing dependence on Helena: 'But follows it, my lord, to bring me down / Must answer for your raising?' (ll.112–13). By his refusal to cooperate, Bertram upsets the smooth operation of a scenario that would allow the king to deflect his dependence by passing it on to the younger man and making him share it.

Helena's relations with the king and with Bertram form parallel actions: in both cases, she meets with resistance which she successfully overcomes by manifesting her superior power. Uneasiness about the triumph of a woman's demand is by no means confined to Bertram. The king's psychological and institutional discomfort is suggested by the lengths to which he goes in his coercion of Bertram. It is as though the king is constrained to deny his own doubts by aggressively suppressing them in Bertram. Yet the completion of the process in which Bertram is 'crush'd with a plot' fails to satisfy the king because it does not bring relief from the fundamental problem of his own dependence on a woman. The king's offer to Diana at the end of the play – 'If thou beest yet a fresh uncropped flower / Choose thou thy husband and I'll pay thy dower' (V.iii.321–2) – is not a simple repetition. Rather, it represents a compulsive effort to redo the plot to make it come out right: this time he, not the woman, seizes the initiative. If the proposal is his, then the male control that he has lost can be reasserted. The irony of this logic is that his proposal is so closely modelled on Helena's original proposition that it testifies to her power rather than to his. But the irony is not a lighthearted one. Though brief, this moment signals a deep and continuing uneasiness with female control.

II

The course of Helena's love in *All's Well That Ends Well* has the effect of reconstituting a combined image of Venus and Diana;[12] she therefore reconnects the female attributes that the poetic sequence from *Venus and Adonis* to *The Rape of Lucrece* had split apart. Helena succeeds, where Venus spectacularly failed, in the conquest of a resistant male. Moreover, Helena also recuperates Lucrece's humility and passivity; for Helena's occasional hesitation and submissiveness, which seem to compromise her assertiveness, act rather as a sign of the virtue that sanctions and strengthens her position. The difference between Venus's and Helena's ambition is that the latter is more difficult, virtually impossible, to fault. Venus's violation carries with it a suggestion of illegitimacy that permits us to label her action as in some sense wrong. Helena's triumph is licensed by a moral justification akin to the merry wives' riddling self-defence that they 'may be merry and yet honest too' (*The Merry Wives of Windsor*, IV.ii.96):

> Why then tonight
> Let us assay our plot; which, if it speed,
> Is wicked meaning in a lawful dead,
> And lawful meaning in a lawful act,
> Where both not sin, and yet a sinful fact.
> (III.vii.43–7)

Two critical formulations lead to an underestimation of Helena's disruptive social significance. The first, exemplified by G. K. Hunter's introduction to the New Arden edition, diminishes the threat of Helena's initiative by stressing her personal submissiveness and her religious reliance on divine agency. Too neatly dividing the play into two parts, Hunter sees Helena's pilgrimage – 'a journey of contrition and abnegation' (p. xxxi) – as the turning point and confines her active role to the first half: 'In the second half of *All's Well*, Helena is a "clever wench" only in the sense in which Griselda is – clever enough to be virtuous, pious, and patient till Destiny and Justice work things out for her' (p. xxxii). Recent feminist critics have challenged and refuted this characterisation of Helena by noting that the consistent forcefulness of her actions impressively outweighs her occasional recourse to passive language or diminutive tone. While acknowledging Helena's mixture of 'aggressive initiative and passivity', Susan Snyder convincingly argues that upon arrival in Florence

Helena 'takes forceful control of the action, persuading the Widow to agree to the bed-substitution, instructing Diana, pursuing Bertram back to France, seeking audience with the king, and through her agent Diana manipulating the final revelation-scene to expose Bertram, prove her fulfilment of the impossible tasks, and claim her reluctant husband all over again'.[13] Helena's oxymorons – 'humble ambition, proud humility' (I.i.167) – apply to her actions at the end as well as the beginning; she is never humble without also being ambitious and proud. There is no mistaking the crisp energy with which Helena manages Bertram's taming: 'But let's about it' (III.vii.48).

A second formulation by which Helena's dominance is tempered is to treat it as a temporary and transitional anomaly whose resolution can be found in the late romances. This motif of the postponed resolution is represented by G. K. Hunter's use of a larger developmental perspective retroactively to solve the problems of *All's Well That Ends Well*: 'Viewed in this context [of the romances], much that seems perverse in *All's Well* begins to fall into focus'; 'much of the perversity of the denouement disappears if we see it as an attempt at the effects gradually mastered in the intervening comedies, and triumphantly achieved in *The Winter's Tale*' (introduction, New Arden edition, p. lv). This approach creates difficulties, however, because it leads in my view to an inaccurate account of *The Winter's Tale*[14] and because it mutes the effect of *All's Well That Ends Well* by recuperating it in terms of another play and thereby reducing our ability to see its own terms. What is lost when *All's Well That Ends Well* is redirected toward and transposed onto the late romances? One answer is that Helena's power is discounted, since the gender dynamic of the romances requires her transformation into an enabling, cooperative heroine. But the Helena of *All's Well That Ends Well* cannot be easily translated and assimilated into the sublime female comfort exemplified by *The Winter's Tale*. In the distinctive play she dominates, Helena makes her own demands and, however cautiously, advances her own power.

The force of Helena's challenge is illustrated by the change in the king's rhetoric about class. Prior to Helena's arrival at court, the king evokes an ideal of hierarchy based on the behaviour of Bertram's dead father:

> So like a courtier, contempt nor bitterness
> Were in his pride or sharpness; if they were,

> His equal had awak'd them, and his honour,
> Clock to itself, knew the true minute when
> Exception bid him speak, and at this time
> His tongue obey'd his hand. Who were below him
> He us'd as creatures of another place,
> And bow'd his eminent top to their low ranks,
> Making them proud of his humility
> In their poor praise he humbled.
>
> (I.ii.36–45)

The witty reversal of 'proud' and 'humbled' in the final two lines depends on the firm, fixed distinction between ranks that admits no ambiguity between 'His equal' and 'Who were below him'. What is striking about this image of clear-cut class structure is that it has no room for Helena. Neither Bertram nor the king can follow this decorum because Helena refuses to accept her position as one of the 'creatures of another place'.

After Helena's decisive intervention in the court world, the king projects a very different image of class relations, now adjusted to reflect the situation into which he has been manoeuvred by the pressure of Helena's upward initiative:

> 'Tis only title thou disdain'st in her, the which
> I can build up. Strange is it that our bloods
> Of colour, weight, and heat, pour'd all together,
> Would quite confound distinction, yet stands off
> In differences so mighty. If she be
> All that is virtuous, save what thou dislik'st –
> A poor physician's daughter – thou dislik'st
> Of virtue for the name. But do not so.
> From lowest place when virtuous things proceed,
> The place is dignified by th' doer's deed.
>
> (II.iii.117–26)

In shifting from his earlier image of 'creatures of another place' who remain in 'their low ranks' (I.ii.42–3) to this more positive version of 'lowest place' (II.iii.125), the king legitimises social mobility instead of ordered stability. In so acting on Helena's behalf, however, he inadvertently names the danger that her advancement as a lower-class woman may 'quite confound distinction'.

The king emphasises his own agency – 'the which / I can build up' – but he is Helena's creation more than she is his. With Helena as prime mover and the king as the figurehead through which she pursues her own ends, the play's action confounds the conventional organising distinctions both of class and of gender.[15] The intertwined gender aspect remains pertinent because while the king enunciates a philosophical endorsement of class flexibility, Helena's practical realisation of her aspiration depends on strong support from female sponsors, one of whom, the Florentine widow, suggests an experience of class that validates Helena's enterprise. The Widow provides a living example of class fluidity, though in the reverse direction ('Though my estate be fall'n, I was well born' [III.vii.4]), and thereby serves as a mediating figure who breaks the barrier between high and low.

Following J. Dover Wilson's suggestion that the class disparity expressed by Helena's view of Bertram as 'a bright particular star / ... so above me' (I.i.84–5) is equivalent to 'the social relationship between Shakespeare and his patron',[16] C. L. Barber develops a parallel between the poet and the young man of the sonnets and Helena and Bertram. According to this analysis, *All's Well That Ends Well* represents an aggressive disengagement from the bourgeois poet's paralysing deference to the aristocratic youth in the sonnets. Feelings about the youth, who is now recast as Bertram, are released in two ways. The first exorcises the poet's adulatory stance by self-critically parodying it in the form of Parolles's empty words of affection for Bertram. The satiric treatment of Parolles is a relatively routine replaying of issues more deeply expressed in the rejection of Falstaff. The second attempts to enact the poet's vindication through Helena's highly charged conquest of the young aristocrat, despite his efforts to ignore and resist her. But this wished-for triumph is secured by a psychological shortcut: since 'Helena's project culminates in the moral aggression expended on Bertram before he accepts marriage to her, we can feel ... that the play is being *used*, rather than that its full human implications are being worked out into the light'.[17]

This interpretation presupposes an alignment between Helena and Shakespeare, who share the same 'moral aggression' against Bertram. I want to modify this version of the balance of forces by emphasising the structural ambivalence of Shakespeare's position. Helena's gender makes impossible any one-sided identification with Helena against Bertram. However enthusiastic Shakespeare's participation in the discomfiting of Bertram, there is also an undertow of residual sympathy for Bertram's plight and concomitant anxiousness over Helena's power.[18] However substantial Shakespeare's promotion of Helena's enterprise, there is no total, unimpeded, unqualified cross-gender identification on his part.[19] Helena's aggression against

Bertram is different from Shakespeare's; the latter is more limited than the former, creating a boomerang effect that pulls Shakespeare's investment in Helena up short and makes his ambivalence run both ways, toward Helena as well as toward Bertram. In this sense it is possible to reverse Barber's formulation and say that the play uses Shakespeare.

Reacting against Helena's triumph, Shakespeare remains in part sympathetically bound to the besieged male positions of both Bertram and the king; the play thereby gives voice not only to the two male characters' discomfiture but also to Shakespeare's. The authorial division that blocks a convincing resolution is significant because it dramatises a much larger cultural quandary: the society's inability to accommodate, without deep disturbance, decisive female control. If the underlying restiveness of *All's Well That Ends Well* gives way in *Hamlet* to open misogynist attack, this shift is made possible in part by the drastic decrease in female power and control. Deprived of the delicate balance between sexuality and purity by which Helena wins her position as wife, the wife in *Hamlet* is left isolated, exposed and vulnerable.

From Peter Erickson, *Rewriting Shakespeare, Rewriting Ourselves* (Berkeley and Los Angeles, 1991), pp. 57–73.

Notes

[This essay is taken from Peter Erickson's full-length study *Rewriting Shakespeare, Rewriting Ourselves* which compellingly takes the reader into historical and more recent debates over the meaning of canon, culture and reading communities. The book was ground-breaking in the early 1990s for offering a model of 'multicultural' literary criticism. In the extract reproduced here Erickson starts by addressing issues of masculinity and military identity, cross-referencing *All's Well That Ends Well* with the figure of Henry V and exploring the relationship between Shakespeare's work and the haunting historical figure of Essex. Questions of identity are to the fore in terms of class, gender and power in this reading of *All's Well That Ends Well*, which remains one of the most original and thought-provoking interpretations of the play. References are to the New Arden editions of Shakespeare's plays. Ed.]

1. The date for *All's Well That Ends Well* is uncertain. G. K. Hunter gives 'a tentative dating' of 1603–4 in the New Arden edition of the play (London, 1959), p. xxv; Anne Barton specifies 1602–3 in *The Riverside Shakespeare* (Boston, 1973), p. 502; David Bevington indicates a range of 1601–4 in his Bantam edition (1988), p. 263. Given the uncertainty, it

may be possible to view the play both in Elizabethan and in Jacobean terms. My goal, however, is to place the play in its Elizabethan context.

2. G. P. V. Akrigg, *Shakespeare and the Earl of Southampton* (Cambridge, MA, 1968), pp. 255–6.

3. S. Schoenbaum, *William Shakespeare: A Compact Documentary Life* (New York, rev. edn 1987), p. 179. Schoenbaum similarly denies any significant connection between Shakespeare and Essex. Reviewing the circumstance of the staging of *Richard II* prior to Essex's revolt, Schoenbaum finds no involvement on Shakespeare's part (*Documentary Life*, pp. 217–19; 'Richard II and the Realities of Power', *Shakespeare and Others* [Washington, DC, 1985], pp. 86–90).

4. Mervyn James, 'At a Crossroads of the Political Culture: The Essex Revolt, 1601', *Society, Politics and Culture: Studies in Early Modern England* (Cambridge, 1986), pp. 416–65. Also relevant is James's earlier essay on honour culture, 'English Politics and the Concept of Honour, 1485–1642', pp. 308–415, which shows how in response to 'the facts of social mobility' a redefinition of honour occurred that tended 'to present honour, virtue and nobility as detachable from their anchorage in pedigree and descent' (p. 375). The struggle between Helena and Bertram is in part a conflict between new and old ideas of honour.

5. I do not discount the critical perspective on Henry V built into the play, which I have discussed in ' "The fault / My father made": The Anxious Pursuit of Heroic Fame in Shakespeare's *Henry V'*, *Modern Language Studies*, 10, 1 (Winter 1979–80), 10–25, and in chapter 2 of *Patriarchal Structures in Shakespeare's Drama* (Berkeley and Los Angeles, 1985), pp. 39–65. My concern here, however, is to emphasise the relative contrast between Henry V and Bertram.

6. There is a line of criticism – from Clifford Leech's 'The Theme of Ambition in "All's Well That Ends Well" ', *English Literary History*, 21 (1954), 17–29, to Richard A. Levin's *'All's Well That Ends Well*, and "All Seems Well" ', *Shakespeare Studies*, 13 (1980), 131–44 – that provides ample testimony to the perception of Helena's ambition and power. However, in the absence of a feminist perspective, the cultural significance of her ambition is lost and this criticism amounts to a restatement of male complaint. Feminist interest in the reversal of customary gender roles whereby Helena becomes the active pursuer rather than the pursued leads to a wholly different emphasis on Helena as the centre of the play's action. See Carol Thomas Neely, chapter 2, 'Power and Virginity in the Problem Comedies: *All's Well That Ends Well*', in her *Broken Nuptials in Shakespeare's Plays* (New Haven, CT 1985), pp. 58–104; Carolyn Asp, 'Subjectivity, Desire and Female Friendship in *All's Well That Ends Well*', *Literature and Psychology*, 32, 4 (1986), 48–63 [reprinted in this volume. Ed.]; Lisa Jardine, 'Cultural Confusion and Shakespeare's Learned Heroines: "These are old paradoxes" ', *Shakespeare Quarterly*,

38 (1987), 1–18; Susan Snyder, 'All's Well That Ends Well and Shakespeare's Helens: Text and Subtext, Subject and Object', English Literary Renaissance, 18 (1988), 66–77.

7. The expected comparison would be the one between Henry V and Elizabeth with which R. Malcolm Smuts begins his 'Public Ceremony and Royal Charisma: The English Royal Entry in London, 1485–1642', in The First Modern Society: Essays in English History in Honour of Lawrence Stone, ed. A. L. Beier, David Cannadine, and James M. Rosenheim (Cambridge, 1989), pp. 65–93:

> Thus when Henry V returned from Agincourt, the Lord Mayor and Aldermen in scarlet robes, and 300 mounted citizens dressed in coats of murrey (dark purple) with gold chains around their necks, rode out to meet him at Blackheath and accompanied him back to Westminster. More than a century and a half later, in 1584, Elizabeth returned from a progress to an essentially similar welcome.
>
> (pp. 68–9)

Shakespeare's reference to Essex disrupts the continuity by marking the difference between a male king's military campaign in Agincourt and Elizabeth's domestic progresses. Annabel Patterson's discussion of the fifth Chorus, which became available only after I had completed this chapter, overlaps with mine on several points: see 'Back by Popular Demand: The Two Versions of Henry V', chapter 5 in Shakespeare and the Popular Voice (Cambridge, 1989), pp. 71–92.

8. The political tensions between Elizabeth and Essex, which Mervyn James excludes from Shakespeare's presentation, are discussed in Jonathan Dollimore and Alan Sinfield, 'History and Ideology: The Instance of Henry V', in Alternative Shakespeares, ed. John Drakakis (London, 1985), pp. 206–27, especially p. 219.

9. Carol Thomas Neely develops the contrast between the efficacy of female solidarity and the emptiness of male bonds in Broken Nuptials in Shakespeare's Plays, pp. 74–8.

10. This motif also occurs, for example, in As You Like It when Duke Senior performs a similar act of recognition for Orlando. Senior reconstitutes the father–son bond by testifying both to the son's and to his own connection to the deceased father.

11. The age/youth conflict is also enacted in a simplified, one-sided form in the encounter between Lafew and Parolles (II.iii.184–260), but the interaction between the king and Bertram is not reducible to this version. Nor is it accurate to portray Helena as siding with and supporting the older generation: her alliance with the older group serves her interests and values, not theirs.

12. In 'Bed Tricks: On Marriage as the End of Comedy in *All's Well That Ends Well* and *Measure for Measure*', in *Shakespeare's Personality*, ed. Norman H. Holland, Sidney Homan and Bernard J. Paris (Berkeley and Los Angeles, 1989), pp. 151–74, Janet Adelman discusses the psychological tension epitomised by the Venus/Diana motif in *All's Well* (pp. 160–1). I would add that an undercurrent of associations with Queen Elizabeth's female power accentuates this tension.

13. Susan Snyder, '*All's Well That Ends Well* and Shakespeare's Helens: Text and Subtext, Subject and Object', pp. 66–7. Of the four feminist critics cited in note 6, only Lisa Jardine finds Helena's power sharply diminished: 'in the second half of the play, Helena acts out an *atonement* for her "forwardness" ' that implies a 'ritual return to exemplary passivity' ('Cultural Confusion and Shakespeare's Learned Heroines: "These are old paradoxes" ', p. 11). Jardine contrasts Helena with Portia of *The Merchant of Venice:* the latter 'does not resolve the actively knowing heroine into passively tolerant wife' (p. 12). I agree with Jardine's basic point that the traditional marital terms of Helena's quest set limits to her exercise of power, but I want to complicate the comparison by suggesting that Portia's power is also qualified. Her dominance is ensured by her withdrawal to the private sphere of Belmont, her intervention in the social action of Venice having been temporary. Portia does not directly challenge the male power structure invested in the position of the Duke of Venice and she leaves it intact. By contrast, Helena's actions place the already questionable authority of the King of France into further question. Moreover, while the compliant Bassanio presents very little opposition to Portia's designs, Bertram offers determined resistance to Helena's. From this standpoint, Helena appears the more powerful figure: she triumphs over greater opposition. Finally, because she lacks the upper-class status that Portia takes for granted, Helena has to traverse a greater social distance to reach the levers of power; by this measure, Helena alters the balance of power to a degree that Portia does not and her victory is consequently more socially disruptive. This view helps to account for the comparatively more strained ending of *All's Well That Ends Well.*

14. I present an alternative, critical account in chapter 5, 'The Limitations of Reformed Masculinity in *The Winter's Tale*', in *Patriarchal Structures in Shakespeare's Drama*, pp. 148–72. In 'T. S. Eliot and the Creation of a Symbolist Shakespeare' – *Twentieth Century Literature in Retrospect* (Harvard English Studies, 2), ed. Reuben A. Brower (Cambridge, MA, 1971), pp. 191–204 – G. K. Hunter criticises Eliot's treatment, influenced by G. Wilson Knight's *The Wheel of Fire* (1930), of the late romances. However, Hunter's own method recapitulates Eliot's view. Hence the romances demonstrate 'the power of a new poetic vision', 'allowing the recognition scene to be human without infringing the symbolic power of the event' (introduction to the New Arden edition of

All's Well That Ends Well, p. lvi). Reading back from this view of the late romances projects an ideal of harmonious resolution that mitigates and distorts the experience of gender conflict in *All's Well That Ends Well*. Moreover, the ultimate assurance of Perdita's high birth in *The Winter's Tale* eliminates the problem of class difference that Helena presents so sharply.

15. Because of this doubling effect, I would rephrase Muriel Bradbrook's claim that 'by making his social climber a woman, Shakespeare took a good deal of the sting out of the affair' ('Virtue Is the True Nobility: A Study of the Structure of *All's Well That Ends Well*', *The Review of English Studies*, 1, n.s., no. 4 [October 1950], 289–301, quotation from p. 297). Helena's combined lower-class and female status, on the contrary, increases the sting. Technically Helena's power is derived from her father's medical expertise, but her own female initiative quickly outstrips the paternal derivation. Moreover, Helena's spectacular success in curing the king is noteworthy because in England the male Royal College of Physicians in effect excluded women from the medical profession.

16. J. Dover Wilson, *The Essential Shakespeare: A Biographical Adventure* (Cambridge, 1932), pp. 58–9.

17. In *The Whole Journey: Shakespeare's Power of Development* (Berkeley and Los Angeles, 1986), C. L. Barber and Richard P. Wheeler discuss *All's Well That Ends Well* on pp. 15–18, 161, 190–1 and 196; quotation from p. 17.

18. It is indicative of the ideological power of norms – and of Shakespeare's implication in them – that Petruchio's handling of Kate in *The Taming of the Shrew* can appear humorous and beneficial, while the reversal of gender roles results in a mood that is strained and unpleasant: the motif of the dominant woman and the resisting male forbids similar comic treatment. The potential tragic cast of Bertram's situation can be suggested by reference to Coriolanus, whose aristocratic military identity is broken not only by his mother's manipulations but also by vulnerability to a lower-class threat. The difference is that Bertram faces this double gender and class threat combined in the single person of Helena.

19. In 'The Third Eye: An Essay on *All's Well That Ends Well*', in his *The Sovereign Flower* (London, 1958), pp. 93–160, G. Wilson Knight assumes a trouble-free continuity between Helena and Shakespeare by positing a 'creative bisexuality' (p. 156) that they share. Thus Shakespeare's androgynous capacity gives him a direct, unobstructed connection with women: 'Shakespeare's women lovers may be said to have been created from the female element in his own soul' (p. 132). Opposing this line of approach, I argue against an authorial androgyny that enables Shakespeare to transcend gender conflict and in favour of

his problematic involvement as a male author in the sexual political struggles he stages. It is symptomatic of Knight's thinking that he can so easily find the 'new form of society where the female values will be in the ascendent', which he sees prefigured by the play, 'darkly symbolised in the queenship of Shakespeare's age' (p. 160). This concluding bit of idealism ignores complicated questions about Elizabeth's status in a patriarchal culture and about Shakespeare's dramatisation of this dilemma.

4

Subjectivity, Desire and Female Friendship in *All's Well That Ends Well*

CAROLYN ASP

> That man should be at a woman's command and yet no hurt done!
> (I.iii.92)

According to prevailing opinion, *All's Well That Ends Well* is a 'problem play' whose major difficulty is located in the very assertion that the title makes in summarising the action. In the opinions of many critics the play does not 'end well' because the resolution remains on the structural level rather than moving to the psychological level.[1] The frog prince remains a frog until the end and the princess chooses to overlook his slimy skin. If the reader or theatregoer expects the romance of heterosexual coupling that concludes Shakespeare's 'high comedies', disappointment is inevitable.

Singular among the plays in Shakespeare's canon, *All's Well That Ends Well* is written out of the history of the female subject and this history is the history of her desire. The inadequacy of the male as subject is not only NOT repressed; it is emphasised. In this, the play challenges both culture and theory which both subordinate the issue of woman-as-subject-of-desire to the question of male subjectivity and desire. Renaissance notions of female inferiority (and consequent objectification) were largely based on physiological schemes. The cultural stereotypes that mandated female subordination were (and are) often legitimised by the appeal to the irreducible realm of

74

the real, i.e., nature. Both Aristotle and Galen after him declared that the female is characterised by deprived, passive, material traits and is cold and moist (earthy) in her dominant humours. Because the female is less fully developed than the male, her sexual organs have remained internal; she is therefore incomplete in a teleological scheme that aims towards perfection, i.e., the male. Heat, associated with perfection on the physical level, is a male characteristic; it is the lack of heat in the process of generation that causes the genitalia of the female to remain internal and therefore imperfect. The male characteristic of heat thrusts out the genitalia and produces a perfect human specimen.[2] To round off the paradigm, this assumed frailty of body was thought to be accompanied by mental and emotional weaknesses which were the natural justification of the female's exclusion from responsibility and moral fulfilment. Although the explanations used to justify female subordination to patriarchal structures have become increasingly complex in our day, the figure of the female hero in Renaissance drama, a figure who, especially in the comedies, rebels against her 'natural' inferior position (or better yet, pays it no heed), still serves as a model of self-determination, i.e., as the subject of her desire, not the object of another's. Because there was much of the new in the old, much of the old in the new, I wish to use certain paradigms from psychoanalytic theory that are congruent with Renaissance notions of the character and place of the female to discuss the complexities and ambiguities of the central female character in *All's Well That Ends Well*. Viewed from this perspective Helena can be seen as coming to independent womanhood by surmounting attitudes and theories of female deprivation and inferiority.[3] Psychoanalytic theory is a useful tool for such an investigation because it attempts to account for the phenomenon of female inferiority in terms of structural psychic formations and introjected cultural ideals; but it is also limited in that it insufficiently addresses itself to female psychic formation, i.e., to a female version of the Oedipal crisis. Until recently, despite Freud's late interest in the 'pre-Oedipal phase', which stresses the mother–infant relationship,[4] psychoanalytic theory had largely ignored that stage of development. Helena, in her ambiguity, represents a challenging subject for the psychoanalytic critic in that she breaks out of both the cultural (historical) and psychic (transhistorical) strictures applied to women in both her time and our own. She does this by the assertion of desire, the refusal of objectification and by interaction with other women in the play.

According to psychoanalytic theory, particularly Lacanian theory, the inauguration of subjectivity and desire is based upon a male model, the model of the Oedipal crisis. That model stipulates the phallus as the signifier for the needs and drives which the subject must relinquish to gain access to the symbolic order, the order of language, culture, and symbolisation. In the Lacanian scheme the phallus is not identifiable with the penis; it is, however, the signifier for the cultural privileges which define male subjectivity and legitimate his desire within the patriarchal order. The female subject remains isolated from this register, ironically, because she has no penis to lose or exchange for the phallus.[5] As Luce Irigaray comments: 'All theories of the "subject" will always have been appropriated by "the masculine." ... The subjectivity denied to the woman is, without doubt, the condition which guarantees the constitution of any object: object of representation, of discourse, of desire.'[6] The scene of 'castration' has only one subject as the concept of penis envy implies; the little girl sees herself through the eyes of the boy as 'lacking'. The 'truth' of female sexuality, therefore, is 'truth-as-lack'.

The male subject, on the other hand, gives up the penis (direct expression of his own sexuality) to attain the phallus (the privileges of the patriarchal order). The female subject does not succumb to as radical an alienation from sexuality but neither does she enjoy as full a participation in the patriarchal order. Female sexuality, then, is not represented by the phallus (power) but by 'castration' or lack. Since female sexuality cannot be represented (it is lack or absence) it remains 'a dark continent' that, according to male theory, threatens to overpower both the female and the patriarchal order. According to Antonia Fraser, this 'menacing' aspect of female sexuality was well known and greatly feared by seventeenth century males. In addition to the testimony of countless dramatis personae, there is the witness of such men as Thomas Wythorne and poets from Wyatt to Lovelace.[7]

Although there is a nice logic about this paradigm it is contrary to common sense to assume that the female is outside of signification or that her sexuality is any less structured or repressed by culture than is the male's. In entering into meaning and symbolisation the female makes a sacrifice analogous to that of the male, i.e., the sacrifice of the mother and the gratifications she supplies.[8] The difference is that the girl's sexuality is negatively rather than positively defined.[9] This definition occurs on a cultural level which assigns public power and prestige to the male. In developmental processes gender myths of female lack and male fullness are internalised and treated as 'true' and identification with stereotyped characteristics takes place. On this cultural, or symbolic level, then, both men and women are conditioned to think of the male as 'all' and the female as 'not-all'.[10] Prior to the Oedipal crisis, however, the subject is bisexual[11] undetermined by gender myths. Although physiological lack may be used to justify the idea of female inferiority, it is not the cause. Penis-envy, such as it is, is symbolic rather than organic, referring to social power rather than to physical potency. Since the female functions as a signifier of lack in culture the male must accommodate himself to the fact of difference by either establishing the woman's unworthiness or by transforming her into a compensatory object. This objectification of woman (as castrated) is designed to annihilate the threat that she represents. Similar relief is found in the disparagement of women by which the male takes pleasure through control and punishment.

The subject's entry into the Symbolic Order (language, culture, power) displaces the mother as the central object of desire with the father; this transaction is of crucial importance in the constitution of the subject. The son identifies with the father as possessor of cultural power; the daughter with the mother as one who lacks such power. The result of such internalisation is a profound sense of inadequacy both for the male and the female – the son can never be equivalent to the symbolic father (the position with which he identifies and with which he identifies the actual father); the daughter is denied even an identification with that position.[12]

This was especially true in matters of sexuality and marriage in Renaissance England where the role of female desire was widely held to be small, even non-existent. According to Lawrence Stone, the qualities most valued in a woman in the sixteenth and seventeenth centuries were weakness, submissiveness, charity and modesty: 'the theological and legal doctrine of the time were especially insistent upon the subordination of women to men in general and to their husbands in particular'.[13] Ian McLean, after an extensive review of the learned documents devoted to the discussion of women in Renaissance theory, comes to the conclusion that the single greatest force preventing fundamental changes in the notion of women in the Renaissance was the institution of marriage; in the eyes of Renaissance thinkers – all male, by the way – marriage is a divine, natural and social institution and any alternative is considered subversive.[14] Rethe Warnicke states that '... women were expected to marry, and those who did not were denied the respect of their communities'.[15]

Any change in the position of the silent and submissive wife in relationship to her lordly husband would require a new vision of the
mental and physical predispositions of the sexes; this was too radical
even for such Utopian writers as Thomas More and Rabelais.

Renaissance handbooks on marriage speak of the 'choice of a wife'
but never the choice of a husband. It is the man – the suitor – who
seeks, who chooses. He does not expect the woman to seek him or to
take the initiative in declaring her love first. It was generally agreed
by wise heads that both physical desire and romantic love were
unsafe bases of an enduring marriage, since both were regarded as
violent mental disturbances which could only be of short duration.
Women were especially prone to fits of passion; a menacing aspect of
female desire was the woman's suspected carnality as the sixteenth
century mysogynist, Thomas Wythorne, states: 'Though they be
weaker vessels, yet they will overcome 2.3. or 4 [sic] men in satisfy-
ing their carnal appetites'.[16] Women were considered incapable of
making a wise choice in the best interests of marriage. After arguing
against 'enforced marriages' in *The Anatomy of Melancholy*, Robert
Burton adds: 'A woman should give unto her parents the choice of
her husband lest she be reputed to be malapert and wanton, if she
take upon her to make her own choice, for she should rather seem to
be desired by a man than to desire a man herself.'[17] Somewhat later
in the century (1688) Lord Halifax writes in his *Advice to a Daughter*:
'It is one of the disadvantages belonging to your sex, that young
women are seldom permitted to make their own choice; their friends'
care and experience are thought safer guides to them than their own
fancies, and their modesty often forbiddeth them to refuse when their
parents recommend, though their inward consent may not entirely
go along with it. ... You must first lay it down for a foundation in
general that there is inequality in the sexes, and that for the better
economy of the world, men, who were to be law-givers, had the
larger share of reason bestowed upon them, by which means your
sex is better prepared for the compliance that is necessary for the
better performance of those duties which seem to be most properly
assigned to it'[18] i.e., the duties of marriage. This representative
patriarchal statement implies that the duties of compliance and subservience which the marriage doctrine enjoins could only be performed by those limited by nature (biological determinism) to a
lesser level of intelligence than man. As late as 1706 Mary Astell still
laments; 'A woman, indeed, can't properly be said to choose; all that
is allowed her is to refuse or accept what is offered.'[19]

Ruth Kelso, who has surveyed an impressive variety of treatises on female behaviour in *The Doctrine of the Lady of the Renaissance*, finally speculates that such emphasis would probably not have been placed on the submission and obedience of women and the inborn superiority of men if women in general were not asserting themselves in the pragmatic sphere. According to Kelso, the womanly ideal as found in male writings represents a most unrealistic separation of theory from fact.[20] Joan Kelly adds another dimension to the pragmatic argument by quoting Lucrezia Marinella who speculates that the psychology of educated men (the authors and authorities) who both vituperated and idealised women was based on both the necessity of feeling superior to women and the displacement of sexual feelings.[21] The received opinion on the value and place of women in a male world was based on male psycho-sexual experiences, not on observation and truth to experience.[22] Learned treatises on the relations of the sexes and marriage were contaminated by the need to maintain male supremacy even if that meant flying in the face of truth. In the face of such bias, how was a true image of woman to be recovered?

It was in the drama in particular that a new portrait of the female began to emerge during the late sixteenth and early seventeenth centuries. No matter what the various guises in which she appears, this woman has one consistent trait: she does not think of herself merely as an appendage of man; she insists on making her own decisions. It is this insistence that is so threatening to the patriarchal prerogative; it sets her apart from the conventional woman and often subjects her to attack or disapproval. One of the most interesting types of female rebels is the one who, like Helena, insists on the right to choose her own husband, to assert her own desire. This was a radical demand. A woman's right to love and marry according to her own desires could not be admitted without upsetting an established order which regarded women as inferior beings who needed to be governed by the sex for whose pleasure and convenience they had been created. Yet with the recognition that woman as well as man was 'a reasonable creature' came the acceptance of the fact that she should use her reason in one of the most vital concerns of her life – the choice of a marriage partner and her relations with him. To find this type of assertive woman very much alive and extremely articulate in Renaissance drama is surely a surprise given the repressive nature of the tracts and sermons. But it is a surprise that leads to a deeper understanding of what is actually new in what seems old; it

also provides an interesting and often amusing instance of that grad-
ual process by which new attitudes supplant old ones over a period
of time and produce profound societal changes.[23]

Helena, in the opening scene, seems to have internalised the 'lack'
mapped onto the female body; she acquiesces in her own powerlessness as defined by her context and tearfully accepts Bertram's inac-
cessibility as a love object. In this scene she plays out her role as
passive, even masochistic female. This problematic first appearance
can be explained by looking at her behaviour from the viewpoint of
psychoanalytic theory which postulates that female masochism is
connected with gender identity and sexual desire, both social products. When the girl completes the Oedipal crisis, she also, like the boy
must renounce the mother, the first love-object, and turn to the father
who will not affirm the phallus in her (as he does for the boy), but
instead will give it to her. When she turns to the father, she represses
the active part of her libido: 'hand in hand [with turning to the
father]' says Freud, 'there is to be observed a marked lowering of the
active sexual impulses and the rise of the passive ones. ... The transition to the father is accomplished with the help of passive trends
insofar as they have escaped from the catastrophe. The path of femininity now lies open to the girl.'[24] It is this path of powerlessness and
dependence which Helena initially believes she must adopt in regard
to her desire for Bertram.

The ascendence of passivity in the girl is due to her recognition of
the futility of realising her active desire and of the unequal terms of
the struggle. A segment of erotic possibility (female desire) is constrained. This realisation, reinforced by cultural norms, prompts
Helena's excessive and according to the other characters, unspecified
emotional response. The creation of 'femininity' in women as they
are socialised also leaves in them a resentment of the constraints to
which they were subjected, but they have few ways of expressing this
residual anger, even rage. Not only is passivity inculcated in the girl;
masochism is as well. When she turns to the father because she must,
she discovers that 'castration' (lack of power) is the condition of the
father's love, that she must be a woman (signifier of lack) to evoke
his love. She therefore begins to desire to be castrated, or powerless,
trying to turn a disaster into a wish. In finding her place in the sexual
system, then, the woman is robbed of libido and guided into masochistic eroticism.[25]

Although Helena at first seems to embody these psychoanalytic
paradigms of psychic masochism and powerlessness, she struggles at

several points in the play to defy them and moves from tearful and powerless acceptance of her position – and a concomitant construction of herself as object – to an assertive desire of which she is the subject. How does this shift occur? In her bawdy and witty banter with Parolles on the subject of virginity they both speak of sexuality with the metaphors of warfare. This conversation brings wit into contact with aggressivity and narcissism, thus establishing a contact with unconscious desire. Desire can be restricted within the bounds of societal gender myths or it can follow its own trajectory and operate independently of them. Helena quickly shifts into resolve rooted in desire and determines upon cunning, aggressive action: a woman need not always defend her virginity against attack, i.e., remain an object; she may in fact, go on the offensive and 'lose it to her own liking' (I.i.145). Desire here overcomes both gender and class; under the impress of its mobile power the unpropertied, educated female had much to gain even though such a desirous woman was regarded as a usurper of the masculine function and prerogative. Filled with resolve she casts off abjection: 'Who ever strove/To show her merit that did miss her love?' (I.i.218–19).

Helena is not alone in her struggle, however. In a canon in which mother–daughter relationships are so few, this play is unusual in having several. Although Helena is a ward of the Countess, it is obvious that the countess extends to her the love of a mother for a child: 'you ne'er oppressed me with a mother's groan,' she tells Helena, 'yet I express to you a mother's care' (I.iii.140–1). Helena quibbles, rejecting a fraternal relationship with Bertram: not 'daughter' but 'daughter-in-law' is the title she desires. When Helena admits her love to the Countess as well as her scheme to cure the King, the Countess allows Helena to speak of her desire, gives her an empathetic hearing, and bids her success, promising what aid she can. Helena appeals to the Countess' own youthful female experience thus creating a bond of womanly desire that transcends class.[26] It is obvious that the Countess regards Helena as an appropriate wife for Bertram, but leaves the initiative to her (the King as Bertram's guardian, has the right to dispose of the young man). Once Helena has legally secured the reluctant Bertram and he rejects her, she returns to the Countess who verbally castigates her son but can do nothing to change the situation. The Countess functions as an emotional centre who utters the correct – and truly felt – sentiments, but who is ineffectual to help Helena in any way except through verbal support. Albeit a kind and caring woman, a validator of Helena's desire, the Countess limits her effectiveness and accepts her position of dependence within the patriarchal order.

Helena leaves the maternal aegis of the Countess on the strength of her paternal inheritance; 'prescriptions of rare and prov'd effects', male learning passed on to her as her dowry. She must leave the mother-figure to insert herself with a larger, public group and utilise the skill bequeathed her by her father. Armed with the patriarchal legacy of language and learning, she confronts and confounds 'the schools' and attempts the king's cure. By curing the debilitating fistula (a sexually symbolic disease) Helena restores the king's manly vigour upon which the success of her project depends. But prior to the cure, she engages the royal honour: 'Then shalt thou give me with thy kingly hand / What husband in thy power I will command' (II.i.194–5). It is in her best interest to restore power to the patriarchy which she plans to engage in her behalf.

This request, which depends upon patriarchal power for its implementation, paradoxically subverts the very order of patriarchy itself. Throughout history women, not men, have been sexual objects, gifts. The 'exchange of women' expresses the social relations of a kinship system that specify that men have certain rights in their female kin and that women do not have such rights over themselves or their male relatives. In this system the preferred female sexuality is one that responds to the desires of others rather than one which actively seeks an object and a response.[27] We ask: 'What would happen if a woman demanded a certain man as her gift rather than the other way around?' This play shows us what happens. The king's debt to Helena is reckoned in Bertram's flesh; he must become the sexual partner to her to whom he is 'owed' as the reward for the restoration of the king's flesh.[28] Bertram resists this structural 'feminisation' loudly voicing the resentment that accompanies objectification, a resentment that arises from having been given no choice; 'I beseech your highness, / In such a business give me leave to use / The help of mine own eyes' (II.iii.105–7).

The play contains a series of triangular exchange transactions of which this is the first. By power the king provides a substitute sexual partner for Helena who will function as his 'stand in'. It is obvious that he values and desires Helena more than any other male in the play – what man does not love the woman who restores his virility? But Helena is determined to have Bertram and the king, by virtue of his position, is outside the circuit of desire, Subject par excellence! Up to this point Helena attempts to control events less through her own sexuality and desire than through patriarchal gifts to her. These gifts come to her in language: prescriptions, learning, promises that will enable her to possess legally what she desires. Even though she is emboldened by desire, she is unable to evoke the desire of the other (Bertram), the ultimate goal in Lacanian psychic dynamics. So what she gets is a marriage in name only – an ironic reward – a marriage that Bertram never intends to honour with his flesh. The letter but not the spirit of the law is fulfilled. So her scheme has both succeeded and failed. This seems to be the limit for female desire that relies too heavily on even the best-intentioned of men.

After the check of Bertram's rejection Helena initiates a complex and indirect action for attaining her desire, an action in which she relies both on her own cunning and on bonding with other women. Taking up the apparently impossible conditions of Bertram's rejection as a challenge – 'When thou canst get the ring upon my finger, which shall never come off, and show me a child begotten of thy body that I am father to, then call me husband, but in such a "then" I write "never" ' (III.ii.56–9). Helena paradoxically weaves her net of capture by literally following his directives, turning his language into a trap. Her campaign initiatives arise from the very messages he sends denying her. Responding to his refusal to return to his ancestral lands 'till I have no wife' she disguises herself as a pilgrim and sets out for Florence where it is possible she knows he is stationed. Ostensibly she appears submissive to his will, but her submission is also a strategy; her success from this point until the end is linked to her ability to assume a 'feminised' (inferior, powerless) position and yet remain in cognitive control of the situation. This combination of positions is exceedingly potent and establishes her mastery in the second half of the play.

In the early part of the play the ideal that Helena thinks she sees in Bertram is not merely hidden; it is absent, lacking. She eventually must come to terms with this fact. Bertram is not a sufficient representation of the 'virile object' that Helena sees only in her fantasy. We might wonder why she so desires him. In Lacanian terms, Helena is initially trapped in the level of consciousness called the Imaginary, i.e., the register in which opposition and identity are the only possible interrelationships between self and other. This 'other' is usually someone or something which is thought to complete the subject or reflects back to him/her an ideal image.[29] The Imaginary is the register of the ego, a construct that involves a purely dual either/or relationship that resembles that of the Hegelian master/slave paradigm.

The predominance of the Imaginary in relationships results in the conversion of interdependent similarities and differences between man and woman into pathological identities and oppositions (as between images of man and woman). To enter into productive relationships it is necessary to transcend the oppositional relationships and reduce mastery to insignificance by means of this transcendence. During the course of the action Helena traverses this path of development, passing from the register of the Imaginary to that of the Symbolic Order.[30] Early in the play she is almost overwhelmed by opposition in her relationship with Bertram; she can see only unbridgeable separations. Then she swings to the opposite, narcissistically identifying his desire with her own, never doubting her ability to win him. His severe rejection forces her to align herself with the limits of the possible. Finally she comes to a third position within the Symbolic Order, the register of similarities and differences, of the social and the cultural. She must accept the fact that his desire, whatever it may be, may be different from her own. Her original desire for Bertram seems to be displaced by her own maternity and by her return to the mother so that she is inserted into the larger cultural sphere of social and familial engagement. Paradoxically she does this by remaining true to her desire (is this type of maturation initiated, then, by desire within the register of the Imaginary?); as desiring subject she not only gets what she thinks she wants but more. And it is in this 'more', this excess, that Helena's real triumph is located. This excess has to do with her increasing realisation of the pragmatic and psychological support that female bonding provides for her in her erotic adventures.

In contrast to the Countess who is a very real but passive support, the Florentine women, a mother and daughter with whom Helena plots, are active on her behalf. Fallen from fortune, they must make their way in the world and struggle to defend their hard-earned gains. The precious jewel of her treasury is Diana's chastity, a 'commodity' that commands a high price. As a consequence, these women have nothing but distrust and contempt for male language, especially the male language of seduction; instead, they rely on female lore: 'My mother told me just how he would woo, / As if she sat in's heart' (IV.ii.69–70) says Diana, fore-armed against Bertram's vows. When these women show a willingness to believe her story, Helena grasps the opportunity to fulfil the letter of Bertram's law, an opportunity that Bertram's 'sick desires' for Diana give her. In a scene of many exchanges she buys Diana's place with gold while Bertram thinks he is purchasing Diana's 'ring' (genitals) with the patriarchal ring of Rosillon.[31] What occurs is a triangular transaction between women in the possession of a man. In this circuit of desire Diana remains aloof, Helena gets what she wants and Bertram gets what he does not know he does not want. Without cognitive power, Bertram assumes the role of a circulatable commodity; again he is 'feminised'.

In transactions of heterosexual desire, there can be hidden strategies of bonding which seem to occur here; the bond between Helena and Diana is cemented by means of sexual substitution. Earlier in the play (I.iii) there is an odd conversation between Lavatch and the Countess in which Lavatch describes the use he will make of Isbel to create 'friends' for himself. Voluntary cuckoldry creates a bond among men with the 'other' (the partner of the opposite sex) as the object to be exchanged among them. When the Countess remonstrates: 'Such friends are thine enemies, knave,' Lavatch points out to her this new type of bonding: 'He that comforts my wife is the cherisher of my flesh and blood; he that cherishes my flesh and blood loves my flesh and blood; he that loves my flesh and blood is my friend; ergo, he that kisses my wife is my friend' (I.iii.43–7). Lavatch describes a literal series of heterosexual displacements in which implicit homoerotic desire is represented as heterosexual adultery. Isbel will mediate a communion among males. Is Lavatch a fool or a knave or neither? He describes himself as involved in triangular sexual transactions in which he maintains control through knowledge and manipulation. As either thief or distributor he regards women as circulatable commodities, objects of desire. His song invoking Helen of Troy underlines this paradigm of the shared woman, the common ground of male desire.

Helena's sexual experience with Bertram, in which she substitutes her body for that of the desired Diana's, leaves her with the conviction of the impersonality of the act. 'Strange men' – in several senses of that word – make sweet use of what they hate, i.e., the female body with its threatening lack. 'Lust doth play / With what it loathes' (IV.iv.24–5) in the darkness which hides both the particularity (subjectivity) of the woman and the place of castration. Lacan explains this imbalance by commenting that what man approaches in the sexual act is the cause of his desire (lack). The male identifies the woman with what he has repressed in himself and makes love to complete himself in her. Thus the woman's specificity is subordinate to the man's quest for this own fulfillment.[32] Helena seems both shocked and disillusioned by this experience of sexual objectification in which she is not seen and in which she may not speak. Yet from this place of apparent lack (her genitals) and seeming powerlessness she traps the cozened Bertram's wild desires and lures them into consummating the legal bond. Publicly commenting on her experience later in the play, Helena admits that Bertram's sexual performance was 'wondrous kind' (V.iii.305), gentle and natural.

After Helena has fulfilled Bertram's stipulations, the ensuing action is excessive, almost gratuitous. I believe that it is only at this point that Helena moves beyond the Imaginary (projected idealisations) with respect to Bertram and begins to see him as he is. All traces of psychological masochism vanish from her character and she begins to express a residual anger towards him, a desire to punish him for having rejected her desire and objectified her. It becomes clear that she has his public humiliation in mind since she now has achieved a cognitive leverage over him which gives her power. She has sent back word to France that she is 'dead', i.e., she represents 'castration' or loss as the ultimate lack or absence. Paradoxically it is from this position of 'castration' or loss that she is able to achieve her greatest power as an active subject.[33] What is thought to be absent can be ignored; what is regarded as lost can be thought of as without power. Yet the very veil of disappearance allows the subject room to act with impunity. Once again she enlists the aid of the Florentine women to carry out her project.

Having arrived in France Helena sends a letter ahead to the King via messenger. Because of the unforeseen concatenation of events, it becomes clear that this letter had been prepared in advance by Helena although it is signed with Diana's name. It lays claim to Bertram as a fair exchange for the latter's honour. What becomes increasingly apparent is that Helena is preparing a public confrontation between Diana and Bertram based on a non-event, i.e., an absence that will entrap him in a web of signs (rings) and language (lies) from which he will be unable to escape. The effectiveness of Diana's script turns upon an exchange of rings prior to the bed trick. Here the plot becomes increasingly dense since neither the audience nor most of the characters knows the history of the rings. The disclosure that the ring Diana gave to Bertram had been given to Helena by the King is a shocking surprise. What is even more disquieting is the fact that Helena had given it to Diana explicitly to exchange for Bertram's patriarchal ring, a transfer that indicates Helena's intent to entrap, since encoded in this ring is a secret message to the King: she is in need of his help. The sight of Bertram wearing this ring coupled with Helena's fictional account of her own death leads the King to suspect Bertram of foul deeds. On the defensive, Bertram entangles himself more and more tightly in the snare; brazenly lying, he repudiates Diana and denies any knowledge of Helena. As the *pièce de résistance* Diana produces Bertram's ring, alleging that with it he purchased her honour. Although like Parolles, Bertram may play with language, he cannot deny the object, irrefutable proof of his complicity. Publicly revealed as a liar, a coward and a faithless husband, Bertram has no choice but to stand shamed and endure humiliation. At this point Helena enters triumphant as the *dea ex machina* to clarify and forgive.

By reading events of the second half of the play backwards, so to speak, we can see Helena's complex plan to turn Bertram's desires and fears against him and then make his weakness, perfidy and ignorance public through the accusations of others, herself remaining aloof.[34] It is evident that there is little romance in Helena's attitude towards Bertram at the end of the play; when she greets him she merely makes known her fulfilment of his conditions. When he further questions her, her final words to him are distant and almost foreboding: 'If it appear not plain and prove untrue / Deadly divorce step between me and you' (V.iii.314–15). This marriage is an unknown item, a risk whose outcome is to be determined beyond the limits of the play. In contrast her greeting to the Countess is warm and affectionate: 'O my dear mother, do I see thee living?' (V.iii.316). These, her last words in the play, seem to indicate that she has re-adjusted the focus of her desire.

Along with the power shift that occurs in the second half of the play there seems also to be a psychological reversal. I would go so far as to say that lurking behind Helena's apparent psychological masochism of her initial attitude towards Bertram lies its opposite, i.e., anger or rage at having been denied subjectivity by him and a willingness to inflict pain, a psychological form of sadism.[35] In some ways her reversal is quite shocking but it certainly is not an unusual female paradigm. As mentioned earlier in this essay, the constraint of female desire in a patriarchal system leaves a residual resentment and anger in the woman which most women, unlike Helena, do not have the opportunity to act on. Granted, her action is indirect, even cunning, but for all that, it is eminently effective. As Helena moves from object position into subject status, from passive to active (the latter associated with the masculine 'position') she concomitantly exchanges psychological masochism for a certain degree of willingness to inflict pain or humiliation in the assertion of mastery. Shakespeare manages to put Helena in the subject (sadistic) position without depriving her of our sympathy by shielding her behind the accusations and anger of others whom she has convinced to act in her place. Her agency has been displaced, certainly veiled. We cannot deny that Bertram deserves the punishment she arranges; our puzzlement is reserved for the 'reconciliation' on which the play ends. If there is a reconciliation, then how does it come about and whose attitudes must change?

Helena's shift occurs in two phases in an encounter with the Real, i.e., the given field of existence, nature in self and in the world. The first phase is Bertram's rejection and abandonment of her which forces her to see him as he is; the second is her sexual encounter with him which is lustful and procreative rather than romantic. These encounters with the Real shake her out of the narcissism and the false perceptions associated with the Imaginary register and precipitate her into positioning herself within the Symbolic Order as a viable alternative to the delusory projections of the early part of the play. There is loss but there is also gain. Her position in culture and the collective is ratified by her obvious 'wife-li-ness' and maternity. She is the fleshly sign of the link between the generations and as such holds a secure place in the Symbolic Order.[36] Helena has successfully rejected the powerlessness of her original position in the Imaginary, emerging from it at another level, carrying the signs of her transaction. It is she, not Bertram, who has both the ring and the child and she will exchange both for his acceptance of her as his wife and mother of his child. Helena's desire now locates itself within the social order – the child in her womb is the heir – but that order is not exclusively patriarchal. In the process of pursuing her desire for Bertram, Helena has come to experience the loyalty, support, and kindness of women who not only never doubted her but who never failed her. What began as a pursuit of a man developed into a transaction among women. With skill, intelligence and cunning they use Bertram's very desires to bind him to what his position and phallic potency demand of him. Through the trajectory of desire he becomes the victim of the trick. But the paradox does not operate only in Bertram's case. Let us entertain the possibility that in the pursuit of a husband Helena has actually found a mother, has discovered the power of feminine bonding. Although she carries the sign of her heterosexual eroticism and Bertram's potency, her desire seems to have transcended the narrow limits of such eroticism and moved into the larger sphere of female affectivity. Her sexual experiences and her own maternity seem to create a new awareness of and desire for the maternal body.

Is Helena's turning to women at the end of the play unusual in her immediate social context? Or does it signal some kind of change in sensibility that was actually occurring at the time? Although there has not yet been much investigation of primary documents relating to the bonding of women in the Renaissance, there are many collateral sources which refer to this phenomenon, including works of poetry, fiction and drama which depict strong, loyal, and loving relationships between and among women. In addition, it seems likely that in a society so constrained by rigid gender-role differentiations there would be both the emotional segregation of women from the male world and a corresponding development of bonding within the female circle. It is certainly true that biological realities centred around incessant pregnancies and childbirth traumas bound women together in intimacy. Supportive female networks paralleled the social restrictions on intimacy between men and women. Courtesy books, advice books, sermons, and other male-originated texts all stress gender-role differentiations as well as the social segregation characteristic of the culture.[37]

Although generally speaking the mother–daughter relationship is at the heart of the female world, in Renaissance literature we see bonds of kinship and service forming the basis of intense friendships. The literature frequently depicts a 'conspiracy of women' that organises itself around female desire. When the male is indifferent or hostile to such desire, the female characters find support in female kin, friends, or servants. Celia conspires with Rosalind; Emilia defends Desdemona to the death; Paulina refuses to abandon Hermione; Cleopatra surrounds herself with her women in the hour of her final triumph. This woman's world has a dignity and integrity that spring from mutual affection and the shared experiences of being a woman in a man's world. The drama of late sixteenth and early seventeenth century England, then, provides many examples of not only strong women but of strong friendships between women. According to Juliet Dusinberre, the struggles of many of the heroines in Shakespeare's plays are struggles against the male idea of womanhood; they are efforts to be considered human in a world that sees them only as female, i.e., as powerless, 'castrated' devoid of initiating desire. In these conflicts women are intimate not just as individuals but as women; they develop a loyalty to their sex which can express itself in confederacy, even cunning.[38] For example, in the play under consideration, the Countess is more sympathetic towards Helena than she is to her own son. She assures Helena: '... be sure of this/What I can help thee to, thou shalt not miss' (I.iii.248–9).

Helena succeeds in her scheme because she heeds and follows her desire even though the caveats of internalised gender values and the constraints of society make her task seem impossible. Frequently she occupies the so-called male position, the position of knowledge and power, through the very paradox of her 'castration'; in this position she sets up the exchanges upon which society depends for its continuation. By the play's end she has come to value and depend on the world of women whose power Bertram, with some humility, is forced to acknowledge. Her success argues for a re-evaluation of the patriarchal denigration of female desire and a reconsideration of that desire's power and validity in the social order. Through Helena's single-minded action a redefinition of gender prerogatives has occurred and as a consequence the patriarchal order is modified, if ever so slightly.[39] Fired by her desire, Helena refuses to submit to gender myths that link the female with loss unless that loss can be turned to gain. The play ends as well as it can – all only 'seems well' the king states at the conclusion – given the fact that sexual relations will never be harmonious, that psychic unity is tenuous at best.[40]

From *Literature and Psychology*, 32 (1986), 48–61.

Notes

[Caroline Asp's essay first appeared in the journal *Literature and Psychology* and its importance is measured by the fact that this is not the first time it has been republished for new readers. Asp has remained a key theorist of the relationship between literary texts and psychoanalysis, drawing on the work of, among others, Jacques Lacan. This theory concerns itself with the development and behaviour of the gendered subject, and in her essay on *All's Well That Ends Well* she offers a challenging critique of former interpretations of the play, and employs and gives account of the kind of approach current in the mid-1980s. She then produces an original reading of Shakespeare's play that shows that it is possible to see it as proto-feminist in its representation of an assertive female subject, despite the consistent tone of patriarchy that underpins the dramatic world against which such assertiveness has to operate. The concerns and methodologies of Asp's essay are characteristic of its time: the lucidity of her writing and the clarity of purpose make it one of the best examples of this kind of critical approach to Shakespeare. Ed.]

1. P. S. Berggren, 'The Woman's Part: Female Sexuality as Power in Shakespeare's Plays', in Carolyn Ruth Swift Lenz, Galyle Greene and

Carol Thomas Neely (eds), *The Woman's Part: Feminist Criticism of Shakespeare* (Urbana, IL, 1980), pp. 22–3; G. K. Hunter, 'Introduction' to *All's Well That Ends Well* (London, 1959), pp. xxix–xxxi. Hunter also comments that 'in [the problem] plays the strand of psychological realism makes the absence of personal reconciliation seem wanton and careless' (pp. liv–lv). That the ending of the play is not a true resolution but merely a superficial denial of the hero's rebellion is stated by Richard Wheeler, 'Marriage and Manhood in *All's Well*', *Bucknell Review*, 21 (1973), 103–24. R. Warren, 'Why Does it End Well? Helena, Bertram and the Sonnets', *Shakespeare Survey*, 22 (1969), 79–92, faults Shakespeare for failing to provide a 'powerful and reassuring speech' for Helena at the finale, a definite dramatic weakness in his opinion.

2. Ian McLean, *The Renaissance Notion of Women* (Cambridge, 1980), p. 33.

3. Warren sees Helena as 'unbearably poignant' and tends to idealise her masochistic tendencies; my argument follows Hunter's insight that 'to fit Helena into the play or to adapt the play to Helena is obviously the central problem of interpretation' (p. xlix). In his enlightening study of the play, Richard Wheeler, *Shakespeare's Development and the Problem Comedies* (Berkeley, CA, 1981), p. 63, keeps to a middle ground when he asserts both her humble, adoring, love for Bertram and her 'viperous, cunning and determined' pursuit of him. Psychoanalytic theory can provide paradigms to account for her complex attitudes and behaviours.

4. Sigmund Freud, *The Standard Edition of the Complete Psychological Works*, Vol. 22 (London, 1964), pp. 112–35. Nancy Chodorow, *The Reproduction of Mothering* (Berkeley, CA, 1978), has developed this theory in great detail.

5. Jacques Lacan, *Ecrits: A Selection*, trans. Alan Sheridan (New York, 1977), p. 66.

6. Luce Irigaray, *Speculum of the Other Woman*, trans. Gillian C. Gill (Ithaca, NY), p. 165.

7. Antonia Fraser, *The Weaker Vessel* (New York, 1984), p. 4.

8. Elif Ragland-Sullivan, *Jaques Lacan and the Philosophy of Psychoanalysis* (Chicago, 1985), pp. 297–8.

9. Kaja Silverman, *The Subject of Semiotics* (London, 1983), p. 198.

10. Jacques Lacan, *Séminaire III*, ed. Jaques-Alain Miller (Paris, 1973–4), p. 198.

11. *The Standard Edition of the Complete Psychological Works*, Vol. 22 (London, 1964), p. 118.

12. Kaja Silverman, *The Subject of Semiotics* (London, 1983), p. 191.

13. Lawrence Stone, *The Family, Sex, and Marriage in England: 1500–1800* (New York, 1977), p. 199.

14. Ian McLean, *The Renaissance Notion of Women* (Cambridge, 1980), p. 85.

15. Retha Warnicke, *Women of the English Renaissance and Reformation* (Westpoint, 1983), p. 178.

16. Quoted in Antonia Fraser, *The Weaker Vessel* (New York, 1984), p. 4.

17. Robert Burton, *The Anatomy of Melancholy* (New York, 1932), 'Third partition', p. 238.

18. Lawrence Stone, *The Family, Sex, and Marriage in England: 1500–1800* (New York, 1977), p. 278.

19. Ibid., p. 278.

20. Ruth Kelso, *The Doctrine of the Lady in the Renaissance* (Urbana, IL, 1978), p. 208.

21. Joan Kelly, *Women, History and Theory* (Chicago, 1984), p. 81.

22. Ibid., p. 82.

23. Joan Gagen, *The New Woman* (New York, 1954), p. 119.

24. *The Standard Edition of the Complete Psychological Works*, Vol. 21 (London, 1964), p. 239.

25. *The Standard Edition of the Complete Psychological Works*, Vol. 22 (London, 1964), p. 128.

26. Carol McKewin, 'Counsels of Gall and Grace: Intimate Conversations between Women in Shakespeare's Plays', in Lenz, Greene and Neely (eds), *The Woman's Part: Feminist Criticism of Shakespeare* (Urbana, IL, 1980), pp. 117–32.

27. Jacques Lacan, *Séminaire* II, ed. Jaques-Alain Miller (Paris, 1973–4), p. 306.

28. Eve Sedgewick, 'Sexualism and the Citizen of the World', in *Critical Inquiry*, 10 (1984), 223. See also Wheeler, *Shakespeare's Development* (Berkeley and Los Angeles, 1981), pp. 49–51, on the deflection of male sexual interest from women to men.

29. Jacques Lacan, *Ecrits: A Selection*, trans. Alan Sheridan (New York, 1977), pp. 2–4.

30. Jacques Lacan, *Séminaire* I, ed. Jaques-Alain Miller (Paris, 1973–4), p. 215.

31. Alexander Welsh, 'The Loss of Men and the Getting of Children: *All's Well* and *Measure for Measure*', *Modern Language Review*, 73 (1978), 17–28, argues against Wheeler and later Arthur Kirsch, *Shakespeare and the Experience of Love* (Cambridge, 1981), in their emphasis on the 'threat of castration inherent in the Oedipal situation', i.e. Bertram's

identification of Helena with her mother. He asserts that 'inheritance and succession are far more important concerns than Oedipal jealousies' (p. 21). Although my focus is not on Bertram, I agree with Welsh that the Oedipal argument is quite weak and unconvincing. Aside from the 'punning' scene between the countess and Helena, there is no reference to such a motive in the play. In that scene Helena specifically and somewhat playfully, refers to brother/sister incest.

32. Elif Ragland-Sullivan, *Jaques Lacan and the Philosophy of Psychoanalysis* (Chicago, 1985), p. 292.

33. Here I disagree with G. K. Hunter, *All's Well That Ends Well* (London, 1959), p. xxxii, on the power of coincidence and submission to supernatural forces as the dynamic forces of the second half of the play. Helena actively uses and arranges the circumstances that lead to her success.

34. R. B. Parker, 'War and Sex in *All's Well*', *Shakespeare Survey*, 37 (1984), 111–12.

35. Wheeler, *Shakespeare's Development* (Berkeley, CA, 1981), pp. 72–3, states that 'the exposure of Bertram releases a righteous feeling of moral outrage and with it a kind of vindictive pleasure that corresponds to the sadistic attack on the internalised object lost in reality described by Freud'.

36. Alexander Welsh, 'The Loss of Men and the Getting of Children: *All's Well* and *Measure for Measure*', *Modern Language Review*, 73 (1978), 21.

37. Carrol Camden, *The Elizabethan Woman* (New York, 1952), quotes from many such treatises which lead us to believe that women spent a great deal of time together. Henry Parrot, *The Gossips Greeting*, inveighs against talkative and outgoing women. Burton also refers to gossiping among women as 'their merrie meetings and frequent visitations, mutual invitations in good times ... which are so in use'. A Dutch traveller named Van Meteren found this mode of entertainment a notable one among Elizabethan women. He writes: 'all the rest of their time they employ in walking and riding, in playing cards or otherwise, in visiting their neighbours and making merry' (p. 162). Educated women also spent their time carrying on an extended correspondence with their female friends.

38. Juliet Dusinberre, *Shakespeare and the Nature of Women* (London, 1975), p. 282.

39. Even at the end of the play the king proposes to repeat the process he inaugurated with Helena by finding Diana, the professed virgin, a husband. Lafew's daughter is offered to Bertram and then summarily withdrawn without any consultation with her. The tableau of women at the end of the play is intriguing; it ranges from Diana, who has vowed not

to marry, to 'fair Maudlin' who is given and taken back. The widow Countess stands with the newly restored wife-mother, Helena. What seems to be emphasised is the lack of or the problematic nature of heterosexual relationships.

40. Jacques Lacan, *Séminaire XX*, ed. Jacques-Alain Miller (Paris, 1973–4), p. 14.

5

Transgression and Surveillance in *Measure for Measure*

JONATHAN DOLLIMORE

In the Vienna of *Measure for Measure* unrestrained sexuality is ostensibly subverting social order; anarchy threatens to engulf the State unless sexuality is subjected to renewed and severe regulation. Such at least is the claim of those in power. Surprisingly critics have generally taken them at their word even while dissociating themselves from the punitive zeal of Angelo. There are those who have found in the play only a near tragic conflict between anarchy and order, averted in the end it is true, but unconvincingly so. Others, of a liberal persuasion and with a definite preference for humane rather than authoritarian restraint, have found at least in the play's 'vision' if not precisely its ending an ethical sense near enough to their own. But both kinds of critic have apparently accepted that sexual transgression in *Measure for Measure* – and in the world – represents a real force of social disorder intrinsic to human nature and that the play at least is about how this force is – must be – restrained.

J. W. Lever, in an analysis of the play noted for its reasonableness,[1] draws a comparison with Shakespeare's romantic comedies where disorders in both society and individual, especially those caused by 'the excesses of sentiment and desire' are resolved: 'not only the problems of lovers, but psychic tensions and social usurpations or abuses, found their resolution through the exercise of reason, often in the form of an adjudication by the representatives of authority'.

In *Measure for Measure* the same process occurs but more extremely: 'Not only are the tensions and discords wrought up to an extreme pitch, threatening the dissolution of all human values, but a corresponding and extraordinary emphasis is laid upon the role of true authority, whose intervention alone supplies the equipoise needed to counter the forces of negation.' Lever draws a further contrast with *Troilus and Cressida* where 'no supreme authority exists; age and wisdom can only warn, without stemming the inevitable tide of war and lechery'. On this view then unruly desire is extremely subversive and has to be countered by 'true' and 'supreme authority', 'age and wisdom', all of which qualities are possessed by the Duke in *Measure for Measure* and used by him to redeem the State.[2] Only these virtues, this man, can retrieve the State from anarchy.[3]

But consider now a very different view of the problem. With the considerable attention recently devoted to Bakhtin and his truly important analysis of the subversive carnivalesque, the time is right for a radical reading of *Measure for Measure*, one which insists on the oppressiveness of the Viennese State and which interprets low-life transgression as *positively* anarchic, ludic, carnivalesque – a subversion from below of a repressive official ideology of order. What follows aims (if it is not too late) to forestall such a reading as scarcely less inappropriate than that which privileged 'true' authority over anarchic desire. Indeed, such a reading, if executed within the parameters of some recent appropriations of Bakhtin, would simply remain within the same problematic, only reversing the polarities of the binary opposition which structures it (order/chaos). I offer a different reading of the play, one which, perhaps paradoxically, seeks to identify its absent characters and the history which it contains yet does not represent.

Transgression

Whatever subversive identity the sexual offenders in this play possess is a construction put upon them by the authority which wants to control them; moreover control is exercised through that construction. Diverse and only loosely associated sexual offenders are brought into renewed surveillance by the State; identified in law as a category of offender (the lecherous, the iniquitous) they are thereby demonised as a threat to law. Like many apparent threats to authority this one in fact legitimates it: control of the threat becomes the rationale of authoritarian reaction in a time of apparent crisis. Prostitution and lechery are identified as the causes of crisis yet we learn increasingly of a corruption more political than sexual (see especially V.i.316ff). Arguably then the play discloses corruption to be an effect less of desire than authority itself. It also shows how corruption is downwardly identified – that is, focused and placed with reference to low-life 'licence'; in effect, and especially in the figure of Angelo, corruption is displaced from authority *to* desire and by implication from the rulers to the ruled. The Duke tells Pompey:

> Fie, sirrah, a bawd, a wicked bawd;
> The evil that thou causest to be done,
> That is thy means to live. Do thou but think
> What 'tis to cram a maw or clothe a back
> From such a filthy vice. Say to thyself,
> From their abominable and beastly touches
> I drink, I eat, array myself, and live.
> Canst thou believe thy living is a life,
> So stinkingly depending?
>
> (III.ii.18–26)

This is in response to Pompey's observation that such exploitation not only exists at other levels of society but is actually protected 'by order of law' (l.8). This is just what the Duke's diatribe ignores – cannot acknowledge – fixating instead on the 'filthy vice' and its agents in a way which occludes the fact that it is Angelo, not Pompey, who, unchecked, and in virtue of his social position, will cause most 'evil ... to be done'. But, because Angelo's transgression is represented as growing from his desire rather than his authority, his is a crime which can be construed as a lapse into the corruption of a lower humanity, a descent of the ruler into the sins of the ruled. Provocatively, his crime is obscurely theirs.

If we can indeed discern in the demonising of sexuality a relegitimation of authority we should not then conclude that this is due simply to an ideological conspiracy; or rather it may indeed be conspiratorial but it is also ideological in another, more complex sense: through a process of displacement an imaginary – and punitive – resolution of real social tension and conflict is attempted.

The authoritarian demonising of deviant behaviour was common in the period, and displacement and condensation – to and around low life – were crucial to this process. But what made displacement and condensation possible was a prior construction of deviancy itself. So, for example, diatribes against promiscuity, female self-assertion, cross-dressing and homosexuality construed these behaviours as symptomatic of an impending dissolution of social hierarchy and so, in effect, of civilisation.[4] This was partly because transgression was conceived in public and even cosmic terms; it would not then have made sense to see it in, say, psychological or subjective terms – a maladjustment of the individual who, with professional assistance, could be 'normalised'. On the one hand then homosexuality was not considered to be the 'defect' of a particular personality type since 'the temptation to debauchery, from which homosexuality was not clearly distinguished, was accepted as part of the common lot, be it never so abhorred. For the Puritan writer John Rainolds homosexuality was a sin to which 'men's natural corruption and viciousness is prone'. And this was because homosexuality 'was not a sexuality in its own right, but existed as a potential for confusion and disorder in one undivided sexuality'.[5] On the other hand it was distinguished sufficiently to be associated with other cardinal sins like religious and political heresy and witchcraft. This association of sexual deviance with religious and political deviance – made of course in relation to Marlowe by the informer Richard Baines[6] and rather more recently by the British tabloid press in relation to Peter Tatchell[7] – facilitates the move from specific to general subversion: the individual transgressive act sent reverberations throughout the whole and maybe even brought down God's vengeance on the whole.

Stuart Clark has shown how the disorder which witches and other deviants symbolised, even as it was represented as a threat to order, was also a presupposition of it. Contrariety, he argues, was 'a universal principle of intelligibility as well as a statement about how the world was actually constituted' and 'the characterisation of disorder by inversion, even in relatively minor texts or on ephemeral occasions, may therefore be taken to exemplify an entire metaphysic'.[8] On this view then the attack on deviancy was not just a diversionary strategy of authority in times of crisis but an elementary and permanent principle of rule. Nevertheless, we might expect that it is in times of crisis that this principle is specially operative. The work of Lawrence Stone would seem to confirm this. He argues that in the early seventeenth century the family household becomes, at least in contemporary propaganda, 'responsible for, and the symbol of, the whole social system, which was thought to be based on the God-given principle of hierarchy, deference and obedience'. Such propaganda was stimulated in part by the experienced instability of rapid change, change which was interpreted by some as impending collapse. According to Stone then, 'the authoritarian family and the authoritarian nation-state were the solutions to an intolerable sense of anxiety, and a deep yearning for order' and the corollary was a ruthless persecution of dissidents and deviants. Sexuality became subject to intensified surveillance working in terms of both an enforced and an internalised discipline.[9] *Measure for Measure*, I want to argue, is about both kinds of discipline, the enforced and the internalised. Their co-existence made for a complex social moment as well as a complex play.

J. A. Sharpe's recent and scrupulous study of crime in seventeenth-century England confirms this discrepancy between the official depiction of moral collapse among the lower orders and their actual behaviour. Sharpe also confirms that the suppression of sexuality was only 'one aspect of a wider desire to achieve a disciplined society. Fornication, like idleness, pilfering, swearing and drunkenness, was one of the distinguishing activities of the disorderly'. Further, the Elizabethan and early Stuart period marked an historical highpoint in an authoritarian preoccupation with the disorderly and their efficient prosecution.[10] Nevertheless, many of those concerned with this prosecution really did believe standards were declining and the social fabric disintegrating. Puritan extremists like Stubbes saw prostitution as so abhorrent they advocated the death penalty for offenders.[11] But if, as Stone and others argue, this fervour is the result of insecurity in the face of change, then, even if that fervour was 'sincere', the immorality which incited it was not at all its real cause. This is one sense in which the discourse of blame involved displacement; but there was another: while the authorities who actually suppressed the brothels often exploited the language of moral revulsion it was not the sexual vice that worried them so much as the meeting together of those who used the brothels. George Whetstone was only warning the authorities of what they already feared when he told them to beware of 'haunts ... in Allies, gardens and other obscure corners out of the common walks of the Magistrate' whose guests are 'masterless men, needy shifters, thieves, cutpurses, unthrifty servants, both serving men and prentices'.[12] Suppression was an attempt to regulate not the vice, nor, apparently, even the spread of venereal disease, but the criminal underworld.[13] Similarly, in *Measure for Measure*, the more we attend to the supposed subversiveness of sexual licence, and the authoritarian response to it, the more we are led away from the vice itself towards social tensions which intersect with it – led also to retrace several distinct but related processes of displacement.

The play addresses several social problems which had their counterparts in Jacobean London. Mistress Overdone declares: 'Thus, what with the war, what with the sweat, what with the gallows, and what with poverty, I am custom shrunk' (I.ii.75–7). Lever points out that this passage links several issues in the winter of 1603–4: 'the continuance of the war with Spain; the plague in London; the treason trials and executions at Winchester in connection with the plots of Raleigh and others; the slackness of trade in the deserted capital'.[14] Significantly, all but the first of these, the war, are domestic problems. But even the war was in prospect of becoming such: if peace negotiations then under way (and also alluded to in the play – at I.ii.1–17) proved successful it would lead to a return home of 'the multitude of pretended gallants, banckrouts, and unruly youths who weare at this time settled in pyracie'.[15] In this political climate even peace could exacerbate domestic ills.

This play's plague references are especially revealing. Both here and at I.ii.85–9, where Pompey refers to a proclamation that 'All houses in the suburbs of Vienna must be plucked down' there is a probable allusion to the proclamation of 1603 which provided for the demolition of property in the London suburbs in order to control the plague. But the same proclamation also refers to the 'excessive numbers of idle, indigent, dissolute and dangerous persons, and the pestering of many of them in small and strait room'.[16] Here, as with the suppression of prostitution, plague control legitimates other kinds of political control. (Enemies of the theatre often used the plague threat as a reason to have them closed.) As this proclamation indicates, there was a constant fear among those in charge of Elizabethan and Jacobean England that disaffection might escalate into organised resistance. This anxiety surfaces repeatedly in official discourse: any circumstance, institution or occasion which might unite the vagabonds and masterless men – for example famine, the theatres, congregations of the unemployed – was the object of almost paranoid surveillance. Yet, if anything, *Measure for Measure* emphasises the lack of any coherent opposition among the subordinate and the marginalised. Thus Pompey, 'Servant to Mistress Overdone' (list of characters), once imprisoned and with the promise of remission, becomes, with no sense of betrayal, servant to the State in no less a capacity than that of hangman.

Yet those in power are sincerely convinced there is a threat to order. At the very outset of the play Escalus, described in the list of characters as an 'ancient' Lord, is praised excessively by the Duke only to be subordinated to Angelo, the new man. The traditional political 'art and practice' (I.i.12) of Escalus is not able to cope with the crisis. Later, the Duke, speaking to the Friar, acknowledges that this crisis stems from a failure on the part of the rulers yet at the same time displaces responsibility on to the ruled: like disobedient children they have taken advantage of their 'fond fathers' (I.iii.23). Hence the need for a counter-subversive attack on the 'liberty' of the low-life. Yet even as we witness that attack we see also that the possibilities for actual subversion seem to come from quite another quarter. Thus when Angelo resorts to the claim that the State is being subverted (in order to discredit charges of corruption against himself) the way he renders that claim plausible is most revealing:

> These poor informal women are no more
> But instruments of some more mightier member
> That sets them on. Let me have way, my lord,
> To find this practice out.
>
> (V.i.235–7)

Earlier the Duke, pretending ignorance of Angelo's guilt, publicly denounces Isabella's charge against Angelo in similar terms:

> thou knowest not what thou speak'st
> Or else thou art suborn'd against his honour
> In hateful practice ...
> ... Someone hath set you on.
> (V.i.108–10; 115)

The predisposition of Escalus to credit all this gives us an insight into how the scapegoat mentality works: just as the low-life have hitherto been demonised as the destructive element at the heart (or rather bottom) of the State, now it is the apparently alien Friar (he who is 'Not of this country', III.ii.211) who is to blame. The kind old Escalus charges the Friar (the Duke in disguise) with 'Slander to th'state!' and cannot wait to torture him into confession (V.i.320, 309–10). That he is in fact accusing the Duke ironically underpins the point at issue: disorder generated by misrule and unjust law (III.ii.6–8) is ideologically displaced on to the ruled – 'ideologically' because Angelo's lying displacement is insignificant compared with the way that Escalus really believes it is the subordinate and the outsider who are to blame. Yet even as he believes this he is prepared to torture his way to 'the more mightier member' behind the plot; again there is the implication, and certainly the fear, that the origin of the problem is not intrinsic to the low-life but a hostile fraction of the ruling order.

Oddly the slander for which Escalus wants to have this outsider tortured, and behind which he perceives an insurrectionary plot, is only the same assessment of the situation which he, Angelo and the Duke made together at the outset. What does this suggest: is his violent reaction to slander paranoid, or rather a strategy of *realpolitik?* Perhaps the latter – after all, it is not only, as Isabella reminds Angelo (II.ii.135–7) that rulers have the power to efface their own corruption, but that they need to do this to remain in power. And within the terms of *realpolitik* the threat of exposure is justification enough for authoritarian reaction. But the problem with the concept of *realpolitik* is that it tends to discount the non-rational though still effective dimensions of power which make it difficult to determine whether crisis is due to paranoia generating an imaginary threat or whether a real threat is intensifying paranoia. And, of course, even if the threat is imaginary this can still act as the 'real' cause of ensuing conflict. Conversely, terms like paranoia applied to a ruling class or fraction, while useful in suggesting the extent to which that class's discourse produces its own truth and apprehends that truth through blame, can also mislead with regard to the class's power to rationalise its own position and displace responsibility for disorder. Put another way, *realpolitik* and paranoia, in so far as they are present, should be seen to coexist more at a social rather than an individual level. An interesting case in point is George Whetstone's *A Mirror for Magistrates* (1584), a possible source for Shakespeare's play. This work related the story of how the Roman emperor, Alexander Severus, re-establishes order in the State by setting up a system of sophisticated surveillance and social regulation which includes himself going disguised among his subjects and observing their transgressions at first hand. These are denounced with moral fervour and the implication of course is that they are condemned just because they are sinful. But as Whetstone's retelling of the story develops we can see a pragmatic underside to his blameful discourse. In fact, as so often in this period, political strategy and moral imperative openly coexist. The focus of Whetstone's reforming zeal are the 'Dicing-houses, taverns and common stews' – 'sanctuaries of iniquity'. But what gives him most cause for concern is not the behaviour of the low but that of the landed gentry who are attracted to them: 'Dice, Drunkenness and Harlots, had consumed the wealth of a great number of ancient Gentlemen, whose Purses were in the possession of vile persons, and their Lands at mortgage with the Merchants … The Gentlemen had made this exchange with vile persons: they were attired with the Gentlemen's bravery, and the Gentlemen disgraced with their beastly manners.'[17]

Here, apparently, hierarchy is subverted from above and those most culpable the gentlemen themselves. Yet in Whetstone's account the low are to blame; they are held responsible for the laxity of the high, much as a man might (then as now) blame a woman for tempting him sexually whereas in fact he has coerced her. The gentlemen are 'mildly' reproached and restored to that which they have transacted away while the low are disciplined. Whetstone believed that the survival of England depended on its landed gentry; in rescuing them from the low-life he is rescuing the State from chaos and restoring it to its 'ancient and most laudable orders'.[18] A reactionary programme is accomplished at the expense of the low, while those who benefit are those responsible for precipitating 'decline' in the first place. The same process of displacement occurs throughout discourses of power in this period. One further example: one of the many royal proclamations attempting to bring vagabonds under martial law asserts that 'there can grow no account of disturbance of our peace and quiet but from such refuse and vagabond people' – and this despite the fact that the proclamation immediately proceeding this one (just six days before) announced the abortive Essex rebellion.[19] The failure of the rebellion is interpreted by the second proclamation as proof of the loyalty of all other subjects with the exception of that 'great multitude of base and loose people' who 'lie privily in corners and bad houses, listening after news and stirs, and spreading rumours and tales, being of likelihood ready to lay hold of any occasion to enter into any tumult or disorder' (p. 232). For the authoritarian perspective as articulated here, the unregulated are by definition the ungoverned and always thereby potentially subversive of government. At the same time it is a perspective which confirms what has been inferred from *Measure for Measure*: in so far as the socially deprived were a threat to government this was only when they were mobilised by powerful elements much higher up the social scale. Moreover the low who were likely to be so mobilised were only a small part of the 'base and loose people' hounded by authority. In fact we need to distinguish, as Christopher Hill does, between this mob element, little influenced by religious or political ideology but up for hire, and the 'rogues, vagabonds and beggars' who, although they 'caused considerable panic in ruling circles ... were incapable of concerted revolt'.[20] Of course there were real social problems and 'naturally' the deprived were at the centre of them.

Moreover, if we recall that there *were* riots, that fornication *did* produce charity dependent bastards, that drunkenness *did* lead to fecklessness, it becomes apparent that, in their own terms there were also real grounds for anxiety on the part of those who administered deprivation. At the same time we can read in that anxiety – in its very surplus, its imaginative intensity, its punitive ingenuity – an ideological displacement (and hence misrecognition) of much deeper fears of the uncontrollable, of being out of control, themselves corresponding to more fundamental social problems.[21]

Surveillance

In Act II scene i we glimpse briefly the State's difficulties in ensuring the levels of policing which the rulers think is required. Escalus discreetly inquires of Elbow whether there are any more officers in his locality more competent than he. Elbow replies that even those others who have been chosen happily delegate their responsibility to him.

A similar anxiety about the ungovernability of his subjects leads the Duke to put those of them he encounters under a much more sophisticated and effective mode of surveillance; though remaining coercive, it seeks additionally to get subjects to reposition themselves. First though, a word about the Duke's use of disguise. The genre of the disguised ruler generally presented him in a favourable light. But in Jacobean England we might expect there to have been an ambivalent attitude towards it. In Jonson's *Sejanus*, contemporary with *Measure for Measure*, it is a strategy of tyrannical repression; Jonson himself was subjected to it while in jail, apparently with the intention of getting him to incriminate himself.[22] Next there is the question of the Duke's choice of *religious* disguise. As I've argued elsewhere, there was considerable debate at this time over the 'Machiavellian' proposition that religion was a form of ideological control which worked in terms of internalised submission.[23] Even as he opposes it, Richard Hooker cogently summarises this view; it represents religion as 'a mere politic devise' and whereas State law has 'power over our outward actions only' religion works upon men's 'inward cogitations ... the privy intents and motions of their heart'. Armed with this knowledge 'politic devisers' are 'able to create God in man by art'.[24]

The Duke, disguised as a friar, tries to reinstate this kind of subjection. Barnardine is the least amenable; 'He wants advice', remarks the Duke grimly (IV.ii.144) and is infuriated when the offer is refused.

Barnardine is especially recalcitrant in that he admits guilt yet is unrepentant and even disinclined to escape; he thus offers no response on which the Duke might work to return him to a position of dutiful submission. But the Duke does not give up and resolves to 'Persuade this rude wretch willingly to die' (IV.iii.80; cf. II.i.35). A similar idea seems to be behind his determination to send Pompey to prison – not just to rot but for 'Correction and instruction' (III.ii.31). Earlier the Duke had been rather more successful with Claudio. His long 'Be absolute for death' speech (III.i.5ff) does initially return Claudio to a state of spiritual renunciation, but Claudio has not long been in conversation with Isabella before he desires to live again. Isabella, herself positioned in a state of intended renunciation, struggles to restore Claudio to his. She fails but the Duke intervenes again and Claudio capitulates.

The Duke makes of Mariana a model of dutiful subjection. Predictably, he is most successful with those who are least powerful and so most socially dependent. He tells Angelo to love Mariana, adding: 'I have confess'd her, and I know her virtue' (V.i.524). He has indeed, and earlier Mariana confirms his success in this confessional positioning of her as an acquiescent, even abject subject (IV.i.8–20); for her he is one 'whose advice / Hath often still'd my brawling discontent' (IV.i.8–9). His exploitation of her – 'The maid will I frame, and make fit for his attempt' (III.i.256–7) – is of course just what she as confessed subject must not know, and the Duke confirms that she does not by eliciting from her a testimony:

> **Duke**   Do you persuade yourself that I respect you?
> **Mariana**   Good friar, I know you do, and so have found it
> (IV.i.53–4)

Thus is her exploitation recast and indeed experienced by Mariana, as voluntary allegiance to disinterested virtue.

The Duke's strategy with Isabella is somewhat different. Some critics of the play, liking their women chaste, have praised Isabella for her integrity; others have reproached her for being too absolute for virtue.[25] Another assessment, ostensibly more sympathetic than either of these because psychological rather than overtly moralistic, is summarised by Lever. He finds Isabella ignorant, hysterical and suffering from 'psychic confusion', and he apparently approves the fact that 'through four ... acts' she undergoes 'a process of moral education designed to reshape her character'.[26] Here, under the guise of normative categories of psychosexual development, whose objective is 'maturity', moralistic and patriarchal values are reinstated the more insidiously for being ostensibly 'caring' rather than openly coercive. But in the play the coercive thrust of such values suggests that perhaps Isabella has recourse to renunciation as a way of escaping them. When we first encounter her in the nunnery it is her impending separation from men that is stressed by the nun, Francisca. The same priority is registered by Isabella herself when she affirms the prayers from 'preserved souls, / From fasting maids, whose minds are dedicate / To nothing temporal' (II.ii.154–6). She seeks in fact to be preserved specifically from men:

> Women? – Help, heaven! Men their creation mar
> In profiting by them. Nay, call us ten times frail;
> For we are soft as our complexions are,
> And credulous to false prints.
> (II.iv.126–9)

If we remember that in the play the stamp metaphor signifies the formative and coercive power of authority, we see that Isabella speaks a vulnerability freed in part from its own ideological misrecognition; she conceives her weakness half in terms of women's supposed intrinsic 'frailness', half in terms of exploitative male coercion. Further, we see in Isabella's subjection a conflict within the patriarchal order which subjects: the renunciation which the Church sanctions, secular authority refuses. The latter wins and it is Isabella's fate to be coerced back into her socially and sexually subordinate position – at first illicitly by Angelo, then legitimately by the Duke who 'takes' her in marriage.

His subjects' public recognition of his own integrity is important in the Duke's attempt to reposition them in obedience. Yet the play can be read to disclose integrity as a strategy of authority rather than the disinterested virtue of the leader. The Duke speaks frequently of the integrity of rulers but the very circumstances in which he does so disclose a pragmatic and ideological intent; public integrity legitimates authority, and authority takes sufficient priority to lie about integrity when the ends of propaganda and government require it (IV.ii.77–83). And the Duke knows that these same ends require that integrity should be publicly displayed in the form of reputation. Intriguingly then, perhaps the most subversive thing in the play is the most casual, namely Lucio's slurring of the Duke's reputation. Unawares and carelessly, Lucio strikes at the heart of the ideological legitimation of power. Along with Barnardine's equally careless refusal of subjection, this is what angers the Duke the most. Still disguised, he insists to Lucio that he, the Duke, '*be but testimonied in his own bringings-forth*, and he shall appear to the envious a scholar, a statesman, and a soldier' (III.ii.140–2, italics added). After Lucio has departed he laments his inability to ensure his subject's dutiful respect: 'What king so strong / Can tie the gall up in the slanderous tongue?' (ll. 181–2; cf. IV.i.60–5). If the severity of the law at this time is anything to go by, such slander was a cause of obsessive concern to Elizabethan and Jacobean rulers,[27] just as it is here with the Duke and, as we have already seen, with Escalus.

The ideological representation of integrity can perhaps be judged best at the play's close – itself ideological but not, it seems to me, forced or flawed in the way critics have often claimed. By means of the Duke's personal intervention and integrity, authoritarian reaction is put into abeyance but not discredited: the corrupt deputy is unmasked but no law is repealed and the mercy exercised remains the prerogative of the same ruler who initiated reaction. The Duke also embodies a public reconciliation of law and morality. An omniscience, inseparable from seeming integrity, permits him to close the gulf between the two, one which was opening wide enough to demystify the one (law) and enfeeble the other (morality). Again, this is not a cancelling of authoritarianism so much as a fantasy resolution of the very fears from which authoritarianism partly grows – a fear of escalating disorder among the ruled which in turn intensifies a fear of impotence in the rulers. If so it is a reactionary fantasy, neither radical nor liberating (as fantasy may indeed be) but rather conservative and constraining; the very disclosure of social realities which make progress seem imperative is recuperated in comedic closure, a redemptive wish-fulfilment of the status quo.

In conclusion then the transgressors in *Measure for Measure* signify neither the unregeneracy of the flesh, nor the ludic subversive carnivalesque. Rather, as the spectre of unregulated desire, they are exploited to legitimate an exercise in authoritarian repression. And of course it is a spectre: desire, culturally manifested, is never unregulated, perhaps least of all in Jacobean London. Apart from their own brutally exploitative sub-cultural codes, the stews were controlled from above. This took several forms, including one of the most subtly coercive of all: economic investment. Some time between 1599 and 1602 the Queen's Lord Chamberlain, Lord Hunsdon, appears to have leased property for the establishing of an especially notorious brothel in Paris Gardens, while Thomas Nashe declared in 1598 that 'whoredom (the next doore to the Magistrates)' was set up and maintained through bribery, and Gāmini Salgādo informs us that 'Most theatre owners ... were brothel owners too'.[28]

At the same time in this period, in its laws, statutes, proclamations and moralistic tracts, the marginalised and the deviant are, as it were, endlessly recast in a complex ideological process whereby authority is ever anxiously relegitimating itself. *Measure for Measure*, unlike the proclamation or the statute, gives the marginalised a voice, one which may confront authority directly but which more often speaks of and partially reveals the strategies of power which summon it into visibility. Even the mildly transgressive Claudio who, were it not for the law, was all set to become law-abiding, becomes briefly that 'warped slip of wilderness' (III.i.141). But if Claudio's desire to live is momentarily transgressive it becomes so only at the potential expense of his sister. The same is true of Pompey and Lucio who, once put under surveillance or interrogation by authority voice a critique of authority itself (III.ii.6–8; 89–175), yet remain willing to exploit others in their position by serving that same authority when the opportunity arises. Ironically though, it is Angelo's transgressive desire which is potentially the most subversive; he more than anyone else threatens to discredit authority. At the same time his transgression is also, potentially, the most brutally exploitative. This is an example of something which those who celebrate transgression often overlook: even as it offers a challenge to authority, transgression ever runs the risk of re-enacting elsewhere the very exploitation which it is resisting immediately.

What Foucault has said of sexuality in the nineteenth and twentieth centuries seems appropriate also to sexuality as a sub-category of sin in earlier periods: it *appears* to be that which power is afraid of but in actuality is that which power works through. Sin, especially when internalised as guilt, has produced the subjects of authority as surely as any ideology. At the same time it may be that not everyone, indeed not even the majority, has fallen for this. The 'sin' of promiscuity, for example, has always been defended from a naturalistic perspective as no sin at all – as indeed we find in *Measure for Measure*. But those like Lucio who cheerfully celebrate instinctual desire simultaneously reify as natural the (in fact) highly *social* relations of exploitation through which instinct finds its expression, social relations which, we might say, determine the nature of instinct far more than nature itself:

Lucio	How doth my dear morsel, thy mistress? Procures she still, ha?
Pompey	Troth sir, she hath eaten up all her beef, and she is herself in the tub.

Lucio   Why, 'tis good: it is the right of it: it must be so. Ever your fresh whore, and your powdered bawd; an unshunned consequence; it must be so.

(III.ii.52–8)

And Pompey, whom he refuses to bail, Lucio perceives as 'bawd born' (III.ii.66). Mistress Overdone, her plight as described here notwithstanding, was one of the lucky ones; after all, the life of most prostitutes outside the exclusive brothels was abject. Overdone is at least a procuress, a brothel keeper. For most of the rest poverty drove them to the brothels and after a relatively short stay in which they had to run the hazards of disease, violence and contempt, most were driven back to it.

In pursuing the authority–subversion question, this chapter has tried to exemplify two complementary modes of materialist criticism. Both are concerned to recover the text's history. The one looks directly for history in the text including the historical conditions of its production which, even if not addressed directly by the text can nevertheless still be said to be within it, informing it. Yet there is a limit to which the text can be said to incorporate those aspects of its historical moment of which it never speaks. At that limit, rather than constructing this history as the text's unconscious, we might instead address it directly. Then at any rate we have to recognise the obvious: the prostitutes, the most exploited group in the society which the play represents, are absent from it. Virtually everything that happens presupposes them yet they have no voice, no presence. And those who speak for them do so as exploitatively as those who want to eliminate them. Looking for evidence of resistance we find rather further evidence of exploitation. There comes a time of course when the demonising of deviant sexuality meets with cultural and political resistance. From the very terms of its oppression deviancy generates a challenging counter-discourse and eventually a far-reaching critique of exploitation. That is another and later story.

From Jonathan Dollimore and Alan Sinfield (eds), *Political Shakespeare* (Manchester, 1985), pp. 72–87.

Notes

[Jonathan Dollimore and Alan Sinfield produced one of the most enduring anthologies of Shakespeare criticism from the mid-1980s. This essay shares with its companions in *Political Shakespeare* a sense of the overt political commitment that came to be characterised as 'cultural materialism'. Although some of the critics brought together under this banner sought to distance themselves from such easy or reductive labels, one characteristic of 'cultural materialism' (predominantly a British and Irish phenomenon), was that it was defined against a parallel development in North America and elsewhere. 'New Historicism' was seen as less politically motivated and much less radical than its European counterpart. Certainly Dollimore's essay, much anthologised and widely quoted, has all the political hallmarks of the mid-1980s where Margaret Thatcher's government, through the apparatus of the state, turned against many 'transgressors', ranging from striking coal miners to the gay-rights campaigners. The essay approaches *Measure for Measure* with an eye to historical events as they unfolded in Shakespeare's time, recasting both text and context in the conditions Dollimore found in Britain in the mid-1980s. What emerges is both a fresh approach to Shakespeare, and a signal from the mid-1980s to the mid-2000s that shows just how political Shakespeare remains. Ed.]

1. *Measure for Measure*, ed. J. W. Lever (London, 1965).

2. Ibid., pp. lx and lxxi.

3. For another kind of critic sexuality in *Measure for Measure* continues to be seen as something deeply disruptive though it is the individual psyche rather than the social order which is under threat. Thus for Marilyn French this is a play which 'confronts directly Shakespeare's own most elemental fears' – hence its 'sexual obsessiveness, mixed guilt, abhorrence'. She writes further of 'the hideous and repellent quality sex has throughout the play. It is, it remains, evil, filthy, disgusting, diseased'. See *Shakespeare's Division of Experience* (London, 1982), pp. 195–7.

4. Alan Bray, *Homosexuality in Renaissance England* (London, 1982); Stuart Clark, 'Inversion, Misrule and the Meaning of Witchcraft', *Past and Present*, 87 (1980), 98–127; Christopher Hill, *The World Turned Upside Down: Radical Ideas During the English Revolution* (Harmondsworth, 1975).

5. Ibid., pp. 16–17, 25.

6. For the Baines document, see C. F. Tucker Brooke, *The Life of Marlowe and the Tragedy of Dido Queen of Carthage* (London, 1930), pp. 98–100.

7. Peter Tatchell, *The Battle for Bermondsey*, preface by Tony Benn (London, 1983).

8. Stuart Clark, 'Inversion, Misrule and the Meaning of Witchcraft', *Past and Present*, 87 (1980), 98–127, pp. 110–12.

9. Lawrence Stone, *The Family, Sex and Marriage in England 1500–1800* (London, 1977), pp. 653, 217, 654, 623–4; and F. G. Emmison has estimated that in the county of Essex around 15,000 people were summoned on sexual charges in the forty-five years up to 1603; see *Elizabethan Life: Morals and the Church Courts* (Chelmsford, 1973), p. 1. Commenting on these figures Stone remarks that 'in an adult life-span of 30 years, an Elizabethan inhabitant of Essex ... had more than

a one-in-four chance of being accused of fornication, adultery, buggery, incest, bestiality or bigamy', ibid., p. 519.

10. J. A. Sharpe, *Crime in Seventeenth-Century England: A County Study* (Cambridge, 1983), pp. 57, 70, 215–16.

11. *Measure for Measure*, ed. J. W. Lever (London, 1965), p. xlvi.

12. *Mirror for Magistrates* quoted from Thomas C. Izard's helpful study, *George Whetstone: Mid-Elizabethan Gentleman of Letters* (1942, reprinted New York, 1966), p. 140.

13. See the Proclamation of 1546 ordering London brothels to be closed, in *Tudor Royal Proclamations* (3 vols), ed. Paul L. Hughes and James L. Larkin (New Haven, CT, 1964–9), vol. 1, pp. 365–6; also Wallace Shugg, 'Prostitution in Shakespeare's London', *Shakespeare Studies*, 10 (1977), 291–313, especially p. 306.

14. *Measure for Measure*, ed. J. W. Lever (London, 1965), p. xxxii.

15. Ibid.

16. *Stuart Royal Proclamations*, vol. 1, ed. James F. Larkin and Paul L. Hughes (Oxford, 1973), p. 47.

17. Thomas C. Izard, *George Whetstone: Mid-Elizabethan Gentleman of Letters* (1942, reprinted New York, 1966), p. 135.

18. Ibid., p. 136.

19. *Tudor Royal Proclamations* (3 vols), ed. Paul L. Hughes and James L. Larkin (New Haven, CT, 1964–9), vol. III, p. 233.

20. Christopher Hill, *The World Turned Upside Down: Radical Ideas During the English Revolution* (Harmondsworth, 1975), pp. 40–1.

21. See especially Leonard Tennenhouse, 'Representing Power: *Measure for Measure* in its Time', in *The Power of Forms in the English Renaissance*, ed. Stephen Greenblatt (Norman, OK, 1982), pp. 139–56; David Sundelson, 'Misogyny and Rule in *Measure for Measure*', *Women's Studies*, 9,1 (1981), 83–91.

22. Ben Jonson, *Works*, ed. Charles H. Hereford, Percy Simpson and Evelyn Simpson, 11 vols (Oxford, 1922–52), I, 19, 139.

23. Jonathan Dollimore, *Radical Tragedy: Religion, Ideology and Power in the Drama of Shakespeare and His Contemporaries* (Brighton, 1984; Chicago, 1984), pp. 9–17.

24. Richard Hooker, *Of the Laws of Ecclesiastical Polity* (2 vols), introduction by C. Morris (London, 1969), 2, 19.

25. In the nineteenth century, for example, A. W. Schlegal praised 'the heavenly purity of her mind ... not even stained with one unholy thought' and Edward Dowden her 'pure zeal' and 'virgin sanctity'.

By contrast Coleridge found her 'unamiable' and Hazlitt reproved her 'rigid chastity'. These other passages from earlier critics are conveniently collected in C. K. Stead (ed.), *Shakespeare: Measure for Measure, a Casebook* (London, 1971); see especially pp. 43–5, 59–62, 45–7, 47–9.

26. *Measure for Measure*, ed. J. W. Lever (London, 1965), pp. lxxx, lxxvii, lxxix, xci.

27. See especially Joel Samaha, 'Gleanings from Local Criminal Court Records: Sedition among the inarticulate in Elizabethan Essex', *Journal of Social History*, 8 (1975), 61–79.

28. E. J. Burford, *Queen of the Bawds* (London, 1974); Thomas Nashe, *The Unfortunate Traveller and Other Works*, ed. J. B. Steane (Harmondsworth, 1972), p. 483; Gāmini Salgādo, *The Elizabethan Underworld* (London, 1977), p. 58.

6

London in *Measure for Measure*

LEAH MARCUS

[...] Much has been written about law in *Measure for Measure*. But law in the play is not one single thing, an absolute against which various forms of illicit 'liberty' and transgression are played off. In terms of the play's meaning for London, we need to distinguish between different kinds of law: between 'local' law, which is inscribed in specific places and bound within their limits, and 'unlocalised' law, which operates, sometimes with apparent wilfulness, across boundaries, outside the limits of place. London and its environs were a crazy quilt of different legal jurisdictions, some inextricable from topography; others more global, independent of topographical boundaries. The former would include city ordinances and customary laws. London's liberties and franchises were jealously guarded by her citizens and, in general, protected by English common law. But there was another system of law interlayered with the 'local' law of the city and increasingly in competition with it during the early Jacobean period: that was the amorphous, pervasive, 'unlocalised' jurisdiction associated with ecclesiastical law and the canons of the church, with royal prerogative (increasingly questioned by the advocates of common law, but buttressed by the civil law) and with the royal 'dispensing power' to exempt individuals from the provisions of statute law. Common law and the liberties it guaranteed were specific to England, embedded in its particular 'places' and history; civil and canon law were outgrowths of the Roman law, which was international, operating across boundaries between peoples and places.

The chief area of jurisdictional conflict in the 'Vienna' of *Measure for Measure* is the matter of sexual incontinence – how it is to be defined and how it should be punished. The same matter was also a well-known battle ground between competing legal systems in the London of 1604. Twentieth-century interpreters have taken pains to establish whether, in terms of Renaissance perceptions, the play's various irregular unions would have been understood as fornication or as lawful marriage. But critical consensus on that thorny interpretive issue cannot possibly be reached if only because there *was* no single Renaissance understanding of what constituted valid marriage – at least not in England. Even in terms of the canon law, the line between illegal sexual incontinence and true marriage was very flexible in practice. The ecclesiastical courts did not always operate according to a clear-cut set of invariable principles out of medieval canonists or Justinian. And if their tolerance for exceptions was not complicated enough, there was also the problem that canon law itself had just altered. As a result of the Hampton Court Conference between James I, key bishops, and selected Puritan divines, a new canon revising the definition of lawful marriage took effect in 1604, the same year as *Measure for Measure*.

Moreover, canon law was by no means the only legal code by which contemporaries could measure the validity of marriages. What constituted 'true' marriage was a more nebulous matter in the London of 1604 than it had been for decades because of new and competing initiatives on the part of Crown, church, Nonconformist divines, and agents of city government to impose consistency upon an area of human conduct which had traditionally been subject only to sporadic regulation. In *Measure for Measure*, as in London of 1604, the question of whose authority will dominate in an area of uncertainty and conflicting jurisdiction is a question which is at least as important – probably more important – than the actual punishments meted out for incontinence.

In late Elizabethan and early Jacobean England, marriage was a long, drawn-out process with a number of steps – from the first private promise of marriage *de futuro* between the two parties themselves, to a public contract and the establishment of property settlement, to the actual church wedding (if that step was even taken at all), and, finally, to sexual consummation (if that step had not been taken already). Before the new 1604 canon took effect, the point in the process at which the couple could be said to be married was largely a matter of local custom, varying from one place to another. In some areas, particularly rural communities, sexual familiarity before the finalisation of marriage was tolerated. Couples, in effect, married themselves through the mutual promise of marriage followed by copulation. If, as in the case of Claudio and Juliet in the play, they became parents before their union was publicly acknowledged, they might get hauled before the local 'bawdy court' and required to do perfunctory penance before the congregation or, if they could afford it, charged a fine to commute the punishment.

If they were unlucky, however, such a couple might come to the attention of local justices of the peace, who also had jurisdiction according to a parliamentary statute of 18 Elizabeth over any case of sexual incontinence which produced a child as well as customary jurisdiction over various other sexual offences. According to the canon law before 1604, clandestine marriage was legal but irregular; in common law, it had no legal status at all. Property settlements under the common law required proof of open, public marriage. By the provisions of the parliamentary statute, two justices of the peace acting together could determine the disposition of a bastardy case and impose 'by their discretion' what seemed to them appropriate punishment of the guilty parties. It is easy to see that, given zealous officials, the statute could create a much more severe climate for sexual offenders than the church courts usually did. That, no doubt, was the intent behind the parliamentary initiative. In some areas, justices of the peace and constables actually conducted house-to-house midnight bed checks to scout out illicit sexuality. Offenders could be handed over for trial either to the ecclesiastical or to the secular courts. Some cases of sexual incontinence got bounced from the ecclesiastical to the common law courts and back again, as each legal system tried to assert its jurisdictional predominance over the other.

In addition to that possible double jeopardy, there were other quarters from which correction could come. Puritan ministers often took upon themselves the revelation and punishment of fornicators within their congregations. Their doing so was, strictly speaking, unlawful, since it pre-empted the jurisdiction of the ecclesiastical courts. But the divines who took such measures were usually markedly hostile toward the church courts to begin with, regarding the whole canon law system as a lamentable survival of pre-Reformation 'papal filth' that made 'but a jest' of vice. The public shaming Puritan divines imposed upon wayward members of the congregation might be similar to the sentence which would have been imposed by the church courts, but it would probably not involve the exacting of fines, it would be imposed in an atmosphere of greater severity toward individual transgression, and it would proceed from a competing source of spiritual jurisdiction.

Some Puritan divines were also prone (like Oliver Martext in *As You Like It*) to conduct what the official church condemned as invalid marriages outside the parish church and without banns or licence. Again, part of the point of creating such unions was to circumvent the official system, which would have required 'superstitious ceremonies' like the use of a wedding ring. London liberties with substantial Puritan congregations also tended to be havens for irregular marriage. The new ecclesiastical canons which took effect in 1604 were designed to stamp out such practices by specifying that marriage had to be performed by a duly licensed cleric in the parish church of one of the partners between the hours of eight in the morning and noon, after either the announcement of banns on three consecutive Sundays or festival days, or the procurement of a valid licence from the bishop. Since the new regulations had been passed by convocation as early as 1584, people had had the time to become familiar with them. Even before they were formally adopted as ecclesiastical law, several ministers who had conducted irregular marriages had been censured by the church. With formal ratification, many more prosecutions were impending.

As it transpired, however, clandestine marriage between the parties themselves, without the use of a minister, remained a grey area of the ecclesiastical law. England did not go as far as Catholic Europe had after the Council of Trent, banning clandestine marriage entirely. But the continuing tolerance in practice was not specifically allowed by the canon. In 1604, with the new canons in place and new, stricter plans for forcing conformity upon resisting ministers, there was considerable uncertainty about whether clandestine marriages would have any continuing validity. Certainly they were now further from official acceptability in England than they had ever been before. The pattern of empire, by which 'unlocalised' canon and civil law reached out to encompass and erase local difference, was brought closer than ever to realisation in the area of marriage litigation through the canons of 1604.

In London, as we have noted, there was agitation in some reformist circles for the adoption of the Mosaic code as a basis for civil ordinance. That, if put into practice, would have brought London almost into line with the statutes of Shakespeare's 'Vienna'.

Something very much like the Viennese ordinance was in fact put in place some forty years later, during the Interregnum. Under the Commonwealth government, a second offence of incontinence could be punished by death. In addition, church marriage was abolished and justices of the peace were empowered both to conduct marriages and to dissolve them. But such 'root and branch' upheaval of the traditional system was only a theoretical model in the London of 1604. As it was, London's own customary penalties against sexual offenders – whipping, shaving the head, public carting, and jail – were far more draconian than the punishment prescribed in most other places and in the ecclesiastical courts. The City of London also claimed the 'freedom' of overriding the ecclesiastical laws regulating sexuality with its own customary restraints. For example, London sometimes punished clerics for incontinence according to its own system of penalties, even though that function was in theory reserved to the ecclesiastical courts. As the crackdown against bawds and whores had made evident, reform was very much in the air in London, 1604. The city was taking on a reputation for exceptional vigour against vice. And this was happening at a time when the Crown and Anglican church were exerting their own competing effort to surmount the crazy quilt of local jurisdictions with one overarching standard governing marriage and sexuality.

If Shakespeare's 'Vienna' is a jittery and confused place when it comes to questions of sexual morality, Shakespeare's London could be said to suffer from a similar insecurity. What constituted valid marriage was not some idle legal nicety: it was an issue people had to confront in the most personal terms possible unless they remained totally celibate. Amid the nervous welter of conflicting jurisdictions over the crime of sexual incontinence, contemporaries would have differed sharply in their assessment of the validity of *Measure for Measure*'s clandestine marriages. Their opinions – if they were able to come to a clear-cut opinion at all – would vary according to their degree of familiarity with recent changes in secular and canon law, and according to their general ideological bent. At a time when the Anglican church itself had launched a new offensive against the problem of clandestine marriage, intolerance for the practice did not necessarily make one overbearingly 'precise'. Despite the range of different opinions, however, there was one area in which there would have been substantial unanimity in London, 1604. To anyone who lived from day to day amid the open jurisdictional skirmishes among competing authorities in London, the styles of legal authority played off against each other in Shakespeare's 'Vienna' would have been immediately identifiable in terms of the local conflict.

Angelo, as chief governor of Vienna, is in effect the city's Lord Mayor, and as a London Lord Mayor would, he acts with the powers of a justice of the peace to defend and strengthen the city's local ordinances, in this case, the 'biting' written statute that requires fornicators to be put to death. The duke initially claims that his own goal is also to restore the integrity of the statute – put teeth back into a local code which has fallen into disregard like 'threatning twigs of birch' (I.iii.24) long unused and therefore 'More mock'd, then fear'd' (I.iii.27). But the duke's secret motive is instead to test Angelo – to probe into the workings of city government and the significance of his own delegation of authority by trying the virtue of a 'precise' man whose whole demeanour and life seem dedicated to the rigour of law, specifically to civic government and to the common law. The duke praises Escalus for his knowledge of the '*Cities Institutions*, and the Termes / For Common Iustice' (I.i.10–11). In contemporary parlance, the 'Termes for Common Iustice' is a phrase specifically associating Escalus and city government with expertise in the common law. This is the realm of legal discourse within which Angelo, too, will function.

In *Measure for Measure*, Angelo and Escalus follow the basic pattern of London' civic authorities or justices of the peace, conducting open, informal interrogations and, in accordance with the parliamentary statute of 18 Elizabeth but unlike any of Shakespeare's sources and analogues, working together as a pair to inquire into cases of sexual incontinence and bastardy. The obscure offence committed in Pompey's unsavoury 'house' against Elbow's pregnant wife at least potentially falls within the statute, since she is with child by someone, but the exact nature of the allegation Elbow wishes to make is hopelessly lost in tangles of lexical confusion. He, a constable and therefore an agent of city law and order, is an 'elbow' indeed, incessantly turning the law and language back upon themselves until all possibility for stable meaning is lost. The fact that such an engine for the decomposition of system can hold public office bodes ill for public order in 'Vienna'. Angelo to some extent abrogates his role as a justice in dealing with Elbow's case, at least by the standard of the English parliamentary statute, in that he eventually loses patience with the constable's obscurities and leaves Escalus to deal with the matter alone. Usually he is more punctilious. In the bastardy case of

Juliet and Claudio, the two justices also confer together to determine appropriate punishment and this time Angelo is the more persistent of the two in following through on the case and applying the full rigour of the law. His insistence on the exact letter of the statute makes him close kin to actual London reformers who grounded their campaigns against vice similarly in the powers of surveillance mandated by the '*Cities Institutions*' and 'the Termes for Common Iustice'.

Angelo, of course, proves corrupt in office, counterfeit 'mettle' rather than true coin. For London theatre audiences, part of the game of topicality in 'Vienna' would have been the titillating pleasure of measuring the hypocrisy of Angelo against their own civic authorities. One obvious candidate for resemblance would have been Chief Justice Popham, probably the most prominent common law justice of the time, who had spearheaded the initiative against brothels about London and was called 'bloody Popham' by his enemies. He was known to be so 'precise' in his personal habits that he kept the Sabbath Day meticulously even when he was riding circuit for the provincial assizes. He was also widely suspected of hypocrisy. Another prime candidate might have been Sir Edward Coke, who was already known for his defence of the common law and city 'liberties' and for his interest in reviving the rigour of old statutes, but who had recently entered into a scandalously irregular marriage himself despite his ostensible veneration of the law. As usual, the game of topical identification was juicy and potentially endless: other ripe candidates were available from among the ranks of pompous London authorities – aldermen, recent Lord Mayors, sheriffs, and zealous justices of the peace. The city's crackdown on vice was bound to create friction and resistance, even perhaps among those who advocated London 'liberties' in theory. Other plays of the period make similar capital out of the unveiling of the secret vices of staid, bourgeois officialdom.

But the figure of the duke was just as vulnerable to the game of topical identification. His various personal likenesses to King James I do not require recapitulation here – they are obvious enough to have struck editors and readers of *Measure for Measure* since at least the eighteenth century. As we will note later on, there are several other contemporary figures whom Shakespeare's duke of Vienna could also be said to resemble. What could perhaps bear more attention at this point, however, is the remarkably Jacobean *style* of the duke's activities in the play in terms of the contemporary conflicts over law.

He, like the new king of England, begins by asserting his reverence for local customs and ordinances: they are, he claims, *his* laws, 'our Decrees' (I.iii.27), and he commits himself to giving them more authority. As it transpires, however, the duke is not at all interested in restoring the rigour of the statute against fornication. Instead, he acts in various ways to mitigate it with flexible principles drawn from the civil law and equity. Like James I in London, he acts indirectly and through intermediaries to assert his own ultimate jurisdiction over the city's customary privilege of policing its territory within the walls.

At the end of the play, despite all the initial talk about the rigid enforcement of law, the Viennese statute punishing fornication with death is forgotten. It disappears almost unnoticed amid the splendid theatrics of the public trial before the city gates. Nobody has been executed for fornication, and no one seems likely to be. In the last act, the duke himself in effect becomes the law, the *lex loquens* or speaking law, as the Roman civil code and the speeches of James I would have it, an independent source of legal authority which transcends the city's ordinance, coming down like universal 'power divine' to reveal the defects in a fallible local human system. The pattern was already familiar in the London of 1604; it was to become more familiar with James's continuing intervention in the city's affairs. In *Measure for Measure* local authority is overridden by royal prerogative, by the principles of Roman civil law, which fostered the idea of the monarch as the embodiment of a general, mysterious, ultimate legal authority.

Throughout the play, the duke's style of intervention is associated, not with the common law, but with ecclesiastical jurisdiction in a markedly conservative form. He is garbed as a friar for most of the action, serving as a confessor and spiritual adviser to those in need of his ministrations. He appears and vanishes with mercurial suddenness, operating in hidden ways outside local boundaries and limits. In several instances, his methods correlate with procedure under the Roman law. As was the practice in the canon law courts (in marked contrast to the common law), he gathers testimony by interrogating witnesses in private and in advance of the trial. Given the secret way in which the relevant testimony was obtained, at ecclesiastical trials the truth often emerged with sudden and undeniable éclat once all the evidence was revealed. Much the same effect is achieved in the duke's public exposure of Angelo. The trial scene, with its crowd of unruly onlookers, its attendant 'clerics', and its emphasis on shaming and public reputation, has some of the quality of a trial in the contemporary bawdy courts, with their odd mix of the awesome and the carnivalesque.

In the end, when the duke throws off his ecclesiastical garb to act in his own person to confer validity on the play's irregular sexual unions, he is assuming a prerogative like that which James I and the Anglican church had asserted in 1604 as they tightened up the canon law governing valid marriage by insisting upon the proper licence. Within the Vienna of the play, there are 'outlaw' areas like Angelo's private garden 'circummur'd with Brick' and outlying areas like Mariana's lonely grange which appear analogous to the London suburbs, removed from the regular jurisdiction of the city. The duke's activities penetrate these places apart, redress the anomalous situations which have been tolerated there, and bring them under his authority, much as James I and the church were moving in to bring the London liberties under royal and ecclesiastical control. When the duke commands that Angelo and Mariana be immediately married, he is claiming ultimate authority over the system of ecclesiastical licensing. Ordinarily, by the 1604 canon, Angelo and Mariana would require a licence from the bishop in order to be married 'instantly', without the publication of banns. In this case, the licence emanates not from a bishop but from the ultimate ecclesiastical power above the bishop, the *lex loquens* of the ruler.

There are also resemblances between the duke's style of justice and the English Court of Chancery. Traditionally, the chancellors of England had been clerics and the duke's disguise recalls that connection. Chancery was the final court of appeal in ecclesiastical cases involving matters of property (which often hinged upon the validity of marriage); it frequently reversed the severity of the lower common law courts, just as the duke alleviates the severity of the statute. According to one contemporary description, the chancellor 'doth so *cancell* and *shut up* the *rigour* of the general *Law*, that it shall not breake forth to the hurt of some one singular Case and person'. By abrogating a local statute in favour of 'mercy' and equity, the duke acts, in effect, as his own Lord Chancellor, overriding local justices in the name of the Roman code and the royal dispensing power. The jurisdictional morass has been cleared away; pockets of secret licence have been opened up to surveillance; and the duke has publicly established for himself and for the civil and canon law the ultimate right to adjudicate 'Mortallitie and Mercie in *Vienna*'.

In twentieth-century editions and productions of *Measure for Measure*, the trial scene usually takes place inside the city. The First

Folio itself offers no such certainty as to place. As the scene begins, the duke is approaching the city gates: 'Twice haue the Trumpetes sounded. The generous, and grauest Citizens / Haue hent the gates, and very neere upon / The Duke is entring' (IV.vi.13–16). The folio stage directions which follow specify only that the 'Duke, Varrius, Lords, Angelo, Esculus, Lucio' and 'Citizens' enter 'at seuerall doores' (V.i). In some of the earliest editions of the play specifying the locus of the public trial which follows, the scene of the trial is described as 'a public Place near the City'. That added stage direction is interesting because it suggests that early editors of the play thought of Shakespeare's 'Vienna' in terms of a topography very like London's: the City proper is a self-contained, walled unit surrounded by other urban areas, like the London liberties, which are not strictly part of it. What the scene enacts is the traditional public ritual by which civic authorities greet a visiting monarch. They meet the ruler with fanfare just outside the walls – the entry 'at seuerall doores' suggesting that the different groups have come from different directions – to formally tender up their authority and accompany him through the gates.

In this case, however, the entry is delayed as a result of the duke's proclamation inviting petitioners to approach him publicly for the redress of grievances. The pleas of Isabella and Mariana turn the usual scene of ceremonial transfer of authority into a forum for inquiring into the conduct of the deputy. The duke establishes his superior claim to govern the city from a location just outside the wall, outside its proper jurisdiction; then, much as James I had entered London in triumph in the year 1604, he enters the gates and proceeds in state to his 'Pallace', formally taking possession of the place he has demonstrated a transcendent right to control. That which is merely local has been made to appear small, paltry and corruptible, by comparison with an authority which partakes of the divine and the universal, which cuts through jurisdictional tangles to establish a single, centralised, yet merciful standard of law.

It is easy to see how James I would have relished the play's depiction of victory for the Roman law with which he felt such sympathy and which, in 1604, he still hoped to use as the basis of a united Britain. There are many ways in which the play seems weighted toward the 'Jacobean line'. The city's own authorities are an unimpressive lot: even Escalus is too shortsighted to suspect the vice of Angelo. Unless Claudio is played as an unusually repellent character, he tends to generate audience sympathy, at least by comparison with

Angelo, just as his plight generates sympathy from onlookers within the play. Insofar as an audience takes the part of Claudio against Angelo and the rigour of the statute, they are being invited to side with the duke against the city – recognise the wisdom of the ruler's timely use of equity to redress a reforming zeal which has gone too far.

There were contemporaries who would have agreed with Angelo that death was not an excessive penalty for fornication, but they were the same zealots who were most vehement against the theatre. They would not (it seems safe to say) have been part of the audience for *Measure for Measure*. To the extent that London theatrical audiences resented the reformers' endless campaigns against the public 'enormity' of stage plays, they may have found it easy to applaud the duke's exposure of a civic leader who was overly precise. The place of the duke's highly theatrical trial just outside the jurisdiction of the city was, in London, the place of the stage itself. There is a natural topographical alliance between the theatricality of the duke and the institution which brought him to life on stage on the outskirts of London.

But for at least some members of a London audience in 1604, the play's victory over statute may have looked more like defeat. Whether or not the duke's influence is perceived as salutary depends to a marked degree on the audience's evaluation of the duke himself. For good or for ill, his *modus operandi* in the play is made to appear arbitrary, manipulative, imposed from without. In modern performances, he is often idealised as the wise exemplar of overarching authority called for by the play's 'Jacobean line', a figure whose arbitrary gestures are justified as desperate counters to the rampant crimes of his surrogate. Almost as frequently in modern productions, however, the duke comes closer to Lucio's description of the 'fantastical Duke of darke corners' (IV.iii.147) or Angelo's equally disparaging language: 'In most vneuen and distracted manner, his actions show much like to madnesse, pray heauen his wisedome bee not tainted' (IV.iv.2–4). In modern productions, the duke can be a *deus ex machina* who descends by means of a whirligig, a shadowy trickster who delights in imposing unnecessary gyrations of misery upon his subjects merely to show his power. Like Jupiter in *Cymbeline*, he exists on a perilous boundary between the sublime and the grotesque.

In London, 1604, there may have been nearly as much potential for variability in the portrayal of the duke as there is in modern performance. Because of the heated conflicts over jurisdictional issues in the city, even relatively small alterations in the nervous balance between the duke and his antagonists could markedly have altered the political complexion of the play. Let us take one 'localised' example of the problematics that contemporary performance could – perhaps fleetingly – have exploited. If a London audience saw a parallel between the duke of Vienna and James I as the promulgator of the new ecclesiastical laws regarding marriage, they could easily have been puzzled by his uncanonical behaviour earlier in the play. The 'bed trick' by which Mariana is substituted for Isabella to satisfy Angelo's lust was *not* lawful according to the church's new definition of marriage. The precipitous wedding ordered by the duke between Mariana and Angelo was also uncanonical unless, by some chance, they happened to be married in the parish church of one of them, or unless the duke's verbal 'licence' is taken to cancel out the usual rules. These are small details, perhaps: topicality thrives on what is almost too insignificant to notice. But they suggest that the duke, insofar as he is identified with James I, can be trusted to respect his beloved canon law no more than Angelo does the statute. That perception unleashes potential for contemporary deconstruction of *Measure for Measure*'s Jacobean line. Like King James, the duke acts above the law, freely overriding even his own preferred code when it suits his purpose to do so. Contemporary viewers could surmount the seeming contradiction in the duke's position by making a 'leap of faith' from the law to Christian mercy, by which all legal codes are confounded. As we will note further later on, *Measure for Measure*, like *King Lear*, is associated with St. Stephen's Day, at least through its performance at court, and therefore with the holiday inversion of law and ordinary hierarchy. But to regard the duke as transcending all law would undermine the play's appeal to the ruler as an alternative and superior source of law. In *Measure for Measure*, the rule of law is overthrown by something that may be divine transcendence, but can also look like royal whim, unruly 'license', a mere recapitulation of the abuse it purports to rectify. [...]

From Leah Marcus, *Puzzling Shakespeare: Local Reading and its Discontents* (Berkeley and Los Angeles, 1988), Chapter 4, pp. 171–82.

Notes

[Leah Marcus's essay is an extract from her successful book which might be seen as an example of the kind of American criticism of the mid-1980s that came to be described as 'New Historicism'. There is a strong sense of historical context in Marcus's work, and specifically in this essay, the idea that the Vienna of *Measure For Measure* has much in common with the London of Shakespeare's day. According to Marcus, the London of 1600 was the site of competing legal systems that would have been evoked for audiences of the play as of specific relevance to their own experiences of the law. At stake in particular are the various legal codes and customs that governed (or sought to govern) sexual behaviour, marriage, and the family. One characteristic of the 'early-modern' period was a clash, or at least an overlap, between feudal and modern legal/ethical codes, and Marcus notes these discontinuities in *Measure for Measure*. These concerns have been taken up widely in approaches to the whole canon of Renaissance literature to very good effect since the 1980s. Marcus's essay can be read as an excellent example of a developing critical approach. Ed.]

7

Love's Tyranny Inside-out in the Problem Plays: Yours, Mine, and Counter-mine

RICHARD HILLMAN

It suggests an intuitive grasp of psychic paradox that Christian mythology came to attach the name of Lucifer, the light-bringer, to the guileful Prince of Darkness. In *Measure for Measure* an analogous attachment is at once vigorously promoted – by Lucio, the self-proclaimed 'bur' who will 'stick' (IV.iii.179) to the 'Duke of dark corners' (l.157) – and indignantly resisted.[1] In the end, of course, it is the Duke, self-invested with 'pow'r divine' (V.i.369), who tricks Lucio into bringing to light the very circumstance that will force him back into the shadows. For Lucio, the consigning of sexual and linguistic freedom to the care of the doubly aptly named Kate Keepdown looms as 'pressing to death, whipping, and hanging' (ll.522–3). By pulling off the Friar's hood to make him 'show [his] knave's visage' (l.353), Lucio is made to 'change persons' (l.336) with him and take this term of abuse, as he must acknowledge his child and the slanders spoken 'according to the trick' (ll.504–5) as his own: 'Thou art the first knave that e'er mad'st a Duke' (l.356). A residual sense of the unmasking as a more creative act than the masking – for indeed, '*Cacullus non facit monachum*' (l.262) – shows in Lucio's plea for mercy: 'Your Highness said even now I made you a Duke' (ll.515–16). But the Duke's re-created world cannot tolerate, any more than God's heaven, a rival claimant to the creator's prerogative.[2] Lucio's very defence of his slander contains a *de facto* recantation of numinosity; to use 'trick', as he clearly does, in the sense of 'custom' or 'fashion' is to strip the word of the subversive potency (realised or not) that it typically carries in connection with Shakespearean clowns, fools, and deceptive practices.[3] From this perspective, 'according to the trick' signals, in the guise of disruptive assertion, a fundamental acquiescence in the discourse of counter-subversiveness. His is a 'mystery' (like Abhorson's [IV.ii.28ff.]) in the service of radical de-mystification.

In a play otherwise about conflicting claims less to hegemony than to separateness, in which a source of friction between the comic form and several principal characters is their drive for barricaded self-sufficiency, the silencing of Lucio presses to death the hitherto irrepressible voice of relatedness and contingency. And it does so on behalf of a comic resolution that cannot persuasively speak for itself because its beneficiaries, too, are largely silent. Isabella's is the notoriously problematic example – the more so because it recalls the pivotal moment when Lucio's call at the convent gate led Francisca to inform her further about the 'restraint' (I.iv.4) she was so eager for:

> When you have vow'd, you must not speak with men
> But in the presence of the prioress;
> Then if you speak, you must not show your face,
> Or if you show your face, you must not speak.
>   (ll.10–13)

Isabella's first encounter with Angelo showed her '[a]t war 'twixt will and will not' (II.ii.33), trying to withhold speech. Now, confronted by the prospect of withholding from a man nothing of herself, should her face show her similarly at war? The momentum of the Duke's disclosures, culminating in the revelation (withheld precisely for its impact) that he has saved her brother's life, has co-opted even her silence. It has been transformed from a correlative of self-'restraint' to an index of powerlessness and sexual vulnerability, with the subtextual support of another proverb – 'silence gives consent'. But if it is hers that resonates most strongly, it also joins the successive silences of others. Lucio's is the only voice apart from the Duke's for the last forty-five lines of the play. Even the relief of Angelo is the Duke's creation: 'Methinks I see a quick'ning in his eye' (V.i.495). What Angelo last articulated was a longing for death.[4]

I

The manifold discrediting, outmanoeuvring, scapegoating, and evasion of subversive forces in Shakespeare's middle plays testify to a deep textual anxiety – not something the text concerns, but something that concerns it – centring on the competing claims of order and disorder. One source of such anxiety may be the continuing formal allegiance of comedies and histories alike to the principle of renewal through the very subversion that calls their values and goals into question. In order to maintain their claim on this process, the power of disruptive energy must be conjured and experienced even as it is resisted. Folly, too, must be enlisted in the cause, however marginalised and confined. Rebirth continues to require symbolic death, a return to chaos. There is more to this than a reductively materialist approach allows: one is put in mind of the religious impulse to renew the sense of salvation by confronting, and even temporarily succumbing to, the devil.

This brings us back to *Measure for Measure*. Lucio's subversive tendencies may be illuminating for the audience – he is, after all, *there*, a presence unthinkable in Illyria, where there is 'no slander' and the corruption only 'of words'; they may appear, in one of many ironic applications of the title, a highly fitting recompense for Vincentio's explicit concern with avoiding slander. Yet they scarcely constitute a substantial threat to the latter's control of events: unlike Don John's, Lucio's slanders are, one might say, like water rolling off a Duke's back, even before the final silencing. Nor, apparently, is there any need for the Duke to rally emblems of folly to his purpose: no 'wise fool' is attached to the court of Vienna. As for subversive impulses, even apart from Angelo, instinct and appetite are as thoroughly stigmatised as could be, thanks to Lucio, Pompey, and Barnardine. Claudio and Juliet do little to redeem passion in the cause of romance, while the Duke's interest in Isabella stands at a discreet, if not chilling, distance from the standard irrationality of love; it does not more than superficially contradict his early declaration of immunity: 'Believe not that the dribbling dart of love/Can pierce a complete bosom' (I.iii.2–3).

The fundamental changes in tone and balance of power amount to far more than the cynicism or sexual revulsion widely perceived in the 'problem comedies' and sometimes projected upon their 'disillusioned' author.[5] I propose that in *Measure for Measure* and *All's Well That Ends Well* we have to do with texts that reflect, in their depiction of subversion, a resolution – however partial, unstable, and open to question – of the ambiguity of the middle plays concerning disruptive energy. This resolution is, in turn, reflected in the very susceptibility of the play-worlds to manipulative experts in public (and private) relations. Quite simply, despite Helena's 'love' for Bertram and the sexual trappings of her role as social renewer, the operative (if hardly avowed) assumption of both shapers of narrative – an assumption, moreover, that *works* – is that disruptive energy has no legitimacy and therefore no contribution to make to comic closure. In so far as romantic consummation is necessary to the genre, it can be mechanically produced and perfunctorily gilded: these are the plays of the bed-trick, which is, in this study's sense, no trick at all. It is the radical disjunction between this new attitude and the continuing transformational connotations of comic form that produces the unsettling anti-comic overtones and the radically 'unsatisfying' endings. These are the contradictions of successful repression (in both the political and psychological senses) and overconfidence – contradictions naturally focused in the manipulations of the dominant characters and the vulnerable deformities of their victims.

Troilus and Cressida, too, may usefully be considered in these terms, despite its problematic genre (comitragedy, perhaps?), the seeming absence of a central manipulator, and, above all, the abundant lip-service paid to amorous folly as the source of both spiritual elevation and despair. In fact, these variations help to expose the new dynamic buried (albeit shallowly) beneath the comic form of the other two plays: not the struggle between principles of order and disorder – that is now a 'dead issue' – but the drive on the part of certain characters for a domination extending to the psyches and self-images of others. Difference itself is constituted as subversive. For Ulysses, the reimposition of Degree blatantly involves psychological warfare; the love-agonies of Troilus, I shall be suggesting, amount to a more subtle but more profound hegemonism.

II

An objective glance at the realities of power in the Viennese state suffices to prove the point, promoted by Dollimore and others, that the fictional universe of *Measure for Measure* is hardly endangered by disruptive impulses.[6] Eloquent as he is on behalf of such impulses, Pompey is Costard's *deformed* descendant, and part of his deforming involves stripping him of any real capacity to make trouble – there are no misdelivered letters here. The respectfully sceptical Friar ('doubting'?) Thomas gets no quarrel from the Duke when he credits him with an absolute power to have dealt with the Pompeys and Overdones at will (I.iii.31–4). Angelo's abuse of power is tracked step-by-step by an irresistible force *in potentia*. Only Barnardine's refusal to be executed puts Vincentio in a tight spot, and the Provost and Ragozine – that is, the text itself – immediately step in to extract him. The Duke's disguise – a parody of symbolic losses of identity elsewhere – merely refocuses his withholding of correction, while endowing him with a temporary (but potent) marginality.

Such continuity tends to confirm that, for the Duke, the goal of social reform lags well behind the desire to 'see/If power change purpose: what our seemers be' (I.iii.53–4). Vincentio's project impresses many commentators as essentially a duel between him and Angelo,[7] and since the latter '[s]tands at a guard with envy' (l.51), his opponent is betraying motives considerably more questionable than the 'fault' (l.35) of lax government to which he willingly admits. The political situation speaks for itself, and perhaps with an echo of Puritan-generated tensions in Jacobean society: given the moral negligence of the Duke's rule, Angelo's ostentatious uprightness constitutes an implicit critique, hence a prospective danger. No further revelations come by way of the Duke's words; even in soliloquy, no feelings obtrude on his impersonal, platitudinous cadences, which claim for his discourse the authority of a transcendent wisdom: 'He who the sword of heaven will bear/Should be as holy as severe' (III.ii.261–2). His actions, notoriously, are another story, riddled as they are with dubious manipulations, as he prepares Angelo for the subversive villain's role in the final scene's ritual of public humiliation. There, putting his proverbial/Biblical discourse multiply into practice – beginning with 'Like doth quit like, and *Measure* still *for Measure*' (V.i.411) – he triumphantly re-integrates moral with political power.

This virtual play-within-the-play makes quite a production, as has often been observed, for one who supposedly does 'not like to stage' (I.i.68) himself to the public eye: the Duke is not only playwright and director, but the busy actor of two of the main roles.[8] In contrast with the Fifth-Act festivity of that earlier pageant of love gone wrong, the tragedy of Pyramus and Thisby, this performance is calculated to re-establish boundaries more strongly, and on Vincentio's own terms. And when the part he has written for Isabella is taken into account, it is clear how thoroughly and variously the play's strange versions of love serve the interests of his political theatre. First, the Duke coolly appropriates the results (whatever we may think of them) of Angelo's crackdown on sexual licence. Then, he exposes the deputy's lapse, together with his own duping of Angelo's desire: Angelo has been tricked into giving his sexuality into the custody of a woman he had repudiated – essentially the fate of Lucio. Finally, Vincentio puts himself in the way of taking Isabella's virginity. His multiple hegemony on the sexual level makes an ironic answer to Pompey's rhetorical question: 'Does your worship mean to geld and splay all the youth of the city?' (II.i.230–1).

No longer, it would seem, is the counterfeit trickster concerned to outmanoeuvre disruptive energies while laying claim to their bene-fits; rather, he seeks to redefine the very terms on which characters form bonds with one another. In so far as the Duke is not merely purging but re-creating his world, in pseudo-divine fashion, it is not subversive forces as such that threaten (and so enable) this activity: it is the very existence of 'free' wills, the concept of separateness. Thus the thrust of his project is to reincorporate characters who would have preferred life on the margins. Angelo does not ask for the post of deputy; Isabella has sought formal withdrawal from the world and sexuality in order to serve another deity; and Mariana surely would have been better off musically enjoying her sorrow in her moated grange, Orsino-like, than she is in getting what she thinks she wants. Through Angelo, 'th' ambush of [his] name' (I.iii.41) functions like a dragnet, not only catching up Claudio and Juliet, who merely want to be left alone, but sweeping the suburbs into the prison; in the broadest sense, the likes of Froth are indeed 'drawn in' (II.i.210). Even Lucio's offensive interventions are rooted in a role thereby imposed upon him – that of Claudio's advocate – and, once centred in the Duke's angry gaze ('here's one in place I cannot pardon' [V.i.499]), he is prevented from retreating to the marginal position of 'allow'd fool', by definition slanderless.

Such absolute domination as the Duke practises unapologetically denies the legitimacy of error, instinct, and desire in shaping existence. It also necessitates the breaking and reforging of self-images – a substitute, in effect, for the transformational processes enacted in the early comedies. Vincentio's power (or potency) substantially exceeds Hal's: its emblem is not exclusion, banishment, or even execution – Pompey and Barnardine can be neither reformed nor eliminated – but imprisonment. It is a deeply fascistic vision – perhaps even more so than has been recognised by commentators, such as Dollimore, who are concerned with Renaissance representations of authority,[9] for authority in this play reaches into the most intimate areas of personal experience, the 'dark corners' of the psyche. State affairs and social issues are pervasively intertwined with appetite. This, of course, is the very tainting of which Angelo stands as an *exemplum*, duly punished, in a way that obscures the subtextual presentation of the drive for power as itself a destructive appetite. That concept is more openly (albeit conditionally) expressed by a politician in a neighbouring text:

> Force should be right, or rather, right and wrong
> (Between whose endless jar justice resides)
> Should lose their names, and so should justice too!
> Then every thing include itself in power,
> Power into will, will into appetite,
> And appetite, an universal wolf
> (So doubly seconded with will and power),
> Must make perforce an universal prey,
> And last eat up himself.
> (*Tro.*, I.iii.116–24)

It is precisely this nightmare that will burst through the containment walls of ritualised statecraft into the world and the mind of Lear.

As for the 'appetite' formally exposed and condemned in *Measure for Measure*, the ruthless isolation of sexuality from a more general subversiveness, and from the love-impulse in particular, functions less to stigmatise it, despite critical perceptions of 'the generalised degradation of sexuality' (Wheeler) or the political construction of 'deviance' (Dollimore), than to make it a mechanical substitute for deeper bonds.[10] The Duke hardly denies (Wheeler) or, except for form's sake, 'demonis[es]' (Dollimore) sexuality; it is rather, as with Pandarus, his stock-in-trade.[11] The sordidness of libertinism functions to taint 'liberty' itself, as Claudio's first speech makes clear (I.ii.125ff.), while the role of 'bawd' serves to demean union that is not on the Duke's terms. (After all, the only sexual congress actually effected within the play involves Vincentio and Isabella as go-betweens.) Sex itself emerges as intrinsically neutral, recuperable in the service of the larger design – a sort of glue that, once applied in a bed-trick, sticks fast and applies, however crookedly, the label of romantic fulfilment. Separating love from sex is a job largely done before the play begins, but the punishment and severing of Juliet and

Claudio neatly recapitulate the process. In this, too, Angelo is 'doing the Duke's dirty work'.[12]

So he is even in pitting himself against Isabella's saintly self-image. Isabella, it is often said, learns humanity at the Duke's hands;[13] certainly, he puts her through the motions of comic transformation, with a plausible culmination in her plea for Angelo's life. Even if one ignores the backhanded self-congratulation in this final speech, however – 'I partly think/A due sincerity governed his deeds,/Till he did look on me' (V.i.445–7) – and allows that her earlier lack of charity towards her brother is behind her, it remains obvious that the Duke's handy solution, which she embraced with unsettling haste, has got her off the subversive hook. The cost is that the counter-trickster can then supply a hook of his own: his script takes her well beyond the part she anticipated playing. Ironically, only Angelo undergoes significant inner conflict, confronting his conscience in a way strongly reminiscent of *Hamlet's* Claudius and experiencing a profound despair when exposed: 'I crave death more willingly than mercy:/'Tis my deserving, and I do entreat it' (ll.476–7). Yet this response, as I suggested earlier, is not allowed to lead anywhere. The benignly despotic master of ceremonies applies Portia's tactics in sparing Angelo's body but, in effect, taking his soul: 'By this Lord Angelo perceives he's safe' (l.494).

III

What chiefly complicates the picture in *All's Well* is the status and purpose of the chief manipulator: while Helena has often been recognised as an analogous internal dramatist,[14] her gender, her social dependency, and her emotional obsession all situate her well down from Vincentio on the scale of power. Moreover, her love-longing automatically invokes the powerful mechanisms of romantic comedy on her behalf. The Duke may gain, at most, our approval; Helena at least begins with an abundant supply of sympathy. Undoubtedly, the acquisition of social and political power figures in Helena's case as well – so strongly as to invalidate, for some commentators, her susceptibility to love. Yet to reduce her to a rank hypocrite and fortune-hunter is both to distort the text and to miss the point. A love-relation, for Vincentio, can be an adjunct to and demonstration of other forms of power; for Helena, power can come only through love. As he also does with Portia – whose problem is too much wealth and status, not too little – Shakespeare presents manipulation in the romantic sphere not as calculation, but as a natural response to female powerlessness. He thus exposes the tendency of repressive social structures to foster resistance to disruptive folly even on the part of their victims.

From the first, Helena's consciousness of inferior rank is intermingled with her romantic feelings. This would be normal enough in the circumstances, but the presentation is equivocal and suggestive. As with her namesake in *A Midsummer Night's Dream*, the sense of a fixation doubtfully related to its object is strongly conveyed, although Demetrius' jilting of her focuses the first Helena's thoughts on her own delusion: 'Things base and vile, holding no quantity,/ Love can transpose to form and dignity' (*MND*, I.i.232–3). Her successor's declaration of one-sided passion, which is made a surprise to us by the red herring of her supposed grief for her father, appears more naïve; in her first soliloquy, she lamely idealises Bertram's 'arched brows, his hawking eye, his curls' (*AWW*, I.i.94), evidently incapable of seeing the decidedly earth-bound young man behind the divine image. This is the cataloguing rhetoric of the love- and grief-blinded Imogen, who cannot tell the body of Cloten from that of Posthumus: 'this is his hand/His foot Mercurial, his Martial thigh' (*Cym.*, IV.ii.309–10). It is also Hamlet's mode of idealising his father ('Hyperion's curls, the front of Jove himself,/An eye like Mars' [*Ham.*, III.iv.56–7]) – a parallel reinforced by the *Hamlet*-echoes over Helena's tears. Yet those tears, in most unHamlet-like fashion, she brusquely strips from her father's memory: 'What was he like?/I have forgot him' (*AWW*, I.i.81–2).

Her transcendental rhetoric makes it all the more remarkable that Helena is simultaneously capable of acknowledging her love as a cult: 'But now he's gone, and my idolatrous fancy/Must sanctify his reliques' (ll.97–8). Apparently, it is not that she cannot recognise Bertram for what he is, but that she does not care. What matters is possessing, or, rather, not possessing him. Unlike the first Helena, who, under the spell of romance, can see no farther than the possibility of getting a glimpse of Demetrius or a kind word from him, this heroine thinks practically and, as they are said to say in advertising, globally. Though her theme is despair, her initial analysis of her dilemma in terms of social barriers is already rich with the potential for taking things into her own hands: ' 'Twere all one/That I should love a bright particular star/And think to wed it, he is so above me' (ll.85–7). When Helena goes on to speak of '[t]h' ambition in my love' (l.90), she effectively presents the two impulses as intertwined. The word 'ambition' is bound to resonate powerfully, as it does when it returns in the letter professing guilt for her '[a]mbitious love' (III.iv.5).

In her second soliloquy, Helena ignores Bertram entirely and speaks (again, most unlike Hamlet) only of the gain to be achieved by bold action:

> Our remedies oft in ourselves do lie,
> Which we ascribe to heaven. The fated sky
> Gives us free scope, only doth backward pull
> Our slow designs when we ourselves are dull.
> (I.i.216–19)

The political overtones of such thinking do not depend on the echo of the tempting Cassius ('The fault, dear Brutus, is not in our stars,/But in ourselves, that we are underlings' [*JC*, I.ii. 140–1]). The idea harks back to Tamburlaine and Richard III, and points forward to Edmund: it is heady – and dubious – company. Even more questionable is her appeal to appetite as self-justifying: 'What power is it which mounts my love so high,/That makes me see, and cannot feed mine eye?' (ll.220–1). One is reminded of Aaron's self-injunction to 'arm thy heart, and fit thy thoughts,/To mount aloft with thy imperial mistress' (*Tit.*, II.i.12–13). Helena proceeds to spur herself on to 'strange attempts' (*AWW*, I.i.224) with a rationalising spirit worthy of Lady Macbeth. The discourse of politics and power has strongly emerged from, and all but erased, that of romance.

For Helena, then, love is at least partly a vehicle, not for social climbing, but for achievement and control. It is both a measure of and a response to powerlessness and dependency, at once revealing and filling an existential vacuum. 'Ambition' may describe an aspect, and a consequence, of that response, but it is an inadequate term for the underlying impulse of self-assertion. Helena's love is, rather, a rough counterpart of Hamlet's revenge, which supplies him, willy-nilly, with mission and meaning after the multiple displacements caused by his father's death. In so far as romance is the only sphere of action open to Helena, she is similarly more chosen than choosing. Yet her actions associate, as in *Measure for Measure*, the acquisition of power with the domination of the thoughts and feelings of other characters. And because love becomes something that Helena uses, not something that uses her, its implicit status as the transforming subversive energy of comedy is itself subverted.

Between Helena's soliloquies of impotence and resolution falls the famous dialogue with Parolles concerning virginity. This bantering exchange superficially exemplifies the sort of clowning elsewhere associated with comic processes. Yet Parolles is a thoroughly tainted representative of disruptive energy, as his subsequent career confirms.[15] It is promising that he is a 'notorious liar' (I.i.100), 'a great way fool, soly a coward' (101) – from this alone, one might expect a Falstaff. What disqualifies him is his calculating interest and success in gaining others' (especially Bertram's) high opinion of him:

> Yet these fix'd evils sit so fit in him,
> That they take place when virtue's steely bones
> Looks bleak i' th' cold wind. Withal, full oft we see
> Cold wisdom waiting on superfluous folly.
> (ll.102–5)

The trickster, when he takes on the role of *miles gloriosus*, is transparent. Everybody sensible sees through Falstaff, as he well knows. For Hal's purposes, there is no need for such empty pretences to valour to be taken seriously and punished – quite the contrary. Falstaff's lies – even his claim to the conquest of Hotspur – can safely be encouraged: the final repudiation focuses on other vices. As the texts shift from Falstaff to his successor Pistol, however, the increase in social menace goes hand in hand with an increased potential for imposing upon others, notably Fluellen: accordingly, there must be a public undeceiving. Parolles represents a further evolution in this direction, and his exposure is made correspondingly more pointed and severe. However, like Pistol's, his distinctive dialect merely preserves the outward form of subversiveness. Parolles is voluble without the traditional clown's linguistic spontaneity; in this sense, too, he is true to his name: he is only words, and his lack of originality in manipulating them would be evident to an audience familiar with the affected 'witty' style of the courtier. In fact, lively inventive wit of the sort wielded by Portia and Rosalind, Beatrice and Benedick, is sparse in *All's Well* – as, for that matter, in *Measure for Measure* and *Troilus*. The later plays, it seems, are less concerned to provide even their romantic leads with a verbal screen of subversive energy.

Certainly, Helena's wit in her exchange with Parolles is coldly mechanical, maintaining the distance established by her opening comment. Moreover, it only thinly veils her inversion of her position of powerlessness – a position of which virginity becomes the index.[16] Parolles begins like Lucio accosting Isabella: ' 'Save you, fair queen! ... Are you meditating on virginity' (ll.106–10). But whereas Lucio's parodic *Ave*, 'Hail, virgin, if you be' (*MM*, I.iv.16), initiates a sexual discourse that Isabella perceives as inherently threatening, Helena instead takes up the challenge in its own terms by respond-ing, 'Ay' (*AWW*, I.i.111), and requesting advice for protecting virginity against men. Assured that there is no defence, she turns to thinking offensively: 'Is there no military policy how virgins might blow up men?' (ll.121–2). She regards virginity as an instrument of self-realisation, considering how 'to lose it to [one's] own liking' (ll.150–1) and rejecting Parolles's advice to cast it away: 'Not my virginity yet' (l.165).[17] These obvious anticipations of her strategy with Bertram are interesting for the attitude towards sexuality that they establish. For Isabella, as well, virginity is a source of personal power, but that power consists merely in self-withholding: hence, the implicit challenge she poses to Angelo (whose response to her osten-tatious purity is not so different from the Duke's to his own), as well as her helplessness in the face of the Duke's final proposal. Helena, by contrast, can envisage the timely loss of virginity as a means to an end. This is, of course, the premise of the bed-trick, and her manipu-lation of Diana – we should not forget that she and her mother are paid for their co-operation – becomes emblematic of Helena's exploitation of virginity itself. Even as her role as central manipula-tor links her with the Duke, therefore, she also unites the two aspects of virginity-as-power that are split in *Measure for Measure* between Isabella and Mariana. (The figure of 'pure' virginity – Diana – is left over as a sort of residue, an empty shell.) It is her affiliation with Mariana that most obviously qualifies Helena's triumph. For however she may succeed to her own satisfaction in possessing the body and subduing the psyche of her husband, she too is ultimately putting herself in a legally subordinate and personally unenviable position. Mariana's plea to the Duke is, after all, pitiable in its self-delusion: 'I crave no other, nor no better man' (*MM*, V.i.426).

One problem for women reduced to using their sexuality as an instrument of power is that the 'prize' traditionally defined as a token of power by men is to be given away only once. Isabella's absolutist chastity contains an anxious cognisance of this fact, as does Helena's 'policy'. Yet it is left to the third central female figure in this trio of texts to articulate her predicament in explicit terms of sex-as-power: 'Achievement is command; ungain'd, beseech' (*Tro.*, I.ii.293). Ironically, Cressida's fate involves not only losing control of her sexuality, as does Isabella, but having the power of virginity turned against her, also in the traditional way, by the imposition of the category of 'whore'. Her situation sheds further light on Helena's successful exercise of sexual power. What chiefly distinguishes Cressida from the other two heroines, and ultimately bears responsibility for her downfall, is her susceptibility to a man who desires her. Isabella has at least precluded the dangers of such reciprocity by cutting off her own sexual feelings, although this does not protect her from 'honourable' sexual possession. On the other hand, Helena's conspicuously unrequited love serves her well throughout. Setting her sights, focusing her susceptibilities, on a reluctant object guarantees that her 'honour' will be kept intact and makes possible an identification of self-gratification with self-realisation. She is free to determine the rules of the game, and from the first they pointedly and self-protectively include marriage.

Helena's jests with Parolles contrast, not only with the meeting of Lucio and Isabella, but also with Cressida's banter:

> Pan. You are such a woman, a man knows not at what ward you lie.
> Cres. Upon my back, to defend my belly, upon my wit, to defend my wiles, upon my secrecy, to defend mine honesty, my mask, to defend my beauty, and you, to defend all these; and at all these wards I lie, at a thousand watches.
>
> (*Tro.*, I.ii.258–64)

The theme is the same – the defence of the sexual self – as is the military lexis. Yet beneath her 'wit', to which she assigns a similar distancing and protective function, Cressida is clearly in the grip of a subversive impulse expressed in the contradictory message of sexual openness. That this contradiction is not mere hypocrisy, a 'cover' for a promiscuous appetite, is established by the acute sense of her particular dilemma projected in the ensuing soliloquy and elsewhere. Cressida finds herself responding sexually to real and pressing overtures made on terms – marriage is never mentioned – that (literally) threaten her integrity: 'I have a kind of self resides with you;/ But an unkind self, that itself will leave/To be another's fool. I would be gone' (III.ii.148–50). Given the productive implications of self-loss and amorous folly in the early Shakespeare, the disastrous consequences of this vulnerability would seem to mark a thorough reversal of perspective, although, as my later discussion will stress, the social context and the projections of Troilus must be taken into account. For the moment, what stands out is the radically dissimilar self-command of Helena, whose love is, in effect, pure initiative.

Her guard with Parolles is always up. Her bawdy dialogue issues in a soliloquy of awesome single-mindedness. Bertram, apparently, is a safe and useful vehicle for her impulses of aspiration precisely because he has no interest in her. It helps her cause even that he is such a cipher as a character. He is mere raw material, however unwilling, for her shaping imagination, and in finally shaping him into a husband as acquiescent, at least, as the nonplussed Isabella or the shamed Angelo, that imagination thoroughly reshapes the world around her.

For attached to Helena's scheme are large implications of social and political renewal. This again affiliates her with Vincentio, but again with an inversion reflecting her primary sphere of action: the Duke's renovation of his image and his state is made to depend upon the suppression of sexual activity; Helena's injection of new life into the play's community is represented in sexual terms, in keeping with her later initiating of Bertram. The powerful overtones of sexual revival in her healing of the King – overtones that resonate with ancient myths of the wounded ruler – have been amply documented. What still calls for comment is the way in which this dimension, far from genuinely revitalising the play-world, merely co-opts male power on behalf of Helena's project. To start with, the cure itself involves her adaptation to her own *will* of her father's – a reminiscence of Portia's use of the casket-device to acquire Bassanio. A further ramification here is that, despite having 'forgotten' him emotionally, Helena is pointedly bringing her father's legacy into conflict with Bertram's own inheritance – his social status: 'She had her breeding at my father's charge – / A poor physician's daughter my wife!' (II.iii.114–15). Similarly, having rejected heaven's power – God the Father – in her second soliloquy, Helena makes a show of submission to divinity, and so appropriates it, when it comes to persuading the King: 'But most it is presumption in us when / The help of heaven we count the act of men' (II.i.151–2).

The two defunct earthly fathers have been juxtaposed since the first scene, as they are within the memory of the King, whose body and mind are the arena chosen by Helena for the contest. She gains her opportunity much in the manner of Bassanio, by giving and hazarding all she has, but here sexuality, not wealth, is the language of power. As her reward will be a husband of her choosing, so the first part of her proposed penalty for failure is precisely what Cressida suffers after taking the ultimate risk with Troilus: 'Tax of impudence, / A strumpet's boldness, a divulged shame, / Traduc'd by odious ballads' (II.i.170–2). In binding Bertram's substitute father to her will by her success, she harnesses the authority of patriarchy itself. The King's threatening–reasoning speech to the refractory Bertram supports the lexis of state supremacy – 'I must produce my power' (II.iii.150) – with Biblical cadences evoking the wrathful Father. 'Obey our will' (l.158), he charges,

> Or I will throw thee from my care for ever
> Into the staggers and the careless lapse
> Of youth and ignorance; both my revenge and hate
> Loosing upon thee, in the name of justice,
> Without all terms of pity.
>
> (ll.162–6)

The play-world's need for renewal, figured forth in the King's illness, is notoriously represented by the entropic lassitude of the older generation[18] – once more, the inverse of the corrupt sexual excess that serves as the Duke's excuse for reform in *Measure for Measure*. The world-weariness of the Countess, Lafew, and the King himself is coupled with a melancholy nostalgia for better days and better men (witness Lafew's 'finding out' of Parolles). There is, then, a reminiscence of Illyria, as well as of the contrast between Duke Frederick's court and the 'golden world' of Arden. What France desires, it would seem, is an injection of the erotic energy Helena alone could be said to possess, and this might imply an openness to subversion. Yet France is also of two minds, as is clear from the character who embodies the state. The King is interested in rejuvenation but not transformation. His imposition of Helena upon Bertram, as he attempts to bend human feelings with the apparatus of state power, improbably makes the latter's refusal the truly subversive element in the scene. There is an analogy to the conflict between Cordelia and Lear, whose language the offended King anticipates: 'Do thine own fortunes that obedient right/Which both thy duty owes and our power claims' (II.iii.160–1). The King's adoptive son must, as Cordelia is supposed to do, sacrifice his sense of himself in order to display gratitude; he must also surrender control of his sexuality in order to act out the King's own feelings for Helena, which implicitly exceed gratitude. In short, the King's recovery strengthens rather than disrupts existing social relations and assumptions about power. Sexuality is appropriated by reaction.

The Countess herself, sympathetic though she is as a promoter of romantic consummation, seeks to revive the past at the cost of ignoring present realities and conflicting personal claims. Her son, indirectly identified as a 'second husband' in the play's first lines, can be retained by making Helena her 'daughter'. Helena's objections to the premature gift of this role in Act I, scene iii, ostensibly relate to the obstacle thereby implied to a marriage with Bertram. But the existential aspect of her design lends depth to her violent reaction ('Methought you saw a serpent' [l.141]), as well as to the suggestion of incest. It is one thing for Helena to make the Countess her mother on her own terms, another to accept the subordinate position of, in effect, the Countess's agent and surrogate. Hence, too, her failure to take the Countess into her confidence concerning her journey to Paris. While she solemnly vows to tell the truth ('by grace itself I swear' [l.220]), it is hardly the whole truth. Nor, when she sets off to put her Florentine scheme into practice, does she share her thoughts with the Countess, any more than with the audience. She is even willing to let the kind old woman suppose her dead and suffer a grief as great as '[i]f she had partaken of [the Countess's] flesh, and cost [her] the dearest groans of a mother' (IV.v.10–11). Quite simply, Helena must die as the Countess's adoptive daughter in order to be reborn as Bertram's wife in her own right.

The incest-motif is usually taken up in narrow psycho-sexual terms and from Bertram's point of view. To regard it from his mother's, and to link it with the King's surrogate fatherhood, is to release its broader implications of stagnation and oppression. What is most incestuous about this play-world is its resistance to growth, change, and difference – in short, to the processes of time that are elsewhere allied with the disruptive force of love. Confirmation of this pattern is Lafew's proposal, to which the Countess assents, that his daughter should take the dead Helena's place with Bertram. This is a closed system, seeking to preserve itself intact by allowing renewal only in its own image, and Helena's 'ambition' entails an assault on that system, rather than mere gratification within it. Having appropriated the power of patriarchy, she must then put patriarchy itself in its (subordinate) place. This involves breaking those bonds between mother and son, son and surrogate father, that would keep her the conduit of others' psychic projections.

Like the other late clowns, Lavatch serves as an index of the progressive displacement and enervation of the subversive. He lags behind Feste in verbal energy while exceeding him in jadedness – Lafew aptly terms him a 'shrewd knave and an unhappy' (IV.v.63). His similarly ambiguous position in the household differs from

Feste's in being a matter less of current than of expired licence: 'My lord that's gone made himself much sport out of him. By his authority he remains here, which he thinks is a patent for his sauciness, and indeed he has no pace, but runs where he will' (ll.64–7). Even the impotent disruptions of an 'allow'd fool', it seems, belong to the past – as they do, indeed, in Shakespeare's comic canon. At the same time, there is an anticipation of the Fool in *Lear*, who, since Cordelia's banishment, 'hath much pin'd away' (*Lr*, I.iv.74). Folly and youth are made interdependent by the Countess herself in bantering with the clown: 'To be young again, if we could, I will be a fool in question' (II.ii.38–9). Over the course of *All's Well*, moreover, Lavatch visibly diminishes in sexual energy; his early plan to wed Isbel, in which he was 'driven on by the flesh' (I.iii.29) in the manner of Touchstone, is abandoned after his visit to court, which draws him further into the atmosphere of superannuation: 'The brains of my Cupid's knock'd out, and I begin to love, as an old man loves money, with no stomach' (III.ii.14–16).

The change in Lavatch reflects not only the evolution of Bertram's sexuality (Wheeler), but, more broadly, Helena's neutralising and controlling of disruptive forces, including that sexuality.[19] The letter from Bertram that Lavatch delivers in this scene is brashly assertive and defiant, but this bravado, like that of Parolles, rings hollow and ends with a running-away: 'I have sent you a daughter-in-law; she hath recover'd the King, and undone me. I have wedded her, not bedded her, and sworn to make the "not" eternal. You shall hear I am run away' (III.ii.19–22). The reality of his defeat is contained in 'undone', with its mixed sexual messages. The claim to independence – 'not bedded her' – is syntactically embedded within the restriction of being 'wedded'; the 'not' is over-shadowed by its homonym. Helena's next move will involve forcing Bertram to acknowledge his own subtext, just as Parolles's brave words will be turned against him.

Parolles is, quite implausibly, made a scapegoat for Bertram by characters desperate for the hero's reform, beginning with the Lords who arrange Parolles's exposure as an object lesson. As a ritual cleansing the business is mere travesty, compared to the outcasting of Falstaff by the Prince whom *he* 'misled' or Fluellen's purging of Pistol on behalf of the new socio-political order. Far from stage-managing it, this young reprobate actively resists his own symbolic purification. When his jocular fear that he will 'hear … hereafter' (IV.iii.97) of his amorous adventure is eventually realised, he parades his impenitence. Yet his presumed reformation through the disgrace of Parolles becomes the basis of the rehabilitation proposed for him by his mother, Lafew, and the King. Lafew assures the Countess, 'your son was misled with a snipt-taffeta fellow there' (IV.v.1–2) – that is, essentially, an imitation of true courtiers like himself. In response, her slippery pronouns betoken a readiness to pile the designated victim with her son's most wilful faults: 'I would I had not known him; it was the death of the most virtuous gentlewoman that ever nature had praise for creating' (ll.8–10). Perhaps the most significant fact about the scapegoating is that Helena has nothing to do with it;[20] it marks the emergence of an independent scheme potentially in conflict with Helena's own – a threatening counter-mine.

The older generation's mourning of Helena is superficially touching, a display of emotional sensitivity, but it also confirms that the revival of their world on their own terms depends on her supposed death. Bertram receives the King's approval when he claims to have loved Lafew's daughter before Helena's intervention, even while he shrewdly pays homage to, and claims posthumous affection for, his lost wife. Helena's memory is conveniently appropriated all round, but most convenient of all is her disappearance from the scene. Having failed to renew itself by using her alive, the social order makes the most of her death. In fact, in the language of forgiveness employed by the time-obsessed King ('Let's take the instant by the forward top;/For we are old' [V.iii.39–40], she herself becomes scapegoat-in-chief, by her death making possible Bertram's spotless revival: 'The nature of his great offence is dead,/And deeper than oblivion we do bury/Th' incensing relics of it' (ll.23–5). The effect is to expose Helena's ongoing role, alive or dead, as outsider in this structure, and hence the need for the manipulative magic of her own rebirth to break that structure down. Only then can she emerge, not as the saviour designated by Countess or King, but as the saviour self-created. This time, she must deprive her chosen instrument not only of the liberty to choose, but of free will itself.

This is the impact on her dramatic world of Helena's second miraculous exercise of power, and an explanation for its otherwise unnecessary deviousness and complex orchestration. To the point here are the seemingly superfluous 'follow-up' tricks of analogous manipulators. Portia gains the day by defeating Shylock; she acquires psychological power through the ring-business. Vincentio has Angelo dead-to-rights early in the play, should he choose to reveal himself; the bed-trick hits his opponent, as it were, below the belt.

Even more appositely, the climax of the Duke's pageant – the revelation of Claudio's safety – puts Isabella in a position very like that of Bertram. His much-discussed response to Helena's disclosure – 'If she, my liege, can make me know this clearly,/I'll love her dearly, ever, ever dearly' (V.iii.315–16) – is simply inaccessible as an index of 'real' feelings. The point is that feelings have been made irrelevant, for *ending* well here depends on the suppression of the very capacity for subversion, including even Shylock's capacity to remain unharmonised. Bertram's statement is the equivalent of Isabella's helpless silence, Angelo's constructed relief, and its conditional formulation is less important than his implicit confession of a dependence on Helena for clear knowledge. Like Vincentio, then, Helena succeeds in irresistibly imposing the mechanism of comic transformation. And all the more clearly, paradoxically, because love is her vehicle, she demonstrates that such a resolution has no need of subversive energy – no need, even, to fear it or to crush it, since it is simply beside the point.

As before, the King's role is symbolically central. It was a comparatively easy task for Helena, using her father's remedy, to restore him to health. Now, with her own arts, exercised through Diana, she must reduce him to impotent and infantile foolishness: 'Take her away, I do not like her now./To prison with her; and away with him' (ll.281–2). In much the same way does Angelo throw up his hands before the confusion instigated by Pompey:

> This will last out a night in Russia
> When nights are longest there. I'll take my leave,
> And leave you to the hearing of the cause,
> Hoping you'll find good cause to whip them all.
> (*MM*, II.i.134–7)

The King is already implicated in the puzzle by way of his ring; he is further drawn in through the 'tangled chain' of Diana's riddling sexual accusations. After answering the King, 'By Jove, if ever I knew man, 'twas you' (l.287), she goes on, in accusing Bertram, to weave her knot ('not') to include even Lafew:

> He knows I am no maid, and he'll swear to't;
> I'll swear I am a maid, and he knows not.
> Great King, I am no strumpet, by my life;
> I am either maid, or else this old man's wife.
> (ll.290–3)

The comprehensive absurdity is functional. All are punished. Diana acts as the 'friend' who performs Rosalynde's magic for her in Lodge's novel, embodying Helena's realisation of the desire, which has gone hand-in-hand from the first with her desire for Bertram, for a 'military policy how virgins might blow up men'.

IV

Troilus, of course, may be regarded as precisely so blown up, but to consider him primarily as a victim, even of his own emotions, is to rely on his self-portrait, and this entails accepting the emblematic destinies, too, of Cressida and Pandarus. It is to take as the play's last word – and very few critics now do so – his view of Cressida's false-ness, his scornful repudiation of Pandarus ('Ignominy, shame/Pursue thy life, and live aye with thy name!' [V.x.33–4]), and his moral triumph as monopolistic incarnation of Truth: ' "As true as Troilus" ' (III.ii.182). Closure would thus accrue to his speech of fatalistic yet heroic defiance after Hector's death, his assumption of the role of 'wicked conscience' (V.x.28) to the Greeks – the very posture, in other words, which Chaucer's precursor romance pointedly refuses to accept as closure, taking the reader on to Troilus' death and recog-nition of earthly vanity, including the vanity of his love for Criseyde. Despite his bitterness and disillusion, the play ends on Troilus' own terms, and we might as well accept as conclusive and innocent the final readings imposed on their respective texts by Vincentio and Helena. What the picture chiefly fails to convey is the implication of Troilus in both the shaping of destiny and the sense of ultimate vanity, a sense which in Shakespeare is less formulaic and far more radical than in Chaucer, with no platform of eternal verity to offer a secure spiritual perspective. Only superficially is Shakespeare's fool-for-love the antagonist of the counter-subversive Ulysses. He is an actor in his own right – one who out-Bottoms Bottom in unit-ing two roles in one but without interrogating the premise of his tragic-love script: 'What is Pyramus? a lover, or a tyrant?' (*MND*, I.ii.22).

The subversive status of Pandarus is difficult to fix, hence particu-larly revealing. He is the energetic agent of the sexual impulses of others; there is no mistaking his pleasure both in the role of bawd and in bawdry itself – witness his obscene performance for Paris and Helen in Act III, scene i, with Paris's comment: 'He eats nothing but doves, love, and that breeds hot blood, and hot blood begets hot thoughts, and hot thoughts beget hot deeds, and hot deeds is love' (ll.128–30). Certainly, sexuality is his natural medium – he virtually swims within it, and at the end, with the turning of the tide, he is left high and dry, a fish out of water. It is easy, too, to compare him to Pompey as a debased descendant of the sex-promoting subversives of the earlier plays. Again, the role of bawd, so prominent in the textual imagination of this cluster of plays, *deforms* Puck's role as facilitator of a more broadly based communion. However, in contrast with *Measure for Measure*, where Pompey stands for a sexuality diseased *ab origine*, Pandarus has the excuse, as it were, of the distorting pressures of war, the same pressures that foster the frenzied decadence of the doomed courtiers and render all human bonds desperate and precarious. In this respect, Pandarus is the counterpart of the physically mis-shapen Thersites, the truth-telling fool who seems to be squeezed into one self-discrediting dimension less, for a change, by the stigmatising bias of his text than by the murderous stupidity around him. By contrast, Lucio's slander, however it may hit home at times, comes out of unseen 'dark corners'. Against a lavish background of grotesque war and love, Thersites and Pandarus emerge as more nearly normal – the living refutations, respectively, of the postures of chivalric honour and of Troilus' claim, 'In all Cupid's pageant there is presented no monster' (III.ii.74–5).[21]

But there remains a fundamental and provocative difference between Thersites and Pandarus – a point that equally distinguishes the latter from such spokesmen for a diseased sexuality as Pompey and Lucio. Pandarus' identification with sexual drives is not part of even a superficially disruptive stance: on the contrary, that he fits so smoothly into his debased aristocratic milieu is part of the satirical point. In sharp contrast with the Greek trouble-maker, there is no whiff of the Vice about him. This renders problematic not only his subversiveness, but the very basis of his fictional identity. After all, the sexual forces that constitute Pandarus as a character are located outside him. He initiates nothing. Apart from his dealings with Troilus and Cressida, he appears only in the scene with Helen and Paris, when he is on Troilus' business, and then he puts himself at the service of their lubricity. If he is, as Paris claims, comprised of 'love' (in the sense of 'hot deeds') such composition reflects the doings and desires of others. Notoriously, any 'motive' for promoting the central liaison as energetically as he does is difficult to locate, yet the lack of one is conspicuous.[22] Despite his descent into the 'hold-door trade'

(V.x.51) in his epilogue, where he claims to reflect (and threatens to infect) his '[b]rethren and sisters' (l.51) amongst the audience, Pandarus is clearly not out for material gain. Even if we choose to posit a buried sexual attraction to Troilus, we are dependent on textual suggestions of vicarious pleasure that merely reinforce his derivative status.

It is apparent from the start, and from any critical perspective, that Pandarus offers a down-to-earth counterpoint to Troilus' romanticism.[23] In the first scene, he actually drives the poetically love-sick prince to talk frankly of achieving the 'stubborn-chaste' (I.i.97) Cressida, although Troilus goes on, asking Apollo for inspiration, to paint his longing in vivid colours:

> Her bed is India, there she lies, a pearl;
> Between our Ilium and where she resides,
> Let it be call'd the wild and wand'ring flood,
> Ourself the merchant, and this sailing Pandar
> Our doubtful hope, our convoy, and our bark.
> (ll.100–4)

The counterpoint continues to be heard in Troilus' metaphors, which, stubbornly materialistic and possessive in a way that recalls Bassanio's image of the Golden Fleece, have given pause to many commentators. The blunt fact is that, however loftily he conceives his feelings, Troilus is setting up his own kind of bed-trick, and it is this fact that Pandarus, cutting through the lovers' professions of eternal loyalty, is made textually responsible for articulating: 'Whereupon I will show you a chamber, which bed, because it shall not speak of your pretty encounters, press it to death' (III.ii. 207–9). Troilus' sordid, falsely subversive agent emerges as an index of the displaced darker side, not only of his idealism, but of his very claim of susceptibility to subversive passion, and so of his boast to be 'as true as truth's simplicity,/And simpler than the infancy of truth' (ll.169–70).

Janet Adelman has taken farther than other critics the idea of Cressida's betrayal as produced, even required, by Troilus' psychopathology.[24] She locates his glaring defensiveness in the infantile quality of his love, a fantasy of union with the maternal ideal, whose ambivalence is actualised by sexual consummation; by projecting his sense of 'soilure' upon the real Cressida, Troilus can keep his maternal fantasy alive – hence his notorious insistence on dividing her in his exchange with Ulysses: 'This is, and is not, Cressid!' (V.ii.146).

In Adelman's view, Troilus' sexual ambivalence prefigures Othello's, with the difference that Shakespeare here allows the text itself to be shaped by Troilus' fantasy. However, by putting sex before power, in classic Freudian terms, even Adelman's argument plays into Troilus' self-justifying hands, stressing his openness to subversion (in the form of neurotic helplessness) and down-playing his manipulative aggression. The military context of the love-story might alone suggest that the question of power takes precedence. So does the treatment of sex-relations in the other Problem Plays – especially in the case of Helena, which is forfeited as a parallel if Troilus' psychological dynamic is traced to a gender-specific root. Only by returning the love-affair to its place within a network of intersecting subversive and counter-subversive forces can we appreciate the multiple resonances of Troilus' destructive eroticism. And this leads to a rather different view of the relation between his initial idealisation and eventual demonisation of Cressida.

Whereas love in its subversive aspect entails a disruption of identity, a loss of self, Troilus, in love and out of it, displays, in the guise of vulnerability, a regard for self amounting to narcissism.[25] He is fiercely self-protective, governed by a need to place identity beyond subversion. His obsession with Cressida may be seen as a means to this end – self-aggrandising sexual manipulation comparable to that practised by Vincentio and Helena. Unlike those characters, however, Troilus is not in a position to do much about his dramatic universe, which imposes inordinate demands on the youngest son of Priam and brother of Paris to perform as warrior and lover – related areas of insecurity, as Adelman demonstrates in analysing Troilus' argument that Helen must be kept for honour's sake.[26] Time looms as the deadly enemy of human meaning,[27] even while it is also, paradoxically, the only possible guarantor of that meaning. The sense of futility is reinforced, from outside the text, by the audience's knowledge of history and, from within it, by Cassandra's.

What Troilus can hope to control is his self-image within this confining structure. Given her parallel uncertainties about her situation and identity, Cressida makes the perfect opponent in a one-sided struggle for moral mastery. The adolescent Troilus effectively constructs a *rite de passage* by which he can initiate himself into a secure sense of worthy manhood.[28] This entails integrating himself with his 'timeless' historical–literary destiny, the myth that has formed around him of chivalric perfection and Troy's 'second hope' (IV.v.109) – a myth that, by definition, can come into its own only when the 'first hope' is eliminated. That myth, as retailed (second-hand) by Ulysses, perfectly accords with Troilus' projected self – down to the sense of unrealised promise, doomed to be endlessly deferred:

> The youngest son of Priam, a true knight,
> Not yet mature, yet matchless, firm of word,
> Speaking in deeds, and deedless in his tongue,
> Not soon provok'd, nor being provok'd soon calm'd;
> His heart and hand both open and both free,
> For what he has he gives, what thinks he shows,
> Yet gives he not till judgment guide his bounty,
> Nor dignifies an impure thought with breath.
>
> (ll.96–103)

Yet the myth has a long way to travel from our first encounter with it in the puffery of Pandarus, deflated by Cressida's mockery. That mockery is itself exaggerated, ironically, but it reveals the threat she poses to Troilus by her knowledge of a gap between the person and the persona. Cressida's real disloyalty consists in wanting the self that Troilus must put behind him.

It should now be clear that Pandarus is necessary less because of his persuasive powers than because he protects Troilus from the *truth* of what he is doing, 'going between' in this sense too. Yet as the agent of the first phase of the project – for as with Vincentio and Helena, there are two distinct stages involved – he inevitably becomes the scapegoat for what Troilus chooses to interpret as betrayal, as he moves on to consolidating his moral and spiritual hegemony within a society that, with Hector's death, is as thoroughly doomed as was his love. In martyrdom there is power, as Isabella well knows, and as Helena amply proves. Indeed, in that Troilus will construct his subversion-proof self by repudiating sexuality, he is psychologically linked with Isabella. For his is also, in the final analysis, an erotics of suffering under the cover of self-sacrifice:

> Th' impression of keen whips I'ld wear as rubies,
> And strip myself to death, as to a bed
> That longing have been sick for, ere I'ld yield
> My body up to shame.
>
> (*MM*, II.iv.101–4)

For Isabella, too, the idea of self-sacrifice is intertwined with the need to sacrifice someone else. A major difference is Troilus' access to male prerogatives. Like Bertram, he participates in the character-type of the soldier who acquires power over (hence protection from) women through degrading knowledge of them, carnal and otherwise.[29] Yet he also exploits Cressida's false – superficially, at least – perception of his own behaviour as stereotypically masculine.

Don Juanism is a notion foreign to the courtly-love ethos, which is the ostensible cultural premise of the play-world, thanks partly to Chaucer's poem. For the medieval Troilus, as for Shakespeare, sex forms a natural part of a nonetheless idealised passion. It is 'that a lover most desires', as Ariosto says of the 'faithfull loving' Sacrapant (1.51). However, the English Renaissance version of the romance tradition preferred its heroes chaste, and Shakespeare's presentation – of Troilus himself, of Pandarus, and of the morals and mores of *this* Troy – enforces an opposition between spiritual and carnal aims. Despite his idealising rhetoric, the Shakespearean Troilus, as he sets sail for Cressida's bed, would hardly be capable of the tender (if naïve) consideration displayed by Chaucer's hero:

> 'But herke, Pandare, o word, for I nolde
> That thow in me wendest so gret folie,
> That to my lady I desiren sholde
> That toucheth harm or any vilenye;
> For dredeles me were levere dye
> Than she of me aught elles understode
> But that that myghte sownen into goode.'
>   (Chaucer, *Troilus and Criseyde*,
>   1.1030–6)

His artificial and self-delusive fusion of the romantic and the physical exposes the later figure as, in effect, taking refuge from responsibility in his literary heritage.

This is the context, then, for Cressida's resistance to Troilus' artificial idealism, however much she counts, and stakes, on the depth of his passion. Criticism has amply documented her defensiveness, her sense of vulnerability, her reluctance to become engaged. Specifically, her observation that '[a]chievement is command; ungain'd, beseech' recognises a sexual politics of male conquest in her milieu as she knows it, and as Shakespeare portrayed it. Yet Troilus insists on establishing faithfulness as the currency of psychological power with his extravagant challenge to her to match his own 'integrity and truth', his 'purity' and 'simplicity' (III.ii.165, 167, 169). She responds, 'In that I'll war with you' (l.171), and he eagerly takes up her metaphor: 'O virtuous fight,/When right with right wars who shall be most right!' (ll.171–2). In effect, he manoeuvres her into outdoing his vow by agreeing to be made a model of falsehood if she should fail him. Only Cressida 'must give and hazard all [she] hath', as the subversive power of love requires.

So it is hardly surprising that Cressida should later put Troilus' conduct into the category she feared – and was encouraged to fear – it might belong in.[30] Troilus' detumescence of urgency, his bland eagerness to part after their tryst, fit the 'love 'em and leave 'em' pattern, as she immediately recognises: 'You men will never tarry./O foolish Cressid! I might have still held off,/And then you would have tarried' (IV.ii.16–18). This statement need not be taken as 'chilling in its implication that Troilus is only one of many'.[31] Rather, it marks a return to the wry and wistful wisdom of her early soliloquy – wisdom that hardly needs, in this society, to have been gained by sexual experience. One may compare Desdemona's sighing exclamation, 'O, these men, these men!' (*Oth.*, IV.iii.60) – also a response to a male faithlessness that is being projected upon her.

In the stressful scene of parting Cressida is fearfully alert to signs of Troilus' failure to match her love, and she finds them in his insistence on renewing, despite what for her has been the ultimate proof of commitment, the earlier 'war' of faith. His lack of faith in her clearly indicates his own shallow feelings. Her outburst, 'O heavens, you love me not' (IV.iv.82), arguably constitutes the emotional pivot of the scene. The self has been ventured and lost, her hopes destroyed of a sexual relation different from the cruelly exploitive models around her, as well as of a sanctuary from the broader context of destruction. Adelman aptly notices Cressida's reduction to silence by the end of the scene as the object of competition between Troilus and Diomedes.[32] The 'chance of war' (Prologue 31) has played into both their hands.

The male imposition upon Cressida of the role of wanton, beginning with the kissing episode and Ulysses' subsequent reading of the 'language' (IV.v.55) of her body, has been widely recognised.[33] The other side of the coin is her internalisation – simultaneously self-destructive and self-protective – of Troilus' betrayal. She now blames her own sex – that is, herself – taking the cynicism of men for granted and deploring the intervention of 'error', the disruptive principle: 'Ah, poor our sex! this fault in us I find,/The error of our eye directs our mind' (V.ii.109–10). For his part, Troilus' one-sided interpretation of her scene with Diomed ironically fulfils his earlier promise to 'give [her] nightly visitation' (IV.iv.73). He watches and 'reads' and raves, but he never thinks of communicating with her. His insistence on partitioning her ('This is, and is not, Cressid') – a reminiscence of her earlier self-division for his sake – dramatises his own integrity in the predictable guise of subversion, with his 'soul' (V.ii.147) divided by the 'madness of discourse' (l.142). He is transparently seeking, not union, but separation.

Despite her disillusion and his silence, Cressida writes to Troilus of love. When he tears up the letter with a Hamlet-like contempt for any language but his own – 'Words, words, mere words' (V.iii.108) – he silences her conclusively, in a *reductio ad absurdum* of the principle that, as French puts it, '[i]nconstant women are central to male rhetoric'.[34] But Troilus also commits an act of theatrical violence beyond even his previous mediation of her speech and actions: he actually denies the audience access to her words. This confirms that the stylistic distancing of Cressida in the latter part of the play, far from endorsing Troilus' view, functions as an index of her isolation and suppression. In so far as there is 'a radical inconsistency of characterisation', it is the creation of yet another internal dramatist.[35] Again, there is an instructive contrast with Chaucer's poem, where Criseyde recedes more drastically than in the play, as the narrator retreats into ignorance ('Ther is non auctour telleth it, I wene' [*Troilus and Criseyde*, 5.1088]) and charity ('Ne me ne list this sely womman chyde/Forther than the storye wol devyse' [5.1093–4]). There Troilus writes pleadingly and often to her and longs to believe her coldly evasive responses. The vulnerability, and the narrator, are unequivocally on his side.

The ultimate irony of Cressida's discovery of Troilus as the typical seducer is not that it plays his psychological 'game' and produces the betrayal he seeks, but that it is not true. Unlike Bertram – and of course his own 'shadow' Pandarus – Troilus is far from cynical about the sex-act, which, on the contrary, serves as a focus of romantic fantasy. Thus the mythology of anticipation reaches its climax in explicitly sexual terms, as he waits, at once Romeo- and serpent-like, in Cressida's orchard:

> Th' imaginary relish is so sweet
> That it enchants my sense; what will it be,
> When that the wat'ry palates taste indeed
> Love's thrice-reputed nectar? Death, I fear me,
> Sounding destruction, or some joy too fine,
> Too subtile, potent, tun'd too sharp in sweetness
> For the capacity of my ruder powers.

I fear it much, and I do fear besides
That I shall lose distinction in my joys,
As doth a battle, when they charge on heaps
The enemy flying.

(III.ii.19–29)

This is a speech that might have furnished Jonson with inspiration for the grotesquely solipsistic sexual fantasies of Volpone and Sir Epicure Mammon. Troilus is wholly in the grip of his imagination, but what it imagines is itself. Ominously, his bizarre elaboration of the standard equation of sex with death first brings out the initiatory overtones of the experience, then gives way to the metaphor of combat. Infantile his love certainly is, but in celebrating the self-sufficiency and exclusivity of a transcendental sensuality, he expresses less a desire for the maternal than a nostalgia for the illusion of omnipotence.

As is well known, Troilus' response to the discovery that the lovers must part – 'How my achievements mock me!' (IV.ii.69) – contrasts sharply with Cressida's wild desperation: 'O you immortal gods! I will not go' (94).[36] Yet while he echoes Cressida's earlier complaint that men treat love as conquest, he does so with a tantrum-like frustration, registering an impact on himself of a kind alien to a Don Juan. For Troilus, the 'achievement' itself is not the be-all and end-all, but a means of 'mocking' him into a form of absolute self-sufficiency. His agent, left to impart the news, imparts also the irrelevance of Cressida's response – 'the young prince will go mad' (l.75) – and her exit in helpless tears is abruptly juxtaposed with his return in a false guise, 'acting' for the benefit of Paris, Diomedes, and the rest. This theatrical marking of a new identity accompanies a transfer of his emotional investment from possessing Cressida to giving her up, as he adapts his former rhetoric of anticipated possession to the idea of (self-)sacrifice: 'And to his hand when I deliver her,/ Think it an altar, and thy brother Troilus/A priest there off'ring to it his own heart' (IV.iii.7–9).[37]

Cressida's penalty for mocking Troilus' myth is to be mocked by it. She is not wrong in intuiting that he does not love her. But in view of that fact, she could hardly anticipate that his loss of her would lead, not to a replacement myth of new conquest, but to a more powerful myth of loss and betrayal that remains squarely focused on her. Troilus has put the very principle of emotional responsibility towards another (that is, an Other) – a principle perceived as subverting the stability of the self – safely into the past. There it remains beyond change, part of the pure and secure memory that he himself will shortly become, self-extricated from the 'wallet at his back' (III.iii.145) into which Time, according to Ulysses, that cynical and so ultimately less dangerous arch-manipulator, puts 'alms for oblivion' (l.146).

From Richard Hillman, *Shakespearean Subversions* (London, 1992), pp. 150–79.

Notes

[Hillman's essay is taken from his book *Shakespearean Subversions*, which ranges across examples of subversion in Shakespeare's plays in the form of trickery and the specific figure of 'the Trickster'. In the full volume, there is reference to almost every one of Shakespeare's plays, and Hillman dexterously applies a range of critical approaches, historical research and a theory of carnival derived from the work of Mikhail Bakhtin. The essay reproduced here is a compelling analysis of *Measure For Measure* but has the additional advantage for this volume of including cross-references to the other 'problem plays'. Hillman's subject in this essay, as in much of his other work, is not only subversion, but necessarily the way that the state is represented in Shakespeare's work. His eloquent essay revisits Shakespeare's plays in a political way that has been typical of the last twenty years of Shakespearean criticism – although Hillman's work is also characterised by the subtle and intelligent way that he approaches such issues, resisting dogma or easy rhetoric. References to Shakespeare's works are to the *Riverside Shakespeare*, textual editor, G. Blakemore Evans (Boston, 1974). Ed.]

1. On the association of the two characters, cf. Marilyn French, *Shakespeare's Division of Experience* (New York, 1981), p. 191, Meredith Anne Shura, *The Literary Use of the Psychoanalytical* (New Haven, CT, 1981), pp. 255–6 and Jonathan Goldberg, *James I and the Politics of Literature: Jonson, Shakespeare, Donne and their Contemporaries* (Baltimore, 1983), pp. 236–9.

2. It is the ultimate ironic tribute to Vincentio's success that he is often more-or-less loosely referred to as a trickster, especially in confirming his status as embodiment of righteous power in the play's own terms – see, e.g., Leonard Tennenhouse, *Power on Display: the Politics of Shakespeare's Genres* (New York, 1986), p. 155 and Marilyn L. Williamson, *The Patriarchy of Shakespeare's Comedies* (Detroit, 1986), p. 105.

3. *Oxford English Dictionary*, Vol. 2, pp. 7–8.

4. This point is also made by Philip C. McGuire in *Speechless Dialects: Shakespeare's Open Silences* (Berkeley and Los Angeles, 1985), pp. 69–70, who examines the multiple final silences in detail (pp. 63–96), with an emphasis on the implications for production.

5. Cf. Richard Wheeler, *Shakespeare's Development and the Problem Comedies* (Berkeley and Los Angeles, 1981), who relates the 'problem comedies' to their author's sexual repression; also Kay Stockholder, *Dream Works: Lovers and Families in Shakespeare's Plays* (Toronto, 1987), pp. 66–83 and 223–4.

6. Jonathan Dollimore, 'Transgression and Surveillance in *Measure for Measure*'. [Reprinted in this volume. Ed.]

7. On links between the Duke and Angelo, see Thomas F. Van Laan, *Role-Playing in Shakespeare* (Toronto, 1978), pp. 95–6 and, in terms of a response by the Duke to an inner conflict over sexuality, Wheeler, *Shakespeare's Development and the Problem Comedies*, pp. 135–9, Stockholder, *Dream Works: Lovers and Families in Shakespeare's Plays*, pp. 81 and 224, Alexander Leggat, 'Substitution in *Measure for Measure*', *Shakespeare Quarterly*, 39 (1988), 342–44, 345–6 and Richard A. Levin, *The Multiple Plot in English Renaissance Drama* (Chicago, 1982).

8. The concept of the Duke as internal dramatist has held the status of a critical commonplace since Anne Barton, *Shakespeare and the Idea of the Play* (London, 1962, pub. under the name of Anne Righter), pp. 178–80, who terms Lucio an 'unruly extempore actor' interrupting the Duke's script; cf. Van Laan, *Role-Playing in Shakespeare*, pp. 94–101. This perspective lends itself to New Historicist readings in terms of the theatrics of power – too readily, according to Anthony B. Dawson, in '*Measure for Measure*, New Historicism, and Theatrical Power', *Shakespeare Quarterly*, 39 (1988), 328–4, who argues persuasively that the metatheatrical ending undermines the 'linkage between sex and knowledge, between verbal power, sexual domination, and legal authority' (p. 337). Cf. Leggatt, 'Substitution in *Measure for Measure*' who finds the duke inept as a playwright and therefore considers this aspect of his role primarily ironic (pp. 358–9). However, the audience's distance and insight do not, I think, diminish the Duke's final achievement of moral, political, psychological, and sexual hegemony *within* the play-world, thanks to what Charles Swann, 'Lucio: Benefactor or Malefactor?', *Critical Quarterly*, 29 (1987), 55–70 who stresses the false harmony of the 'shape' imposed by the duke, aptly terms the 'mytified acceptance' of his 'power' (p. 68) by other characters (Lucio being a subversive exception).

9. Jonathan Dollimore, 'Transgression and Surveillance in *Measure for Measure*'. See also Goldberg, *James I and the Politics of Literature: Jonson, Shakespeare, Donne and their Contemporaries*, pp. 231–9 and Tennenhouse, *Power on Display: the Politics of Shakespeare's Genres*, pp. 156–9.

10. Dollimore, 'Transgression and Surveillance in *Measure for Measure*' and Wheeler, *Shakespeare's Development and the Problem Comedies*.

11. Wheeler, ibid., p. 149, Dollimore, ibid., pp. 73–4.

12. A favourite critical phrase – see Shura, *The Literary Use of the Psychoanalytical*, p. 254, A. C. Nuttall, *A New Mimesis: Shakespeare and the Representation of Reality* (London, 1983), p. 130, and Leggatt, 'Substitution in *Measure for Measure*', p. 346.

13. See, e.g., Marjorie Garber, *Coming of Age in Shakespeare* (London, 1981), p. 221, who specifically credits the Duke's withholding of the truth about Claudio.

14. See, e.g., Arthur Kirsch, *Shakespeare and the Experience of Love* (Cambridge, 1981), pp. 115–16.

15. See Alan C. Dessen, *Shakespeare and the Later Moral Plays* (Lincoln, 1986), pp. 113–33 on Parolles as vice, although he comes close to accepting the eventual scapegoating as efficacious.

16. On the place of virginity in a male-determined system of symbolic commodity-exchange, see Luce Irigaray, *This Sex Which Is Not One*, trans. Catherine Porter with Carolyn Burke (Ithaca, NY, 1985), p. 186, much of whose discussion of sexuality as a manifestation of power-relations (pp. 170–97) suits the three Problem Plays. On the sexual politics of this exchange, cf. Marilyn French, *Shakespeare's Division of Experience* (New York, 1981), pp. 174–6 and Carol Thomas Neely, *Broken Nuptials in Shakespeare's Plays* (New Haven, CT, 1985), pp. 58–104.

17. A doubtful line, it should be noted, followed by an apparent gap in sense.

18. See, e.g., G. K. Hunter's introduction to the Arden *All's Well That Ends Well* (London, 1959), p. xxxvi, and Robert Grams Hunter, *Shakespeare and the Comedy of Forgiveness* (New York, 1965), p. 103.

19. Wheeler, *Shakespeare's Development and the Problem Comedies*, pp. 52–4.

20. The persuasive argument of Richard A. Levin that Parolles is 'society's scapegoat' hardly warrants his fabrication of an elaborate conspiracy of which Helena is 'the secret mastermind'. See '*All's Well that Ends Well* and "All Seems Well" ', *Shakespeare Studies*, 13 (1980), 139–42.

21. Cf. John Bayley, 'Time and the Trojans', *Essays in Criticism*, 25 (1975), 55–73, p. 64 on Thersites as uniquely, among Shakespeare's 'cynics and railers', in conformity with his milieu.

22. On Pandarus as motiveless go-between, cf. Richard Fly, *Shakespeare's Mediated World* (Amherst, MA, 1976), p. 38.

23. I am substantially in agreement with French's analysis of the first scene and, in particular, of Troilus' self-absorption in *Shakespeare's Division of Experience*.

24. Janet Adeleman, ' "Anger's My Meat": Feeding, Dependency, and Aggression in *Coriolanus*', in Murry M. Schwartz and Coppélia Kahn (eds),

Representing Shakespeare: New Psychoanalytical Essays (Baltimore, 1980), pp. 129–49.

25. Cf. Robert Ornstein, The Moral Vision of Jacobean Tragedy (Madison, WI, 1960), p. 245 and J. A. Bryant Jr, *Shakespeare and the Uses of Comedy* (Lexington, MA, 1986), p. 199.

26. Adelman, ' "Anger's My Meat": Feeding, Dependency, and Aggression in *Coriolanus*', pp. 134–6.

27. See Bayley, 'Time and the Trojans', Charles R. Lyons, *Shakespeare and the Ambiguity of Love's Triumph* (The Hague, 1971), pp. 69–99, and R. A. Yoder, ' "Sons and Daughters of the Game": An Essay on Shakespeare's *Troilus and Cressida*', *Shakespeare Survey*, 25 (1972), 15–16.

28. There is an intriguing resemblance between Troilus's sexual initiation, with the help of a 'wise' older male, and the structure of various primitive rituals that effect the transition to manhood and a symbolic death to childhood. See Mircea Eliade, *Patterns in Comparative Religion*, trans. Rosemary Sheed, org. title *Traité d'histoire des religions* (London, 1958), *passim*.

29. Linda Woodbridge notes that the 'most prominent stage misogynists are or have been soldiers', including Troilus and Claudio in *Much Ado About Nothing*. See *Women and the English Renaissance: Literature and the Nature of Womankind, 1540–1620* (Urbana, IL, 1984), p. 279.

30. Cf. Yoder, ' "Sons and Daughters of the Game": An Essay on Shakespeare's *Troilus and Cressida*', pp. 22–3, Bryant, *Shakespeare and the Uses of Comedy*, pp. 197–200, and René Girard, 'The Politics of Desire in *Troilus and Cressida*', in Patricia Parker and Geoffrey Hartman (eds), *Shakespeare and the Question of Theory* (London, 1985).

31. Adeleman, ' "Anger's My Meat": Feeding, Dependency, and Aggression in *Coriolanus*', p. 136 n. 21.

32. Ibid.

33. See Bayley, 'Time and the Trojans', pp. 67–71, Gayle Greene, 'Shakespeare's Cressida: "A Kind of Self" ', in Carolyn Ruth Swift Lenz, Gayle Greene, and Carol Thomas Neely (eds), *The Woman's Part: Feminist Criticism of Shakespeare* (Urbana, IL, 1980), pp. 143–5, Yoder, ' "Sons and Daughters of the Game": An Essay on Shakespeare's Troilus and Cressida', p. 22, M. M. Burns, '*Troilus and Cressida*: The Worst of Both Worlds', *Shakespeare Studies*, 13 (1980), 105–30, pp. 122–7, Grant L. Voth and Oliver H. Evans, Cressida and the World of the Play', *Shakespeare Studies*, 8 (1975), 231–9, p. 236, Emil Roy, 'War and Manliness in Shakespeare's *Troilus and Cressida*', *Comparative Drama*, 7 (1977), 107–20, pp. 112–13. Marianne Novy, *Love's Argument: Gender Relations in Shakespeare* (Chapel Hill, NC, 1984), p. 119,

Dollimore, 'Transgression and Surveillance in *Measure for Measure*', pp. 47–9, and Caroline Asp, 'In Defense of Cressida', *Studies in Philology* 74 (1977), 306–17, pp. 413–14, who emphasises Cressida's self-image as a psychological influence throughout.

34. French, *Shakespeare's Division of Experience*, p. 159.

35. Adelman, ' "Anger's My Meat": Feeding, Dependency, and Aggression in *Coriolanus*', p. 120.

36. While the bedroom exchange earlier in the scene parodically recalls the parting of Romeo and Juliet in III.v – 'Wilt thou be gone? It is not yet near day' (1ff) – this is close to Juliet's desperate response to Friar Lawrence: 'Go get thee hence, for I will not away' (V.iii.160).

37. On Troilus' conduct here, cf. Yoder, ' "Sons and Daughters of the Game": An Essay on Shakespeare's *Troilus and Cressida*' (1972), pp. 20–1, Burns, '*Troilus and Cressida*: The Worst of Both Worlds', pp. 121–2, and Girard, 'The Politics of Desire in *Troilus and Cressida*', p. 194.

8

'Tricks We Play on the Dead': Making History in *Troilus and Cressida*

HEATHER JAMES

When Troilus hears that Cressida is to be handed over to the Greeks, he exclaims, 'How my achievements mock me!' and inadvertently confesses the extent to which he considers her to be a quite unromantic extension of himself. She is a sign of his labour and value, and Troilus is stunned to find that she has become part of larger negotiations that pre-empt his interests.[1] At the very centre of the play, Troilus and Cressida act out what I call their 'trope-plighting' scene: they swear to become the tropes for faithful and faithless lovers that are their literary destinies. Troilus wishes to become 'truth's authentic author to be cited', declaring, ' "As true as Troilus" shall crown up the verse / And sanctify the numbers' (3.2.180–1). He achieves the illusion of self-authorisation through Cressida, whose defection guarantees his own transcendence. Troilus is liberated from his indeterminate identity, however, only when Cressida enters the Greek camp to assume her tropical role. He is then able to read his superfluity and ambivalence in her and define himself as simple truth. The 'speculations' that prevail in the Greek camp also dominate the romance plot, with the difference that Helen comes 'between men' and Cressida mediates Troilus' relations with himself.

Troilus invents coherent interiority for himself by reading Cressida as a page on which he writes his lyric devotions.[2] The play reserves for Cressida enigmatic and compelling representations of selfhood

159

and, simultaneously, strenuous insistence on scripted identity. She emerges as lively and self-possessed in her first appearance, when she bests Pandarus in skirmishes of wit, yet concludes that scene by instructing herself in her contingent worth:

> Women are angels, wooing:
> Things won are done; joy's soul lies in the doing.
> That she belov'd knows naught that knows not this:
> Men prize the thing ungain'd more than it is.
> That she was never yet that ever knew
> Love got so sweet as when desire did sue.
> Therefore this maxim out of love I teach:
> 'Achievement is command; ungain'd, beseech.'
> (I.ii.291–8)

Left to soliloquise, Cressida anticipates and personalises Troilus' question about value: the illusion of an unknown and unachievable interior is functional, she claims, for it defers her inevitable exhaustion by another's desire.

Cressida realises that she belongs to herself tenuously, at best. In a moment of tantalising disclosure, she tells Troilus,

> I have a kind of self resides with you,
> But an unkind self, that itself will leave
> To be another's fool.
> (III.ii.146–8)

Her ambiguous words speak to her liminal state between past and present tenses, a closed and open book. On the one hand, her oracular words predict that she will abandon the self stamped by Troilus in favour of one marked by Diomed: they anticipate her conflation with Helen of Troy, the 'contaminated carrion-weight' whose impure body bears the signatures of two men and two nations. Simultaneously – taking the second line as apposite to the first – she says that she must abandon herself and become generically 'unkind' to herself in order to become Troilus' lover: she must exchange her interests for his. She fulfils this role in an unexpected fashion when she learns that she is to be traded for Antenor. Exhibiting desperate selflessness, she cries out:

> I have forgot my father;
> I know no touch of consanguinity,
> No kin, no love, no blood, no soul so near me
> As the sweet Troilus. O you gods divine,

> Make Cressid's name the very crown of falsehood,
> If ever she leave Troilus! Time, force, and death,
> Do to this body what extremes you can;
> But the strong base and building of my love
> Is as the very centre of the earth,
> Drawing all things to it.
>
> (IV.ii.99–108)

In this petition, which recalls the one that prefaces her trope-plighting, Cressida enters fully into her role and appears determined to see Troilus' desires through to their completion. An uncannily perfect Elizabethan wife, she bases her internal coherence on Troilus and seeks to reproduce his will: her willingness to donate her name as a sign of falsehood testifies to the magnetic draw of her love and identity as Troilus' and the tradition's kind of self.[3] Cressida continues to pose problems of agency, because she *seeks* to copy Troilus' will and because the closer she comes to her tropical role, the more she displays an agency that 'is, and is not' hers. The sense that she has deepened characterologically comes partly from a shift in her rhetoric: she has a phenomenological intuition, rather than an oracular knowledge, of her literary destiny.

Paradoxically, Cressida fulfils her vow of selfless devotion to Troilus when she enters the Greek camp and is 'kiss'd in general' (IV.v.21) by a receiving line of commanders. Cressida is silent while Agamemnon sets precedent for Nestor, Achilles, and Patroclus to step up, boast or insult his predecessor, take his kiss, and name himself. Their competition is so overt that Patroclus – by claiming to be Paris and interrupting Menelaus' kiss – jokingly suggests that the commanders are replaying the Trojan war with Cressida/Helen as the 'theme of all our scorns' (l. 30). When Cressida finally speaks, it is with a cool and pert familiarity that draws Ulysses' withering condemnation:

> Fie, fie upon her!
> There's language in her eye, her cheek, her lip –
> Nay, her foot speaks; her wanton spirits look out
> At every joint and motive of her body.
> O, these encounterers, so glib of tongue,
> That give accosting welcome ere it comes,
> And wide unclasp the tables of their thoughts
> To every ticklish reader. Set them down
> As sluttish spoils of opportunity
> And daughters of the game.
>
> (IV.v.54–63)

Ulysses' censure comes, appropriately, at the moment Cressida is consigned to tradition as its most frequently handled figure for wantonness. The role of a censor – he wants to snap shut the pornographic book's covers – may help Ulysses get the better of the discomfort she causes him. Her nonchalant management of the merry Greeks prompts him to describe her as a solicitous blazon[4] in which her wanton agenda appears in every term of her body – eye, cheek, lip, and unpetrarchan foot. Ulysses successfully depicts Cressida as an emblem of feminine incontinence, largely by presenting her as a gaudy poem that Puttenham might compare to the extravagant fashion statements made by upstart courtiers, or as a deliberate violation of the poetic decorum in which 'the skinne, and coat' of language, as Jonson writes, ideally 'rests in the well-joyning, cementing, and coagmentation of words; when as it is smooth, gentle, and sweet, like a Table, upon which you may runne your finger without rubs, and your nayle cannot find a joynt'.[5] He less convincingly asserts Cressida's full responsibility, since it takes a 'ticklish reader' to find so much solicitation in so many joints and rubs. The 'motive' of her body – an exclusively Shakespearean usage of the word – expresses the complicated state of agency and instrumentality that distinguishes Cressida: are those 'motives' inward promptings and impulses? Or overinterpreted joints?[6]

Cressida's textual conversion is characterologically impoverishing in a way that Achilles' textual breakdown is not. John Bayley notes that 'Cressida *does* strike us as a real person, in spite of her role as a commonplace in the play's externalised and intellectual scheme' and 'when Ulysses calls her a daughter of the game we may feel obscurely that he is wrong, and, if we feel so, it is at this moment that she gives some sort of impression of personality'.[7] Bayley's account rings true, despite the facts that Cressida has never been less comprehensible or coherent and that Ulysses' bitter summary of Cressida is unnervingly accurate: only moments ago, Cressida was a different woman. *Troilus and Cressida* displays the shocking lengths to which it will go to deliver its characters into the hands of a tradition whose final moves are to eradicate what Joel Fineman calls 'subjectivity effects' and replace a characterological function with a rhetorical one.[8] When Cressida's character vanishes, a retrospective sense of her subjective possibilities emerges and is felt as loss.

Troilus himself paves the way for Cressida's conversion in the trope-plighting scene, in which he appears more eager for his own tropical resolution than for sexual consummation. Evidently yearning to be free of *Troilus and Cressida*'s epistemologically mired world, he indirectly requests that Cressida relieve him of his burden of doubt:

> O that I thought it could be in a woman –
> As, if it can, I will presume in you ...
> Or that persuasion could but thus convince me
> That my integrity and truth to you
> Might be affronted with the match and weight
> Of such a winnowed purity in love –
> How were I then uplifted! but alas,
> I am as true as truth's simplicity,
> And simpler than the infancy of truth.
>
> (III.ii.156–7, 162–8)

Troilus is almost swept up, ungrammatically, in his hopes for release from his scepticism. This is the speech of a fallen idealist whose fears about his lover's reciprocation are overwhelmed by a greater anxiety over his incapacity for the faith that should 'convince' and 'uplift' him. Logically, when Troilus exclaims, 'but alas', his dejected admission should be, 'but I cannot believe'. What he does instead is fall back on the very axiom that he is testing – his traditional simplicity – and redefine 'truth's simplicity' as the failure to achieve the complex state of mind required for unverifiable faith in one's lover.

In the plighting of oaths, Troilus predicts his future as a trope for the amorous simplicity and integrity that he described as a consummation devoutly to be wished. In their 'trope-plighting', Troilus and Cressida construct their future identities in the negative image of the other. Troilus swears that

> True swains in love shall, in the world to come,
> Approve their truth by Troilus; when their rhymes,
> Full of protest, of oath, and big compare,
> Wants similes, truth tir'd with iteration
> (As true as steel, as plantage to the moon,
> As sun to day, as turtle to her mate,
> As iron to adamant, as earth to th' centre)
> Yet, after all comparisons of truth,
> As truth's authentic author to be cited
> 'As true as Troilus' shall crown up the verse
> And sanctify the numbers.
>
> (III.ii.171–81)

Troilus' speculations are fantasies of an integrated self which he jubilantly greets as his 'ideal ego'. He formally exchanges the weakness of infancy – his first complaint of the play – for the infancy of truth, the trope for original devotion. Anticipating his future value, Troilus constitutes himself as a source and author of truth and – by virtue of his status as a citation – a creature presumed to be an 'authentic' self.[9]

Cressida assumes the negativity of the doubts Troilus casts off when he resolves to be the essence to which all positive lyrical comparisons will refer:

> If I be false, or swerve a hair from truth,
> When time is old and hath forgot itself,
> When water-drops have worn the stones of Troy,
> And blind oblivion swallow'd cities up,
> And mighty states characterless are grated
> To dusty nothing – yet let memory,
> From false to false, among false maids in love,
> Upbraid my falseness! When they've said 'As false
> As air, as water, wind, or sandy earth,
> As fox to lamb, or wolf to heifer's calf,
> Pard to the hind, or step-dame to her son' –
> Yea, let them say, to stick the heart of falsehood,
> 'As false as Cressid.'
>
> (ll. 182–94)

Cressida's oath, conditional and subjunctive, differs from Troilus' predictive precedent. She utters an indirect command, a proleptic performative which fulfils Troilus' fantasy of fixed identity, if only as figures of speech.

To become 'true as truth's simplicity', Troilus must await Cressida's entrance into the Greek camp. He implores Pandarus to be his 'Charon / And give me swift transportation to those fields / Where I may wallow in the lily-beds / Propos'd for the deserver!' (III.ii.9–12). Sexual achievement furnishes Troilus' first anxious steps towards his literary future but does not itself secure for him the integrity and simplicity that he seeks in passing over the river Styx. In the aubade scene, he is so desirous to be gone that his very tenderness menaces: 'To bed, to bed. Sleep kill those pretty eyes / And give as soft attachment to thy senses / As infants empty of all thoughts' (IV.ii.4–6). Cressida laments his readiness to abandon her: 'O foolish Cressid! I might have still held off, / And then you would have tarried' (ll. 17–18). Lost to the amnesia of literature, this scene cannot enter the annals, where Troilus is to stand for truth. According to the play's mechanics of troping, however, he may assume exemplary fidelity only when Cressida enters the Greek camp.[10]

In the camp and in her father's tent during her meeting with Diomed, the divisions we have witnessed in Troilus are formally inscribed on Cressida:

> Troilus, farewell! one eye yet looks on thee,
> But with my heart the other eye doth see.
> Ah, poor our sex! this fault in us I find:
> The error of our eye directs our mind.
> What error leads must err; O then conclude,
> Minds sway'd by eyes are full of turpitude.
>   (V.ii.106–11)

Her lines, which as Carol Cook aptly notes, sound 'like an effect of ventriloquism', are so conclusive of her fault that one forgets, as the tradition will, that Troilus had stopped wanting to 'tarry' once he had achieved the grinding, the bolting, and the leavening of the cake.[11] The couplet form highlights the scriptedness of Cressida's last words, an effect further enhanced by the metaphor of printing that the men watching and reading her employ. Thersites comments that 'A proof of strength she could not publish more, / Unless she said "My mind is now turn'd whore" ' (ll. 112–13). Troilus himself lingers to 'make a recordation to my soul / Of every syllable that here was spoke. / But if I tell how these two did co-act / Shall I not lie in publishing a truth?' (ll. 115–18).

Troilus gives full voice to the 'madness of discourse', as he names it in his notoriously opaque soliloquy:[12]

>   This is, and is not, Cressid.
> Within my soul there doth conduce a fight
> Of this strange nature, that a thing inseparate
> Divides more wider than the sky and earth;
> And yet the spacious breadth of this division
> Admits no orifex for a point as subtle
> As Ariachne's broken woof to enter.
> Instance, O instance! strong as Pluto's gates:
> Cressid is mine, tied with the bonds of heaven.
> Instance, O instance! strong as heaven itself:
> The bonds of heaven are slipp'd, dissolv'd, and loos'd;
> And with another knot, five-finger-tied,
> The fractions of her faith, orts of her love,
> The fragments, scraps, the bits and greasy relics
> Of her o'er-eaten faith, are given to Diomed.
>   (V.ii.145–59)

He maintains, if barely, his integrity by referring his internal chaos to spiralling epistemological doubts which he inscribes onto Cressida. He is later able to distil his characterological upheaval into a more concise linguistic theory: Cressida, who sends 'Words, words, mere words, no matter from the heart' (V.iii.108), signifies the fickleness of language. We never learn the contents of Cressida's letter. Troilus' condemnation rings with an authority that pre-empts any possibility that Cressida might pursue a narrative and characterological reversal. Such defiance of tradition would introduce intolerable and undermining complications. Cressida is necessarily a sign of fragmentation in the tradition and in Troilus. In *Troilus and Cressida*, no authority, origin, or integrity is allotted to the Troy legend or its eponymous hero, and Troilus' trauma serves as an extreme representation of the internal division of the tradition and the cultural legacy inherited by Elizabethan England.

The mystery in the soul of state: drama, politics, and treason

Ulysses spots a mutiny in the closet theatre going on in Achilles' tent, and asserts that Patroclus' unlicensed theatrical imitations for his patron 'take degree away', leaving hapless members of the commonwealth wondering 'what plagues and what portents, what mutiny ... Commotion in the winds, frights, changes, horrors, / Divert and crack, rend and deracinate / The unity and married calm of states / Quite from their fixture' (I.iii.96–101). What cultural conditions prompt Shakespeare, in *Troilus and Cressida*, to multiply the damage caused by imitation and, taking representational disturbance much further than Patroclus, contaminate the Troy legend?

Explanations may begin with the appearance of Chapman's Homer and the fall of the Earl of Essex. For all the novelty of restoring a neoplatonised Homer to his privileged seat at the head of the Trojan banquet, Chapman anachronistically refeudalises the power structures and the classical idioms that had come to proliferate in the London market of the late Elizabethan period.[13] *Troilus and Cressida*, in contrast, reflects a developing capitalist society which promoted social mobility and generated strong tensions among rivals for economic and cultural capital. Unlike Chapman's Homer, Shakespeare's play cheapens the coin of the realm by delivering it over to London merchants: the play is appropriate to a city in which a chapman could have a Homer of his own. When Meres sought for native equivalents for classical talents in *Palladis Tamia*, and Jonson announced his personal identification with Horace, they suggested that poetic authority was necessary to the establishment of England as a nation with an imperial destiny: poets are bearers of political authority rather than mere conduits for its passage to the crown and court. When Jonson dons his guise as Horace in *Poetaster*, his upgrading of the playwright's status is analogous to *Poetaster*'s politically transgressive Ovid, who usurps Augustus' identification as Jupiter at his profane dinner of the gods.[14]

The second occasion for Shakespeare's revaluation of the Troy legend is the rebellion and fall of the Earl of Essex, 'an overmighty subject, a noble resistant to royalty and centralisation, on the one hand, and to market evaluation, on the other', in Engle's words for Chapman's Achilles.[15] In Achilles' private theatre Shakespeare places dramatic versions of the questions of feudal rights that Essex imprudently asked Egerton:

> Dothe religion enforce me to serve? doth god require it? is it impietie not to doe it? why? cannot princes Erre? and can not subiectes receyve wronge? is an earthlie power an authoritie infinite? Pardon me, pardon me, my lorde, I can never subscribe to these Principles.[16]

Whereas Essex was condemned 'to be drawn on a hurdle through London streets and so to the place of execution ... [to] be hanged, bowelled, and quartered',[17] Achilles strikes the set of his closet theatre when he discovers the power of the state over its subjects' basic prerogatives. At the height of Achilles' identity crisis, Ulysses invokes the 'providence that's in a watchful state':

> There is a mystery, with whom relation
> Durst never meddle, in the soul of state,
> Which hath an operation more divine
> Than breath or pen can give expressure to.
> All the commerce that you have had with Troy
> As perfectly is ours as yours, my lord ...
> (III.iii.200–5)

Ulysses introduces a politically topical form of the speculations and eye metaphors involved in the constitution of social subjects: spying. The state gains a divine soul – its *arcana imperii* – when it uses intelligence agencies to search into, appropriate, and reform its citizens.

Shakespeare and Ulysses are punning, although to different effect, on the meanings of 'mystery' as 'profession' and something shielded from public view – what Hamlet calls the 'heart of my mystery'. Achilles' theatre is impotent in the face of the 'providential' knowledge that makes his commerce with Troy as 'perfectly' known to the government as to himself; defeated, Achilles abandons his subversive theatre and plays his part in the Trojan war. Shakespeare, however, does not capitulate to the spectre of power in quite the obliging manner of his glorified thug. Instead, he comments on the censors, state officials, and delators who adopt theatrical tactics – disguise, plots, and entrapping dialogue – to keep citizens from overmighty lords to recusants, printers, players, or rogues and vagabonds from 'meddling' with state practices. Taking Ulysses' lines as a point of departure, it is possible to see how *Troilus and Cressida* engages the aftermath of the Essex rebellion, suffered by the citizens of London as well as Essex himself.

Throughout Elizabeth's reign, direct assaults against state power with 'breath' and 'pen' tended to end in the speaker's and author's imprisonment, interrogation by the Star Chamber, and punishment. Speech and writing fell under Elizabethan treason laws, which included 'compasses, imaginations, inventions, devices, or intentions' and sought out persons who 'maliciously, advisedly, and directly publish, declare, hold opinion, affirm, or say by any speech express words or sayings' (p. 414) prejudicial to Elizabeth's sovereign authority.[18] On the issue of succession, Elizabethan treason laws extended to those who 'set up in open place, publish, or spread any books or scrolls to that effect', or who attempted to 'print, bind, or put to sale, or utter, or cause to be printed, bound, or put to sale, or uttered, any such book or writing wittingly' (p. 416). Rigorous and comprehensive, Elizabethan treason laws reversed the greater liberality of Edward VI and Mary Tudor, both of whom had begun their reigns by repealing Henry VIII's expansion of treason from deeds to speech and writing. At no time does Elizabeth's government express Mary Tudor's concern (for Catholic martyrs) that certain laws and statutes are made

> whereby not only the ignorant and rude, unlearned people, but also learned and expert people minding honesty, are often and many times trapped and snared, yea, many times for words only, without other fact or deed done or perpetrated.
>
> (p. 406)

or Edward VI's government's attempt to lighten treason laws:

> as in tempest or winter one course and garment is convenient, in calm or warm weather a more liberal race or lighter garment both may and ought to be followed and used, so we have seen divers strait and sore

laws made in one Parliament, the time so requiring, in a more calm and quiet reign of another Prince by like authority and Parliament repealed.

(p. 401)

The political crises that led both Mary and Edward to rescind their clement policies[19] and the constant pressure of plots against the Protestant Queen taught Elizabeth I's government to word its treason laws severely.[20] Her government at all times found criminality in speech and writing as well as deeds. In a famous example, John Stubbs paid for his exposure of the 'Gaping Gulf' threatening England with the hand that wrote his treatise. Yet what is striking about the range of treasonous activities under Elizabeth I is the inclusion of thoughts and unarticulated motives. With the rise of the secret service, the mystery that lent divinity to the 'soul of state', the government fully undermined Sir Thomas More's claim that 'God only ... [is] the judge of our secret thoughts'.[21] Many Londoners of the late Elizabethan reign may have agreed with Cressida that it was increasingly difficult not to be 'unsecret to ourselves'.

While Essex engaged in overt treason, Ulysses' surveillance and exposure of Achilles bear on those whose thoughts were not yet 'perfectly' known to the state. The Essex rebellion led to a zealous searching out of further accomplices and sympathisers among London's inhabitants. In February 1601, Elizabeth I announced the arrest of Essex along with Rutland and Southampton in a proclamation that concluded with exhortations and warnings, admonishing her 'good people' that the 'open act' of rebellion.[22]

> cannot yet be thoroughly looked into how far it stretched and how many hearts it hath corrupted, but that it is to be presumed ... that it was not without instruments and ministers dispersed in divers places to provoke the minds of our people to like of their attempts, with calumniating our government ... that they shall do well (and so we charge them) to give diligent heed in all places to the conversation of persons not well known for their good behavior, and to the speeches of any that shall give out slanderous and undutiful words or rumors against us and our government; and they that be in authority to lay hold on such spreaders of rumors; and such as be not in authority to advertise those thereof that have authority to the end that by the apprehension of such dangerous instruments, both the drift and purpose of evil-minded persons may be discovered, their designs prevented ...

Within a week, her government placed London vagabonds (once again) under Martial Law on the grounds that they, unlike 'the loyal and true hearts and settled and unmoveable affections as well as the rest of our subjects as specially of our citizens of London', were more likely 'to lie privily in corners and bad houses, listening after news and stirs, and spreading rumors and tales'. On April 5, she issued a further proclamation

> to signify to all manner of person and persons that whosoever shall in any sort either openly or secretly discover and make known to any of the lords or other of our Privy Council, or to the Lord Mayor of our said city, the name of any of *the authors, writers, or dispersers of any of the said libels*, whereby the offenders therein the sum of £100 of current money paid and delivered unto him by the Lord Mayor ...

One thinks of the unscrupulous courtier in John Donne's fourth satire, bent on exhibiting the court's dirty laundry: he recounts 'More then ten Hollensheads, or Halls, or Stowes, / Of triviall houshold trash' until, Donne's speaker claims, 'I ... felt my selfe then / Becomming Traytor, and mee thought I saw / One of our Giant Statutes ope his jaw / To sucke me in' (ll. 97–8, 130–3). Howard Erskine-Hill notes that an early manuscript mentions the treason-happy agent, Richard Topcliffe.[23] After Essex's rebellion cast London under a pall of suspicion and surveillance, Elizabethans grew eager for the next regime to restore the golden age lost in the queen's final years. Pressures from 'foreign Enemies, Domestical Discontents' ultimately led Edward Phelips, the new Speaker of the House of Commons who addressed the newly crowned James I, implicitly to criticise Elizabeth I's cultivation of favourites who advanced by denouncing their rivals: 'Virtue is now no Treason, nor no man wisheth the Reign of *Augustus*, nor speaketh of the first Times of *Tiberius*.'[24]

Despite his brush with the Star Chamber over the Essex rebels' sponsorship of a new performance of the old play, *Richard II*, Shakespeare continued to test the political issues raised by the rebellion: the liberties of the subject and the sometime greater freedom of speech, writing, and private thought from relation, or delation, to the authorities. Shakespeare was fortunate to work unscathed by censorship and interrogation, unlike his colleague, Ben Jonson, imprisoned for his part in *The Isle of Dogs* and interrogated by Topcliffe. Jonson recalled the episode in conversation with Drummond:

> jn the tyme of his close Imprisonment under Queen Elizabeth his judges could gett nothing of him to all yr demands bot I and No, they placed two damn'd Villans to catch advantage of him, wt him, but he was advertised by his Keeper.

For his revenge, 'of the Spies he hath ane Epigramme'.[25] He suffered interrogation again over *Sejanus his Fall*, for despite Jonson's efforts copiously to annotate and document his sources, ancient histories had become almost as suspect as modern ones.[26] Because Shakespeare had the forethought to produce Ulysses' toe-lining speech on degree, bedrock of the *Elizabethan World Picture*, or perhaps simply because *Troilus and Cressida* was never 'clapper-clawed', Shakespeare himself did not face the interrogations endured by his fellow playwright or his character Achilles.

Yet his theatre, where he filters his sociopolitical critiques through the literature supporting political iconography, warrants close scrutiny. By the end of *Troilus and Cressida*, the late Elizabethan audience should mortally fear that England has indeed inherited its national identity from the Troy legend. The diseased and leering Pandarus, with his 'Winchester goose' of a syphilis sore, is altogether too close: at the play's end he stands in what Nashe called 'this great Grandmother of Corporations, Madame Troynovant',[27] and specifically in the Southwark brothels, situated on land that fell under the Bishop of Winchester's jurisdiction. The Troy legend made abundant surrogate authorities available for exploitation and analysis: Ulysses himself demonstrates the use of authoritative texts to bolster and mystify the sources and coercive effects of authority. Through surrogate authorities, it is possible to bring into view the institutional mechanisms cloaked by classical reference. Shakespeare investigates, with surprising vigour, the degree to which identity and thought are impinged on by politically authoritative codes ranging from statutes to hortatory norms. All citizens, like Achilles, may consider what it means for their identities to be as fragmentary and conflicted as the cultural codes that inform their social possibilities.

Shakespeare's political readers within his plays suggest that class does not determine the ability to decode the political content of classical signs. Shakespeare dishes up the events and exemplars of the Troy legend as 'greasy orts' not 'caviar to the general'. His uses for the Vergilian–Marlovian line of classicising dramaturgy do not require an elitist reader like Prince Hamlet: Ulysses and Thersites outperform Nestor, Agamemnon, and Ajax as interpreters and Tamora and Aaron are skilled in reading political significance in imperial Roman icons, texts, or performances, while Tamora's sons are failures. *Titus Andronicus'* unfortunate Clown is an unmistakable sign of the consequence of small Latin and worse political cryptography: hanging for treason.

Classical figures and events, moreover, were available to anyone hungry for a ballad or broadside: genre stamped the seal of class distinction on the social coordinates of Ajax, Cressida, Aeneas, or Dido ('A Jakes', 'Cresset-light', 'Any-ass' and 'Die-doe' to the irreverent).[28] The sliding scale of class to which Trojans and Romans were susceptible does not mean that late Elizabethan purchasers of a broadside were unaware that upscale models were available in other venues of London. On the contrary, critics need to imagine the circumstances in which a classical allusion would inflame rather than glaze the eye: classics appealed to all because social and political values were at stake, as Chapman knew when he dedicated his *Iliades* to Essex and as Topcliffe knew when he questioned Jonson over *Sejanus*. Censors and secret service agents suspected the subversive power of staging events from the classical past, yet the very range of their available meanings rendered the figures and events of the *translatio imperii* a resilient mirror that Shakespeare might hold up to socially eclectic audiences. Should the need arise, the players might adapt their text or performance to suit the court, the Inns-of-Court, or audiences of the Globe. Yet in any venue, Shakespeare invites his audiences to be Hamlets, and to study, mull over, appropriate, and act on his play.

From Heather James, *Shakespeare's Troy: Drama, Politics and the Translation of Empire* (Cambridge, 1997), pp. 106–18.

Notes

[Heather James's essay is an extract from her full-length volume *Shakespeare's Troy: Drama, Politics and the Translation of Empire*. The book shows how the legend of Troy, derived in the early-modern period from Virgil, Ovid and other sources, was used variously in the official ideologies of the Elizabethan and early-Stuart states. In this detailed analysis James discusses the Troy legend in relation to *Troilus and Cressida*. She shows how the play reflects and interrogates the changing status of the Troy myth and how it reveals the anxieties apparent in the utilisation of myth in the developing ideological apparatus that was to play an important role in the evolution of empire. Ed.]

1. With delightful acerbity, Raymond Southall, '*Troilus and Cressida* and the Spirit of Capitalism', *Shakespeare in a Changing World*, ed. Arnold Kettle (New York, 1964), pp. 217–32, insists that critics stop romanticising the quality of Troilus' love: 'It is extraordinarily difficult' to find 'any intensity in the love of Troilus, or rather any love in the intensity of Troilus', p. 216. Southall's focus on the bankruptcy of petrarchan language relates to his Marxist reading of economics and capitalism in the play.

2. Leading defenders of Cressida are Gayle Greene, 'Shakespeare's Cressida: A Kind of Self', in *The Woman's Part: Feminist Criticism of Shakespeare*, ed. Carolyn Ruth Swift Lenz, Gayle Green and Carol Neely (Urbana, Chicago and London, 1980); Carolyn Asp, 'In Defense of Cressida', *Studies in Philology*, 74 (1977), 406–17; Grant L. Voth and Oliver H. Evans, 'Cressida and the World of the Play', *Shakespeare Studies*, 8 (1975), 231–9; and Janet Adelman, ' "This is and Is Not Cressid": The Characterization of Cressida', *The (M)other Tongue*, ed. S. N. Garner, C. Kahane, and M. Sprengnether (Ithaca, NY, 1985), pp. 119–41. By psychologising her motivations, the critics attempt to combat Cressida's literary fate. Their sympathy with Cressida confirms the sense that Shakespeare is concerned with the costs to the subject of representational tactics meant to transmit authority to a privileged reader. Douglas Bruster, however, attractively argues that Cressida gains agency: 'realising that she is seen as a commodity, Cressida decides to take control of her commodity function', *Drama and the Market. In the Age of Shakespeare* (Cambridge, 1992), p. 98.

3. Janet Adelman analyses Shakespeare's use of tragedy to meditate problems of uniting separate wills and minds in marriage: 'Is thy Union Here?: Union and its Discontents in *Troilus and Cressida* and *Othello*', *Suffocating Mothers: Fantasies of Maternal Origin in Shakespeare's Plays, Hamlet to The Tempest* (London and New York, 1992).

4. Noting the speech's relation to the petrarchan blazon, Cook relates it to pornography, 'Unbodied Figure of Desire', *Theater Journal*, 38 (1986), 49–50. Bruster, *Drama and the Market*, p. 103, develops the relationship of petrarchism to commerce, with particular reference to the image of the merchant-adventuring ship that Spencer, Donne, and Drayton adapt from Petrarch.

5. Quoted from Ben Jonson, *Works*, ed. Charles H. Hereford, Percy Simpson and Evelyn Simpson, 11 vols (Oxford, 1922–52), II, p. 271. Jonson further exhorts the poet not to let 'the skin and coat' of language become 'horrid, rough, wrinkled, gaping, or chapt' – the kind of language Shakespeare represents in Pandarus. Puttenham's comparison of poetic to courtly decorum, particularly in dress, appears in the *Arte of Poesie* III.xxv.

6. The *O.E.D.* defines 'motive' as a moving limb or organ and specifies that this is an exclusively Shakespearean meaning. The other instance of this usage also meditates a complex state of agency and instrumentality: Bolingbroke swears that he will bite off his tongue as 'the slavish motive of recanting fear' if he obeys King Richard's order to withdraw from combat with Mowbray (*Richard II* I.i.193). Rather than allow his tongue to be the instrument of Richard's will, Bolingbroke would bite it off as a traitor to his own will.

7. John Bayley, *The Uses of Division: Unity and Disharmony in Literature* (London, 1976), p. 205.

8. 'Shakespeare's *Will*: The Temporality of Rape', *Representations*, 20 (Fall 1987), 25–76.

9. Troilus' ecstatic greeting of his ideal ego is, as Cook notes, reminiscent of Lacanian ideas of ego-formation, and particularly the role of 'speculation'. The great Myrmidon, however, can hardly be said to greet his identity 'jubilantly': when he resumes his heroic identity by taking credit for Hector's death, Achilles goes about his business grimly.

10. To focus on the aubade scene calls for the audience or reader to tug against the play's and Troilus' pull toward closure and coherence. See Adelman, *Suffocating Mothers* and René Girard, 'The Politics of Desire in *Troilus and Cressida*', ed. Patricia Parker and Geoffrey Hartman, *Shakespeare and the Question of Theory* (New York and London, 1985), pp. 188–209, for detailed readings of this curiously misplaceable scene.

11. Cook, 'Unbodied Figures of Desire', pp. 34–52, and 54.

12. J. Hillis Miller, 'Ariachne's Broken Woof', *Georgia Review*, 31:1 (1977), 47–60, describes Troilus' shifts from illusory unity to doubling and finally fragmentation. Jonathan Dollimore reads the speech's linguistic and philosophical implications in terms of a disintegrating society in *Radical Tragedy* (Manchester, 1985).

13. For a discussion of early modern London's neofeudal character and emerging capitalist market, see Lawrence Manley, *The Literature and Culture of Early Modern London* (Cambridge, 1995). Also relevant to my concluding section are the studies of Lars Engle, Richard McCoy, and Raymond Southall, and Jean-Christophe Agnew, *Worlds Apart: The Market and the Theater in Anglo-American Thought, 1550–1750* (Cambridge, 1986).

14. Jonson adapts the scene from Suetonius, where it is Augustus who presides over the bacchanalian dinner. In *The Boke Named The Governour* (London, 1907), Sir Thomas Elyot describes the ignominy which spurred Augustus to self-reformation:

> The noble Emperor Augustus, who in all the residue of his life was for his moderation and temperance excellently commended, suffered no little reproach, forasmuch as he in a secret supper or banquet, having with him six noblemen, his friends, and six noble women, and naming himself at that time Apollo, and the other men and women the names of other gods and goddesses, fared sumptuously and delicately, the city of Rome at that time being vexed with scarcity of grain. He therefore was rent with curses and rebukes of the people, insomuch as he was openly called Apollo the tormenter, saying also that he with his gods had devoured their corn. With which liberty of speech, being more persuaded than discontented, from thenceforth he used ... frugality or moderation of diet ... (III.xxii)

15. Lars Engle, *Shakespeare's Pragmatism: Market of his Time* (Chicago, 1993), p. 155.

16. Quoted from A. R. Braunmuller (ed.), *A Seventeenth Century Letter-Book* (London, 1983), pp. 66–7.

17. William Cobbett, T. B. Howell et al., *A Complete Collection of State Trials*, 42 vols (London, 1816–98), vol. 1, pp. 1333–60. Essex was grateful to escape public execution: after his abrupt shift from honour-bound self-righteousness to pious self-condemnation, Elizabeth's government granted his request for a private execution in the Tower.

18. All references are to J. R. Tanner, *Tudor Constitutional Documents, 1485–1603* (Cambridge, 1922), 'The Law of Treason', pp. 375–451.

19. The body counts of these early Tudor rebellions were high: D. M. Loades, *Two Tudor Conspiracies* (Cambridge, 1965), pp. 73, 113–14, notes that sixty to seventy men died in battle during Wyatt's rebellion and as many were executed for treason.

20. Alison Plowden discusses Walsingham's development of his secret service in response to Catholic plots, domestic and international, against the queen's life in *The Elizabethan Secret Service* (New York, 1991). In *Treason in Tudor England: Politics and Paranoia* (London, 1986) Lacey Baldwin Smith surveys educational, political, and behaviour manuals as well as court politics to establish the culture of suspicion in England, and devotes several chapters to Essex. Drawing on seminal work in Keith Thomas, *Religion and the Decline of Magic* (New York, 1971), Carole Levin, *'The Heart and Stomach of a King': Elizabeth I and the Politics of Sex and Power* (Philadelphia, 1994), pp. 91–120, describes less publicised or clearly motivated conspiracies of commoners against the queen.

21. Quoted from Tanner, *Tudor Constitutional Documents, 1485–1603*, p. 435.

22. Paul L. Hughes and James F. Larkin, *Tudor Royal Proclamations*, 3 vols (New Haven and London, 1969).

23. I quote Donne from H. J. C. Grierson, *Donne's Poetical Works*, 2 vols (Oxford, 1912). In *The Augustan Idea in English Literature*, a valuable guide to the literary, political, and religious contexts in which the renaissance understood the Augustan age, Howard Erskine-Hill notes the significance of the early manuscript reading (p. 81). His emphases on the law and politics in the chapter on Donne's satires furnish stimulating groundwork for understanding *Troilus and Cressida* as a translation of empire.

24. I quote from Howard Erskine-Hill, *The Augustan Idea in English Literature* (London, 1983), p. 130, who takes the allusions to Augustus and Tiberius as reference to a providential pattern of rise and decline.

Blair Worden elaborates Erskine-Hill's discussion of the late Tiberian–Elizabethan political scene in 'Ben Jonson among the Historians', *Culture and Politics in Early Stuart England*, ed. Kevin Sharpe and Peter Lake (Stanford, CA, 1993), pp. 67–90. Malcolm Smuts, 'Court-Centered Politics and Roman Historians', published in the same volume, pp. 21–43, stresses that Roman history reminded early seventeenth-century Englishmen of the vulnerability of 'ancient constitutional forms', and notes that the collapse of the Republic and establishment of the empire, an intensively studied period of Roman history under Elizabeth and James, was 'a story of constitutional instability and subversion' (p. 41).

25. Herford and Simpson, vol. 11, p. 574. On the institutional censorship of drama, see G. E. Bentley, 'Regulation and Censorship', *The Professions of Dramatist and Player in Shakespeare's Time* (1971; rpt. Princeton, NJ, 1984), pp. 145–96, and V. C. Gildersleeve, *Government Regulation of the Elizabethan Drama* (New York, 1908; rpt. New York, 1961).

26. Anticipating political misconstructions, Samuel Daniel burned his history of Cleopatra and Camden deferred his history of Queen Elizabeth's reign. John Hayward was imprisoned for publishing his *Life and Reign of King Henry IV* (1599), which 'was interpreted as a parallel with recent events, and was alleged to be an apology for the Earl of Essex and an incitement to Elizabeth's subjects to overthrow her, as Henry IV had overthrown Richard II', Worden, 'Ben Jonson among the Historians', p. 75. Suspicions were well-placed: Hayward dedicated the history to Essex and published it in 1599, just before Essex left for Ireland. Tacitean historiography, practised by Hayward, Savile, and Bacon, found a home in the Essex circle. See Mervyn James, *Society, Politics, and Culture Studies in Early Modern England* (Cambridge, 1986), ch. 9. The author and printer were brought to the Star Chamber, and the licenser, Samuel Harsnett, wriggled out of responsibility: see W. W. Greg, *London Publishing Between 1550 and 1650* (Oxford, 1956), pp. 61–2.

27. Quoted from Manley, *London in the Age of Shakespeare*, pp. 277–8.

28. Frank Kermode notes the puns on Dido and Aeneas in Middleton's *The Roaring Girl* (1607/8) in the Arden edition of *The Tempest* (London and New York, 1958), p. 47n. Samuel Rowlands dubs Cressida 'Cresset-light' in *The Letting of Humors* (Glasgow, 1880), and Sir John Harington commemorates the scatological joke on a 'jakes' in *A New Discourse of a Stale Subject, Called the Metamorphosis of Ajax* (1596).

9

Invading Bodies/Bawdy Exchanges: Disease, Desire, and Representation

VALERIE TRAUB

The discourses that have contributed to the global crisis of AIDS demonstrate the extent to which the body can be constructed as a vulnerable enclosure, with its erotic apertures positioned as sites of and conduits for contamination. Representations of AIDS also testify to the tendency to place blame for epidemics on those others who are vulnerable by virtue of their erotic practice or racial/national origin.[1] Such twentieth-century preoccupations are prefigured by early modern constructs of venereal disease in which gender, erotic, and nationalist anxieties were managed by conferring blame on those who, by reference to their social status or geographical location, could be considered not merely inferior but inherently contaminated. The early modern terminology of syphilis, for instance, points to an endless deferral of origin and cause: in a dizzying displacement of culpability, syphilis made its way into the British vocabulary as the 'French pox' or 'morbus gallicus'; the Parisians alternately rerouted the disease to be Germanic or Italian in origin – 'morbus Germanicus' or 'la maladie Napolitiane'; the Germans placed the blame on the Italians and the French: 'mal de Naples', 'morbus gallicus', 'malafranzcos' or 'Franzosenkrankheit'. The Turks pointed the finger to *their* others, 'male dei cristiani', while Africans blamed the Jews who had been driven out of Spain.[2] In each case, xenophobia protected the nation, if not the nation's bodies, from disease.

Itinerants – Jews and gypsies – were the primary focus of scape-goating until 1539, when the origin of syphilis was further displaced onto the New World: according to this new theory, the disease was introduced to Europe by Spanish sailors who engaged in sexual rela-tions with Haitian women during the second of Columbus' voyages.[3] Whatever the possible facticity of the 'Columbian hypothesis' – and it remains a matter of debate in the medical community today – it is clear that early modern 'America' functioned in the European imagination much as does 'Africa' in some Western minds today: a foreign, 'primitive' continent, inhabited by 'savages' practising exotic and diseased sexual behaviours.[4]

Many contemporary critics have argued that the orifices of the body metonymically figure the vulnerabilities of the gendered psyche and the nation.[5] The specific ways in which bodies are constructed can thus be read as maps of both the subject's and the state's self-representation. *Troilus and Cressida* provides a particularly telling rendition of the vulnerabilities of the erotic body and the body politic. In this play, faithlessness to nation is synonymous with faith-lessness to love, as the position of Helen so palpably indicates: whether she remains in Troy or is forcibly carried back to Greece, her transfer of affection from Menelaus to Paris suggests that the mobil-ity of her person goes hand in hand with the mobility of her desire. Likewise, erotic mobility is clearly the main stake in Cressida's movement from Trojan walls to Grecian camp, and the subsequent transformation of her identity from Trojan beauty to 'The Troyans' [s]trumpet' (IV.v.64).[6] Within the nationalist framework of the play, at issue for both women is whether they are to be positioned as idealised or degraded objects of male desire – in the vernacular of the play, as 'pearls' or 'plackets'[7] – and the answer depends, in part, on which nation (and which man) claims their allegiance.[8]

Questions of nationalist and erotic identity, then, are consistently intertwined: it is those 'merry Greeks', after all, defined as morally and sexually loose, who seek to penetrate the walls of a Troy also already defined via Paris' abduction of Helen as sexually licentious.[9] Much in the play contributes to a linking of war and sexuality: early on, Cressida quips that she will lie 'Upon my back, to defend my belly' (I.ii.262), and she continues this line of reasoning when she tells Troilus she will 'war with' him over the ability to remain honest (III.ii.169). On a more cynical level, Thersites sums up the Greek/Trojan conflict thus: 'all the argument is a whore and a cuckold' and 'war and lechery confound all' (II.iii.71–4). Indeed,

René Girard argues that metaphorically embodied in the Greek/Trojan war is the very essence of sexuality: a 'mimetic desire' for the object of one's rival, in which identity is constructed through the envious gaze of the other.[10] More recently, Linda Charnes intriguingly argues that within the play's circularity of desire and aggression is a male homosocial ethos that produces a *myth* of heterosexuality. Whereas many critics view the homoerotic relation of Achilles and Patroclus as the ultimate corruption of sexuality, with sodomy carrying the signifying burden of the 'unnatural', Charnes views male homoerotic aggression as one moment in an endless cycle of exchange producing the Trojan war.[11]

To my mind, however, it is less male homoeroticism than sexual exchange *per se* that signifies psychic dis-ease in this play, as literal venereal disease is posed as the necessary outcome of all erotic liaisons. That is, just as the equation between war and sexuality sums up erotic relations in *Troilus and Cressida*, so too does a further tropological substitution specify the empty content of 'sexuality'. If war equals sexuality, then sexuality equals syphilis. If state-sponsored masculine aggression fundamentally motivates (and provides the appropriate metaphor for) erotic encounters, then 'penetration' is not merely represented by the 'invading bodies' of the Trojans, but also by the 'invaded bodies' of those afflicted with venereal disease.

'Diseases' is the final word of *Troilus and Cressida*, and metaphors of disease are invoked to describe all the major problems in the play, from Nestor's comment that 'all our power is sick' (I.iii.139); to the 'infection' of 'plaguy' self-pride charged against Achilles and Ajax (I.iii.187, II.iii.176) and the 'envious fever' of emulation that spreads throughout the Grecian camp (I.iii.133); to Troilus' characterisation of his love for Cressida as 'the open ulcer of my heart' (I.i.55). Contagion is not only the imagistic base, but the goal of Thersites' curses:

> the rotten diseases of the south, the guts-griping, ruptures, catarrhs, loads o' gravel i' the back, lethargies, cold palsies, raw eyes, dirt-rotten livers, wheezing lungs, bladders full of imposthume, sciaticas, limekilns i' th' palm, incurable boneache, and the rivell'd fee-simple of the tetter, take and take again such preposterous discoveries!
>
> (V.i.17–24)

A rhetoric of contagion not only 'contaminates' the action of the play, it supplies the central signifier of desire: desire *is* disease, the play seems to say, and both are posed as a military problem, defined in terms of attack and defence.[12] The play in fact presents three interconnected fantasies of invasion: the prophesied (and, for the audience, legendary) Greek penetration and destruction of the walled city of Troy, the syphilitic infection of individual bodies, and the incursion of the 'diseased' (Pandarus, Cressida, and prostitutes generally) into the body politic.[13] The multiple deployment of these fantasies renders desire not only contagious, but deadly.

Let us return to Thersites' remark in full: 'All the argument is a whore and a cuckold, a good quarrel to draw emulous factions and bleed to death upon. [Now the dry serpigo on the subject, and war and lechery confound all.]' (II.iii.71–4). Syphilis – the 'dry serpigo' – is invoked both as a description of the subject (the argument, the war) and as a curse upon it. Thersites is merely repeating what he said 50 lines earlier: 'After this, the vengeance on the whole camp! Or rather, the Neapolitan bone-ache! For that, methinks, is the curse depending on those that war for a placket' (II.iii.17–19). Those that fight over a woman – woman defined as a 'slit in the petticoat' and thereby through her genitals – deserve for their foolishness the 'Neapolitan bone-ache'. Here, aching bones becomes a symptom not only of disease but of male heterosexual desire and, in Charnes' terms, the male homosocial desire that fuels the continuation of the war. Thersites' use of the equivocal 'depending on' suggests that disease not only *threatens* but *depends on* those who em-body the co-incidence of sexuality and war. Through such 'bawdy exchanges', syphilis becomes a displaced signifier for the anxieties potentially inhering in *all* bodily exchanges.

The exchange of bodies is a primary thematic and structuring principle of the play: not only is Cressida traded 'in right great exchange' for the Trojan prisoner Antenor (III.iii.21; IV.ii; IV.iv), and then passed from one kissing Greek to the next (IV.v), so too the possibility of giving Helen back to the Greeks is forcefully argued between Troilus and his brothers (II.ii). Not only does Cressida allegedly 'substitute' Diomedes for Troilus (V.ii), but the entire war is fought over Helen's purported 'exchange' of Menelaus for Paris.[14] And, what is war, if not the exchange of live bodies for dead? Bodily exchange forms the basis of the play's representation of both sexuality and war; it symbolises, in fact, the interchange between sexuality and war that serves as the play's pretext.[15] In this context the bawdy exchanges about venereal disease take on a special significance, metaphorically and metaonymically replicating and enhancing the play's irreducibly interwoven erotic and militaristic significations.

What is at stake, ultimately, in the mutual implication of disease, desire, and bodily exchange is the identity and relation of subject and state. Insofar as the body metonymically represents the subject as a whole, the body's vulnerabilities to both disease and desire demonstrate the tenuousness of a subjectivity constructed in relation to social processes. Indeed, the intersection of desire and disease intimates the extent to which subjectivity can be 'spoiled' by forces external to it. Not only does syphilis transform the body into something alien, something repulsively other,[16] it introduces a biological and social force into the state that could not, in those days, be managed or contained.[17] Like those desires that initiate the Greek/Trojan war, early modern syphilis seemed paradigmatically excessive, not only in its ravages of the individual body, but in its epidemic march across the polity. Like leprosy, syphilis was, in Steven Mullaney's terms, an 'incontinent disorder', an illness that 'exceeded the bounds of community and classification'.[18] And like the symptoms of leprosy in the culture at large, the symptoms of syphilis in *Troilus and Cressida* function as

> manifestations of a disorder that [is] both particular and pervasive, signs of disease in an individual body and signs whose frame of reference extend[s] to the culture as a whole, signalling on a figurative level a disorder to which the body politic itself [is] vulnerable.[19]

As invasion of body and state, as symbol of erotic and social incontinence, syphilis demands, within the defensive logic of *Troilus and Cressida*, corresponding military action.

In his assertion of 'mimetic desire' as the primary mode of exchange in *Troilus and Cressida*, René Girard remarks:

> Pandarus, the go-between, the mediator of desire ... plays no political role but ... nevertheless rightly appears as the symbol of everything in the play, the alpha and the omega of *Troilus and Cressida*. He is on stage at the beginning, and he is on stage again at the end. In his Rabelaisian epilogue he bequeaths to the spectators a venereal disease that had not been mentioned earlier, and that seems to turn him almost into an allegory of the contagious power of mimetic desire.[20]

Syphilis, however, *had* been alluded to earlier, not only in the above statements of Thersites, but also in Hector's allegation that Grecian women are 'sunburnt' (I.iii.282), and in puns on 'sodden business' and 'stew'd phrases' (III.i.41).[21] Girard's effacement of such references, and in particular references to the disease's vivid material reality, seems to serve his effort to translate syphilis into a disembodied allegory of mimetic desire. Contagion in Girard's schema is pre-eminently psychological, an epidemic of envy and emulation: 'Emulation is mimetic rivalry itself. It creates many conflicts but it empties them of all content.'[22] But what if we were not to allegorise Pandarus or syphilis, but to take both quite literally and materially, resisting the structuralist urge to empty the epidemic of content, and instead placing the dramatic representation of syphilis within the historical discourses of the sixteenth century? The epidemic of syphilis that 'invaded' Europe a century before Shakespeare's play continued well into the Tudor period; and insofar as no cure had yet rendered the disease less fatal – Thersites calls it the 'incurable bone-ache' (V.i.22) – it is likely that its ravages were the focus of considerable anxiety.

At the same time, the meaning of syphilis was, from its inception, ideologically constructed. Indeed, as Bruce Boehrer argues, the *discovery* of syphilis is also an *invention*.[23] That is, while it seems true that a possibly new disease emerged in epidemic form in Naples in 1494, and quickly made its deadly way across Europe (reaching England by 1498 and Japan about twenty years later), it is also true that the English discourses in which the symptoms and possible treatments of 'morbus gallicus' were described worked as more than description: not only were the names given the disease a signifier of nationalist sentiment, but the terms by which the medical and legal discourses defined the victims, carriers, and healers of the scourge were also ideologically invested. Boehrer's analysis of early modern representations of syphilis concludes:

> syphilis is invented as a new medical category and various treatments are explored when the illness becomes a recognised challenge to the power elite. ... [It] comes into being *as a treatable ailment* only when it is associated with those figures at the heart of the political and social order. ... When identified with the poor and socially undistinguished, the disease almost ceases to be a disease at all; instead, it emerges in its concomitant character as an instrument of discipline and punishment – that is, as an appendage of government itself.[24]

Gender as well as nation and class affected the representation of syphilis: women were uniquely figured as carriers of the disease, perhaps because of their perceived immunity – a common belief supported by the less visible symptomology on female genitalia in comparison to the penile sores and painful urination of men.[25] More to the point, this positioning of women as vessels but not victims of syphilitic contamination draws upon the cultural reservoir of disgust which animates other early modern representations of women's erotic desire. Add to this disgust the image of syphilis as a threat not only to man, but ultimately to nation, and we find gender, nationalistic, and erotic anxieties converging in a powerful demonstration of othering: through a particular ideological slippage, the possibly diseased 'woman' comes to equal the potentially invasive 'foreigner'.

The history of syphilis, then, is the history of the construction of various *boundaries* of disease, formulated along mutually reinforcing nation, class, and gender lines. These material boundaries served a psychological function of defence: by drawing lines of differentiation between victims and carriers, elite males both enhanced their own sense of medical emergency and freed themselves from responsibility for transmission.

If, as Boehrer argues, early modern syphilis emerges not simply as a medical crisis but as a 'managed political event', then it makes sense to ask what ideological work Shakespeare's play performed in its own time.[26] It is hardly incidental that syphilis had from its inception been figured through literary constructs: many surgeons poeticised the disease, and in the sixteenth century the poet-surgeon Girolamo Fracastoro wrote the Latin poem whose depiction of the shepherd Sifilo gave the disease its modern name.[27] Indeed, this mutually sustaining relation between aesthetic, political, and medical events forms the basis of Shakespeare's representation of syphilis in *Troilus and Cressida*.

In a culture so dedicated to displacing blame for disease, and in a play so concerned with the need to affirm nationalist boundaries, it would not be surprising to see venereal disease projected onto the foreign others against whom the identity of the state is maintained. Although the Greek and Trojan warriors do not employ such metaphors, privileging instead the language of chivalry to mediate their conflict, the primary observer of and commentator on battle does, as Thersites indifferently heaps curses upon Greek and Trojan alike. As spokesman against lechery who imagines it lurking everywhere, Thersites embodies the quality of *projection*.[28] Since there is 'nothing but lechery', 'Lechery, lechery, still wars and lechery; nothing else holds fashion', he indifferently flings curses on both camps: 'A burning devil [venereal disease] take them' (V.i.98; V.ii.198–200).[29] Finally, in a powerful conflation of the physical wasting of disease that owes much to the early modern confusion between syphilis and leprosy, he observes: 'lechery eats itself' (V.iv.35).[30]

What is less expected, perhaps, is that as much as the disease is projected outward, the inverse is equally true: syphilis in *Troilus and Cressida* is the foreign disease that is paradoxically always already *within*. 'Syphilis is Us', Pandarus intimates at the end of the play, as, having crossed over onto the liminal ground of the blood-soaked plains outside Troy, he invites the audience into a bawdy partnership of prostitution and venereal disease:

> A goodly medicine for my aching bones! O world, world, world! Thus is the poor agent despis'd! O traders and bawds, how earnestly are you set a-work, and how ill requited! Why should our endeavour be so lov'd and the performance so loath'd? What verse for it? What instance for it? Let me see:
>
> > Full merrily the humble-bee doth sing,
> > Till he hath lost his honey and his sting;
> > And being once subdu'd in armed tail,
> > Sweet honey and sweet notes together fail.
>
> Good traders in the flesh, set this in your painted cloths:
> As many as be here of Pandar's hall,
> Your eyes, half out, weep out at Pandar's fall;
> Or if you cannot weep, yet give some groans,
> Though not for me, yet for your aching bones.
> Brethren and sisters of the hold-door trade,
> Some two months hence my will shall here be made.
> It should be now, but that my fear is this,
> Some galled goose of Winchester would hiss.
> Till then I'll sweat and seek about for eases.
> And at that time bequeath you my diseases.
>
> (V.x.35–56)

How has the bee lost his phallic sting? His impotence, the rest of the passage implies, is caused by syphilis, its distressing material effects graphically represented in decaying eyes, aching bones, and the sweating cure.[31] Pandarus' repetition of venereal references constructs himself as a walking em-body-ment of syphilitic interchange, while his construction of the audience-as-bawds (Brethren and sisters of the hold-door trade) assumes, indeed depends upon, their prior contamination. The 'trader in the flesh' who constantly bewails his aching, syphilitic bones (V.iii.105) thus gives voice to the underlying anxiety of the play: we are all already infected.

This paranoid fantasy is related to the discourse of prostitution which 'infects' the play, and of which Pandarus comprises a major part. In *Troilus and Cressida*, prostitutes are vessels and primary agents of disease;[32] they have presumably contracted their illness by some means, but that means is never specified, instead lurking murkily in the play's non-dramatised pre-history. This dramatic strategy reproduces the dominant paradigm of disease in which moral sign and physical manifestation are one: as agents of moral corruption, prostitutes are 'naturally' agents of physical corruption as well. That this unidirectional causality is asymmetrical in its gender alignments is obvious: female prostitutes infect men, never the other way around, and men are uniquely vulnerable by means of their excessive lust. It is this vulnerability to lust and disease – or the lust that *is* disease – that is displaced onto Pandarus: as voyeur of and procurer for *other* men's lusts, he is implicated, not only in prurient pleasure at other men's pleasures, but in the infectious dangers to which their desires are subject. Add to this heterosexual vulnerability Pandarus' role as instigator of female corruption – his function as pimp – and he comes to represent simultaneously the male victim and the female cause of disease. The effect of this doubling is the enormous power of the horrific fantasy he expresses, a power incommensurate with his putative function in the plot.

Victim and agent, Pandarus represents both the manifest sign and the psychic *internalisation* of the disease. By giving Pandarus the final say, the play, however uncomfortably, positions him as authority, summing up from the other side Thersites' denunciations of war and lechery. By means of these characterisations, *Troilus and Cressida* holds in tension two fantasised trajectories: on the one hand, Thersites' representation of the Greek/Trojan conflict dramatises the tendency to project outward the threat of contagion, to expel it and attach it to others. On the other hand, Pandarus gives voice to the fear that impels such projective desire: contamination already lurks within the perpetually vulnerable body. Seemingly oppositional, these fantasies are in fact two aspects of a mutually sustaining mode of defence, each diacritically necessitating the other.[33] Despite their diametrical positioning as bawd and anti-bawd, Pandarus and Thersites are in essential agreement about the nature of desire. Any tension between their two responses collapses, as Pandarus and Thersites adopt opposite yet symmetrical strategies to psychically manage the threat that the 'venereal' *is* disease. Between the articulations of these two spokesmen, *Troilus and Cressida* denies the possibility of 'choosing' between alternative 'viewpoints'; insofar as each term and each response is integrally constitutive of the other, the system of representation governing the play allows no escape from the circularity of disease and desire, projection and internalisation. Hence the sense of suffocation, of claustrophobia we feel when reading or watching this play.

It is a claustrophobia which would have been experienced even more acutely by Shakespeare's audience, for the play's representation of desire and disease is informed by an awareness of the theatre's status as site of contamination. If, as Sander Gilman suggests, 'The fixed structures of art provide us with a sort of carnival during which we fantasise about our potential loss of control, perhaps even revel in the fear it generates within us, but we always believe that this fear exists separate from us',[34] then Pandarus' transgression of the usual epilogic function (inviting the audience's consumption and approval) transgresses the conventional function of drama as well. Rather than offering a psychic strategy of separation, distance, projection, and hence imagined safety, Pandarus forces audience members to confront their own position within the representational nexus of the play, and thus their own possible hopes and fears: that in partaking of the 'common' pleasure of dramatic spectatorship they will be implicated in the desire and disease, prostitution and corruption, circulating throughout and around the 'place of the stage'.[35] Under Pandarus' auspices, not only the play, but the audience as well, is re-figured as a potentially 'syphilitic body'. In short, his speech elicits an uneasy recognition of the very vulnerabilities we rely on art to manage and control, vulnerabilities even more palpably experienced within the socially porous walls of the early modern theatre.

And yet, despite Pandarus' powerful final appeal to a fantasy of internalisation, much of the play has already endorsed the strategy of projection; indeed, projection structures the two central 'exchanges' in the play. For what is Troilus' response to Cressida in the Greek camp if not projection, in which he 'reads' the 'worst' in Cressida's actions, eliminating the possibility of ambiguity, ambivalence or even adroit manipulation in her vacillating responses to Diomedes? Occupying Thersites' position of voyeur, Troilus – 'O Cressid! O false Cressid! False, false, false!' – comes to the same conclusion as Thersites: 'A proof of strength she could not publish more,/ Unless she said "My mind is now turn'd whore" ' (V.ii.182, 116–17).

But such a conclusion was already in the process of being implemented in the play. After Cressida is traded for the prisoner Antenor, and is physically passed from one kissing man to the next (in a scene that reads very close to gang rape), Nestor praises her quick and bawdy wit. Ulysses, however, powerfully responds with this enraged outcry:

> Fie, fie upon her!
> There's language in her eye, her cheek, her lip,
> Nay, her foot speaks; her wanton spirits look out
> At every joint and motive of her body.
> O, these encounterers, so glib of tongue,
> That give a coasting welcome ere it comes,
> And wide unclasp the tables of their thoughts
> To every ticklish reader! Set them down
> For sluttish spoils of opportunity
> And daughters of the game.
>
> (IV.v.55–63)

As elsewhere in Shakespeare, female glibness of tongue is made to correspond to a veritable 'body language', in which women's oral facility signifies sexual wantonness. Indeed, her very body 'speaks' a language, with 'wanton spirits' emerging from every orifice, every 'joint and motive of her body'. Like Gertrude, Ophelia, Desdemona, Hermione, and Falstaff, Cressida becomes representative of the 'grotesque body': impure, open, loose, transgressive. Too open in speech, excessively inviting in body, Cressida becomes positioned – is projected – as a member of the 'hold-door trade', a 'slut', a 'daughter of the game', incontinent inciter of her own rape. By this moment in the play we all know with what 'sluttish spoils' prostitutes contaminate their clients – and just in case we miss it, Pandarus' departing reference to 'some galled goose of Winchester' [syphilitic prostitute] reiterates the point (V.x.54).[36] Indeed, with this representation of the disease that, in its circulation throughout the erotic body mimes its circulation throughout sexual society, we encounter the most paranoid version of the 'grotesque body' as 'a subject of pleasure in processes of exchange ... never closed off from either its social or ecosystemic context'.[37] Here, though, neither the imposition of death nor ritual expulsion are upheld as possible resolutions of psychic distress; instead, the play lingers over the guilt it layers onto the female contaminant. As Cressida is blamed as agent of contamination, the circulating meanings of sexual exchange become located, even fixed, in her physical being. Her body is transfigured into an 'encounterer', the projected site of exchange of the desire that *is* disease. Reduced from subject to object, a veritable 'spoil' of war, Cressida-as-encounterer serves the psychic function for the male characters of localising and thus holding at arm's length the paranoid fantasy of diseased erotic circulation. Once Cressida's erotic being is so fixed, all that remains to take place is Troilus' and Thersites' interpretations, excoriations, and individual attempts to expel it. That Troilus does so through a tortured disavowal and splitting of Cressida's 'identity' – 'This she? No, this is Diomed's Cressid. ... This was not she. ... This is, and is not Cressid' (V.ii.136–50) – speaks tellingly both of the inordinate powers of projection and the tragic costs of expulsion.

If the 'exchanges' of Cressida's erotic body scapegoat her in a fashion familiar to those who study the social effects of epidemic disease, so too does the language of bawdy defend against the anxieties occasioned by venereal dis-ease. At the risk of privileging heterosexuality for the sake of a pun, what is bawdy if not 'verbal intercourse'? But what distinguishes bawdy from other (economic, theological, romantic) tropes of sexuality – its signifying difference if you will – is its consistent re-materialisation of the body. Evident aurally through the verbal pun bawdy/body, this materialisation insists on body parts and functions as more than signs and symbols of something else, rather, as pleasurable and/or offensive in the body's own terms. Bawdy references in *Troilus and Cressida* do not merely *express* a contaminated sexuality; they also mediate the anxieties of syphilitic contagion. Bawdy functions here in much the same way as do cuckold jokes in other Shakespearean plays – expressing male hostility and fear, but also acting as compensation, revising male powerlessness. As Carol Cook argues:

> The telling of cuckold jokes ... restores the male prerogative: it returns the woman to silence and absence, her absence authorising the male raconteur to represent her in accordance with particular male fantasies, and produces pleasure through male camaraderie.[38]

Cuckold jokes, however, are unavailable in this play due to Menelaus' status as cuckold *originaire*: cuckoldry can no longer function as a joke when it is the sole cause of a lengthy and unpopular war.[39] Instead, 'bawdy' jokes take their place as the primary means to manage social anxieties stemming from gender, erotic, and national conflict. That is, bawdy jokes about syphilis not only express the isomorphic relations between war, desire, and disease, but also *defend against* the perceived vulnerabilities of the warring body politic and the erotic body. If the 'heroes' of the war – Achilles, Hector, Ajax – assert power and masculine selfhood through violent fantasies of another's loss of identity and power (as when Achilles says to Hector, 'Tell me, you heavens, in which part of his body/ Shall I destroy him? Whether there, or there, or there?' IV.v.242–3), the non-participants of battle – Thersites and Pandarus – consistently use bawdy as a less dangerous mode of defence. Both bawdy jokes and militaristic posturing mediate the vulnerability occasioned by erotic and military 'exchange'.

With erotic and nationalist identities under strain, bawdy works in conjunction with militarism to reassert boundaries between self and other, Us and Them. It is hardly coincidental that this mode of separation is also a dominant social response to epidemic disease.[40] To our earlier formulation, 'war equals sexuality, sexuality equals disease', we can circle back again to the equation, 'response to disease equals war'. Asserting such an enclosed circuit of desires, *Troilus and Cressida* defies any effort to imagine a sexuality that is not defensive or diseased – in short, a desire that is not already thoroughly anxious.

Except, perhaps, one. Insofar as male homoeroticism interrupts the war, it threatens to short-circuit the mutually sustaining relations of disease, desire, and violence. Indeed, the representations of male-male love here register a yearning less for homoerotic relations *per se* than for an erotic modality uncontaminated by the equation of desire and disease. As Achilles substitutes dallying with Patroclus 'Upon a lazy bed the livelong day' (I.iii.147) for martial engagement on the battlefield, erotic bonds between men threaten to disrupt the persistent homosocial equation between martial and erotic 'arms'. Though male homoeroticism exists contiguously with male homosocial militarism, it instigates neither projection nor internalisation, remaining remarkably non-defensive, untainted by the logic of disease pervading other erotic relations.

This non-infectious mode of sexuality, however, is ultimately abandoned, as Patroclus, under male homosocial pressure, adopts the militaristic perspective, encouraging Achilles to take to the field:

> To this effect, Achilles, have I mov'd you.
> A woman impudent and mannish grown
> Is not more loath'd than an effeminate man
> In time of action. I stand condemn'd for this;
> They think my little stomach to the war
> And your great love to me restrains you thus.
> Sweet, rouse yourself, and the weak wanton Cupid

Shall from your neck unloose his amorous fold,
And, like a dewdrop from the lion's mane,
Be shook to air.

(III.iii.216–25)

Despite Patroclus' obvious tenderness here, male homoeroticism becomes refigured as military battle, as Achilles defines Hector's proposed engagement with Ajax as a 'maiden battle' (IV.v.87) void of penetration and bloodshed, clearly preferring his own bloody fantasies of penetration and dismemberment which are finally roused to action by Patroclus' death. All difference collapses between Hector's homosocial invitation to embrace martial 'arms' (I.iii.265–79) and the playful, intimate embraces occurring within Achilles' tent. Ultimately, representations of homoeroticism remain confined within, and the language of bawdy reasserts, the circularity of war, desire, and disease.

But to focus on homoerotic desire as such goes against the erotic ethos of the play itself. For *Troilus and Cressida* declines to differentiate types of desire. Both Achilles and Troilus are 'effeminised' by their desires; both temporarily avoid the military action that in this play constitutes the masculine subject. The difference, of course, is that Troilus' preoccupation with Cressida matters little to anyone on the field, whereas Achilles' defection constitutes a threat to the entire operation of the war. Yet desire presents not only an interruption of the war; it is finally shown to be the animating impulse for it. The literal or figurative 'death' of the beloved impels both warriors back into battle: Achilles to kill Hector, that 'boy-queller' (V.v.45), and Troilus to fight the man who wears his love-token in his helm.[41] The overarching sense of rage surrounding Patroclus' death and Cressida's 'betrayal' dissolves any possible distinction between types of desire in the heat of violence; indeed, the play displays an *in-difference* to the gender of erotic object.

It hardly seems fortuitous that this erotic in-difference takes place within an obsessive resurrection of other distinctions. For the play's recurrent anxieties about disease and desire overlay another fear, circulating throughout, of nondifferentiation. Ulysses' rhetorical set-piece regarding degree, for instance, pleads the necessity of hierarchical distinction; without degree, all is chaos:

Then every thing includes itself in power,
Power into will, will into appetite;
And appetite, an universal wolf,

So doubly seconded with will and power,
Must make perforce an universal prey,
And last eat up himself.
(I.iii. 119–24)

Appetite, an Elizabethan commonplace for desire, is presented as oral self-destruction, in an image that introduces the paranoia that 'infects' all bodily references in this play, and specifically prefigures Thersites' use of the lechery/leprosy conflation: 'lechery eats itself.' The categorical implosion of the dyads lechery/leprosy, lust/disease apparent throughout the play is vividly alluded to in this passage in the image of the voracious, passionate body *eating itself*. Taken together, desire, lechery, leprosy, and syphilis are shown to enact a relentless march toward the body's extinction. And disease, like appetite, is the terror within, precisely because it does not differentiate, does not know distinctions.

So too with war. Although the rhetoric of war is conventionally dependent on distinctions (self/other, general/foot soldier, valiant/cowardly), the actuality of battle abolishes all difference in indiscriminate carnage. Thus it is entirely in keeping with the play's portrayal of disease and desire that Achilles ambush and massacre Hector, for with that action all moral claims based on the distinction between self and other vanish. The militarism that in this play frames and impels desire is just as vigorous in its pursuit of death, which itself involves the loss of distinction, the reception of the body back into the boundlessness of an eternal void. The terror of this insight generates the defences employed against it, the psychic mechanisms by which distinctions of gender, status, health, and finally, life are reinscribed.

In closing, it is crucial to realise that my reading of *Troilus and Cressida* is itself 'contaminated' by the discursive history of syphilis. That is, it is almost impossible to bracket off or ignore the ideological baggage that accompanies, indeed has constituted, the meaning of sexually transmitted disease in early modern and contemporary cultures. The problem, I hope to have shown, is not merely one of biology, but of representation. Any distinction between the material and the psychological is blurred in the hermeneutics of disease. If desire can seem to leave a material mark on the body – an open sore, an ache in the bones, blindness – it is because the body makes palpable the intimacy of the relation between the biological and the cultural. Because of this intimacy, however, the meanings of desire and disease are not fixed; they are formulated through a process of discursive inscriptions, of ancillary meanings that are mobilised and put to use by dominant structures of power, knowledge, and exchange. The feelings of horror *we* experience at the final moment of Pandarus' invitation to indulge in diseased prostitution, as he bequeaths to us *his* diseases, is out of proportion to the 'real' impact of syphilis on *us*, for whom that particular disease is no longer fatal. Our response is in part due to the constellation of anxieties which continues to overdetermine the intersection of erotic desire and disease.

Troilus and Cressida makes no attempt to reconfigure disease, its representation of syphilis remaining thoroughly claustrophobic, even nihilistic. And yet, the impact of contemporary discourses on AIDS suggests that it is imperative that we find ways to represent disease *differently* – neither as divine retribution, nor, in the liberal tradition of which *Troilus and Cressida* is a part, as military invasion. As the rhetoric of 'protected' intercourse and 'safe' sex reformulates the body as military fortress, defending against the 'invasion' of 'foreign' bodily fluids, we find ourselves once more in a situation – in a system of signification – in which 'we' protect ourselves from 'them'. But who are 'we', if not also 'them'? What is projection, if not a futile attempt to defend against the diseased significations we have internalised as inhering in sexuality? Our bodies *are* vulnerable: disease is an unhappy function of our mortality. But that mortality is neither curse nor punishment; it is an inescapable fact, for which the rhetoric of blame is an impoverished and inappropriate mode of defence. Unfortunately, it remains to be seen if we can refigure the ideological nexus of desire and disease, to de-moralise and de-mobilise the defensive meanings of their still fatal 'exchange'.[42]

From Valerie Traub, *Desire and Anxiety: Circulation of Sexuality in Shakespearean Drama* (London, 1992), pp. 71–87.

Notes

[Valerie Traub's work in the area of psychoanalysis and social theory has been internationally recognised for its originality and purpose. This essay, taken from a full-length volume, traces the historical relations between the body, disease and desire in a way that reflects upon *Troilus and Cressida* historically but roots itself methodologically in the present, starting with references to AIDS and other sexually transmitted diseases. The essay places desire and disease at the heart of Shakespeare's play with reference to its military overtones and anxieties about sexuality in relation to the state. Noting that 'diseases' is the final word of *Troilus and Cressida* Traub points out that this is appropriate since metaphors of disease have been used to evoke all the problems of the play. Traub's work is challenging and uncomfortable, but the anxieties it announces, for Shakespeare's times and our own, make the play a 'problem play' in a way that is very distanced from the fairly mild disquiet of the earlier critics. Ed.]

1. In addition to the works cited below, particularly insightful analyses of the representation of AIDS are Paula A. Treichler, 'AIDS, Homophobia, and Biomedical Discourse: An Epidemic of Signification', *October*, 43 (Winter 1987), 31–70; Lee Edelman, 'The Plague of Discourse: Politics, Literary Theory, and AIDS', *South Atlantic Quarterly*, 88:1 (Winter 1989), 301–17; Cindy Patton, *Sex and Germs: The Politics of AIDS* (Boston, 1985); Allan Brandt, 'AIDS and Metaphor: Toward the Social Meaning of Epidemic Disease', *Social Research*, 55:3 (Autumn 1988), 413–32; and Elizabeth Fee and Daniel M. Fox (eds), *AIDS: The Burdens of History* (Berkeley, 1988).

2. According to Dorothy Nelkin and Sander Gilman, 'Placing Blame for Devastating Disease', *Social Research*, 55:3 (Autumn 1988), 361–78, every early modern European nation 'defined syphilis as a disease of other nations' (p. 365). This view is corroborated by Anna Foa in 'The New and the Old: The Spread of Syphilis (1494–1530)', *Sex and Gender in Historical Perspective*, ed. Edward Muir and Guido Ruggiero, trans. Margaret A. Gallucci et al. (Baltimore, 1990), 26–45.

3. Sander L. Gilman, 'AIDS and Syphilis: The Iconography of Disease', *October*, 43 (Winter 1987), 87; Susan Sontag, *AIDS and its Metaphors* (New York, 1988), 47–8. Many medical historians question whether syphilis was a novel disease when it broke out in epidemic proportions. In *History and Geography of the Most Important Diseases* (New York, 1965), 117–27, Erwin H. Ackerknecht presents evidence that syphilis had long been present among the labouring classes, and was new only to the learned surgeons who limited their clinical practice to the elite. He mentions prescriptions for antisyphilitic drugs that were prescribed by barber surgeons in 1457 in Germany, 1470 in Italy, and 1475 in England. For a summary of early modern medical theories about the origin of syphilis, and their current status within the medical profession, see Danielle Jacquart and Claude Thomasset, *Sexuality and Medicine in the Middle Ages* (Princeton, NJ, 1988), 177–83; William H. McNeill, *Plagues and Peoples* (New York, 1976), 218–20; and Thomas Parran, *Shadow on the Land: Syphilis* (New York, 1937). According to Nelkin and Gilman, to the early modern European, 'syphilis *had* to come from the New World: it was the final sign of the cataclysmic changes of that period. ... As it became necessary to distinguish the goals of European colonialism from those of the indigenous population, Indians became not only diseased, they were defined as the source of disease' ('Placing Blame', p. 364). In

this light, Eric Partridge's gloss on 'malady of France' is particularly instructive for its characterisation of origins: 'Syphilis seems to have come to England from France; to France from Italy; to Italian ports ... from the Levant; and perhaps the disease-breeding filth of the Levant received its accretion from the pullulating populousness of the farther East', *Shakespeare's Bawdy: A Literary and Psychological Essay and a Comprehensive Glossary* (New York, 1969), 144. I particularly call attention to the tone of disgust animating 'disease breeding filth' and 'pullulating populousness'.

4. See Foa, 'The New and the Old', for the way the Indian functioned as the other in Italian discourses of disease.

5. See, for instance, the work of Mary Douglas, Peter Stallybrass and Gail Kern Paster.

6. Arthur Rossiter first noticed this aural pun in *Angel with Horns and Other Shakespearean Lectures*, ed. Graham Storey (London, Green, 1961), p. 133.

7. I.i.103, II.iii.19. Bevington glosses 'placket' as 'a slit in a petticoat; hence (indecently) a woman'.

8. Paris, for instance, says of Helen, 'But I would have the soil of her fair rape/Wip'd off, in honorable keeping her' (II.ii.148–9).

9. Bevington glosses 'merry Greek' as slang for a frivolous person, loose in morals. As such, it stands as a signifier of sexually licentious behaviour.

10. René Girard, 'The Politics of Desire in *Troilus and Cressida*', *Shakespeare and the Question of Theory*, ed. Patricia Parker and Geoffrey Hartman (New York, 1985), 188–209.

11. Linda Charnes, ' "So Unsecret to Ourselves": Notorious Identity and the Material Subject in Shakespeare's *Troilus and Cressida*', *Shakespeare Quarterly*, 40:4 (Winter 1989), 413–40. Charnes' complex argument posits the following circuit of desire: 'possession of Helen generates desire for war, desire for war generates desire for Helen, desire for Helen generates mimetic desire, mimetic desire generates competitive identification between Greek and Trojan men, competitive identification generates homoerotic aggression, homoerotic aggression generates desire for more war, and finally, desire for more war reproduces desire for Helen' (p. 437). In 'Emulous Factions and the Collapse of Chivalry: *Troilus and Cressida*', *Representations*, 29 (Winter 1990), 145–79, Eric S. Mallin employs a homosocial grid to argue that a 'submerged axis' of male homosexuality, narcissism, and misogyny animates the play. Assuming a 'natural' correlation between homosexuality and antifeminism leads Mallin to employ a normalising psychoanalytic model of male narcissism in the interest of a feminist critique. Both Charnes and Mallin tend to conflate male homoeroticism and homosociality, seeing the first as the logical extension of the second. For instance, Charnes'

term 'homoerotic aggression', which I take to mean male-male rape and eroticised battle, comes to represent all homoerotic desires in the play, including the relationship of Achilles and Patroclus. My view is somewhat different, as I am concerned to show the possible divergences of male homosocial and homoerotic desire.

12. The equation between desire and disease is evident in others of Shakespeare's plays, notably *Hamlet, Twelfth Night, Measure for Measure*, and in a lighter vein, *As You Like It*.

13. Mallin, 'Emulous Factions', interestingly places this 'neurosis of invasion' in the Elizabethan context of Britain's political fortunes and the Queen's personal symbology.

14. For an excellent analysis of how Cressida is positioned as whore, see Janet Adelman, ' "This Is and Is Not Cressid": The Characterization of Cressida', in Garner et al. (eds), *The (M)Other Tongue: Essays in Feminist Psychoanalytic Interpretation* (Ithaca, NY, 1985), 119–41.

15. Other types of exchange, especially mercantile commerce, are also important to the signification of desire in the play.

16. According to Sontag, *AIDS and its Metaphors*, syphilis and leprosy were the first two diseases to be described as repulsive.

17. Debate exists as to whether early modern syphilis and its modern counterpart are the same disease. Both lack of resistance on the part of the European population and the exceptional virulence of the early strain combined to produce the following symptoms: high fever, delirium, violent headaches, bone pains, sores, bone ulcers, and death. However, part of this virulence may have been due to other accompanying diseases and malnutrition. At least some of the epidemics of syphilis correspond to periods of famine.

18. Steven Mullaney, *The Place of the Stage: License, Play, and Power in Renaissance England* (Chicago, 1988), 37.

19. Ibid., 32.

20. Girard, 'Politics of Desire', 208.

21. According to Partridge in *Shakespeare's Bawdy*, 'sunburnt' meant infected with venereal disease, and 'soddon business' and 'stew'd phrases' refer to brothels and the sweating treatment for syphilis.

22. Girard, 'Politics of Desire', 202. Mallin, in 'Emulous Factions', follows Girard in viewing the plague metaphorically, but he places the illness of emulation and factionalism within the historical context of the Elizabethan court.

23. Bruce Boehrer, 'Early Modern Syphilis', *Journal of the History of Sexuality*, 1:2 (Autumn 1990) 197–214.

24. Ibid., 200, 209.

25. Women's sores were usually on the hidden lip of the cervix. See Charles Dennie, *A History of Syphilis* (Springfield, IL, 1962), and Jacquart and Thomasset, *Sexuality and Medicine*, 181, 189–90.

26. Boehrer, 'Early Modern Syphilis', 213. For later 'inventions' of syphilis as moral category, see Allan M. Brandt, *No Magic Bullet: A Social History of Venereal Disease in the United States since 1880* (Oxford, 1985).

27. Geoffrey Eatough (trans.), *Fracastoro's 'Syphilis'* (Liverpool, 1984).

28. I am told that in a recent Royal Shakespeare Company production at Stratford, Thersites wears surgical gloves – an obvious insertion of AIDS discourse into the play.

29. This sense of lechery as 'burning' within the body is repeated in Thersites' aside, 'Fry, lechery, fry!' (V.ii.58–9).

30. For the confusion between leprosy and syphilis, see Jacquart and Thomasset, *Sexuality and Medicine*, 177–93, and Foa, 'The New and the Old', 37–42. In addition to the fact that the rise of syphilitic infection temporarily coincided with the abolition of the Order of Lazarus and the scattering of 19,000 leper houses, the aural similarity between leper and lecher should be acknowledged as contributing to this conflation. Foa also argues that Jews were used as a mediating term between leprosy and syphilis. The language by which syphilis was described confused it not only with leprosy, but also with the bubonic plague and typhus. For a powerful rendition of this conflation, see Robert Henryson's medieval poem, 'Testament of Cresseid', which transforms Cressida into an itinerant leper, an image that makes explicit the need to imagine the infected as carrying off the disease, *Testament of Cressed*, ed. Denton Fox (London, 1968).

31. Bleeding, purging, sweating, and applications of mercury were the standard therapeutic treatments for syphilis. Baths were valued for their palliative effect on aching bones.

32. For the coincidence of syphilis and prostitution in other plays, see in *Henry V* the references to powdering tubs and tub-fasts, and the particularly interesting invocation of Cressida as leprous whore: 'to the spital go,/ And from the powd' ring tub of infamy/ Fetch forth the lazar kite of Cressid's kind,/ Doll Tearsheet she by name' (II.i.75–8); indeed, it is reported that Doll Tearsheet dies of 'a malady of France' (V.i.81). In *Timon of Athens*, Timon says to Timandra: 'Be a whore still. They love thee not that use thee;/ Give them diseases, leaving with thee their lust./ Make use of thy salt hours. Season the slaves/ For tubs and baths; bring down rose-cheek'd youth/ To the tub-fast and the diet' (IV.iii.84–8).

33. Sander L. Gilman alludes to precisely this dynamic in *Disease and Representation: Images of Illness from Madness to AIDS* (Ithaca, NY, 1988): 'It is the fear of collapse, the sense of dissolution, which contaminates the Western image of all diseases ... But the fear we have of our own collapse does not remain internalised. Rather, we project this fear onto the world in order to localise it and, indeed, to domesticate it. For once we locate it, the fear of our own dissolution is removed. Then it is not we who totter on the brink of collapse, but rather the Other. And it is an-Other who has already shown his or her vulnerability by having collapsed' (p. 1).

34. Ibid., 2.

35. For an excellent analysis of the theatre as site of such contamination, see Mullaney, *The Place of the Stage*. For an examination of the theatre as site of sexuality, see Colin MacCabe, 'Abusing Self and Others: Puritan Accounts of the Shakespearean Stage', *Critical Quarterly*, 30:3 (1988), 3–17.

36. According to Ann Haselkorn, the Bishop of Winchester had jurisdiction over financial gains from prostitution, and women inmates of Bankside Street, Southwark, located near the Bishop's palace, were known as 'Winchester geese', *Prostitution in Elizabethan and Jacobean Comedy* (Troy, NY, 1983). See also E. J. Burford, *Bawds and Lodgings: A History of the London Bankside Brothels c. 100–1675* (London, 1976). Foa 'The New and the Old', also alludes to the alleged role of prostitutes in the dissemination of syphilis in depictions from sixteenth-century Italian fabulae.

37. Peter Stallybrass and Allon White, *The Politics and Poetics of Transgression* (Ithaca, NY, 1986), 22.

38. Carol Cook, ' "The Sign and Semblance of Her Honor": Reading Gender Difference in *Much Ado About Nothing*', *PMLA*, 101:2 (1986), 189.

39. Thersites, of course, does joke about Menelaus, calling him 'the primitive statue and oblique memorial of cuckolds', but his humour is moderated by his repugnance: 'Ask me not what I would be, were I not Thersites; for I care not to be the louse of a lazar, so I were not Menelaus' (V.i.54–5, 63–5).

40. See in particular David F. Musto, 'Quarantine and the Problem of AIDS', and Guenter B. Risse, 'Epidemics and History: Ecological Perspectives and Social Responses', in Fee and Fox, *AIDS: The Burdens of History*, 33–85.

41. Troilus' sleeve, like Othello's handkerchief, operates as an emblem of the circulation of desire.

42. Unlike Sontag (*AIDS and its Metaphors*), I do not believe that disease can be totally de-metaphorised; indeed, I believe that such a desire is born of precisely the self-protectiveness I try to question. However, I do believe that we must metaphorise sexually transmitted diseases differently. Leo Bersani makes some provocative comments on the conflation of desire and disease in 'Is the Rectum a Grave?' *October*, 43 (Winter 1987), 197–222.

10

Fragments of Nationalism in *Troilus and Cressida*

MATTHEW GREENFIELD

Literary critics largely agree that Shakespeare's history plays raised troubling questions about who qualified as a member of the national community.[1] Problematic cases include: the Scots, the Welsh, and the Irish; bastards; ethnic half-breeds; foreign brides; women generally; and sometimes all non-aristocrats. Still, though, despite these questions and anxieties, Shakespeare's tetralogies and the other English history plays move toward closures in which the nation heals and the dream of community reasserts its claim.

Troilus and Cressida explores a more pessimistic political argument. If Shakespeare's histories maintain an investment in some idea of national community, *Troilus and Cressida* works programmatically to reveal the nation as a collection of fictions. Where the histories construct genealogies for England, projecting a new social formation backward into the past, *Troilus and Cressida* attacks the very idea of genealogy. In *King John* the bastard Faulconbridge represents the real England: he embodies the principle of legitimacy in all but the most literal sense. In *Troilus and Cressida*, on the other hand, the bastard Thersites speaks from a cosmopolitan, extranational perspective. During the climactic battle he cheers alternately for the Trojans and for the Greeks. His illegitimacy liberates him from the ideological claim of the nation, whose central trope imagines citizens as brothers. Where Faulconbridge functions as a synecdoche for the nation, Thersites stands outside its borders. Thersites emblematises the project of *Troilus and Cressida*: much of the play's continuing power to disturb derives from its relentless attack on nationalism's narratives, its tropes, its strategic amnesia, and its assumptions about human character and agency.[2]

Troy and the origin of the English

Most political scientists locate the origin of nationalism in the eighteenth century: their theories carefully distinguish political units centred on monarchs from those defined by allegiance to what Benedict Anderson calls 'imagined communities'.[3] In these theories neither ethnicity, a shared language, religion, nor territorial boundaries constitute national identity – they are its raw materials. The moment of nationalism arrives when citizens see the state as a reflection of their will, as an expression of the collective sovereignty of the people. Nationalism is not a fact of political structures but a way of understanding oneself and one's social environment. The citizens of a nation imagine themselves as a community, and they imagine this community as invested with a sovereign power. Citizens must forget the differences of rank and wealth that divide them, and they must repudiate ties that bind them to those outside the boundaries of the nation.[4] Liah Greenfeld argues that this moment arrived in England earlier than elsewhere.[5] Whether or not Greenfeld's chronology is correct, English nationalism certainly developed unevenly. Some Protestant intellectuals, drawing on an older, religious conception of community, expressed a passionate nationalism early in the sixteenth century. One can also detect a quieter nationalist discourse in the language of the civil servants who staffed the new, rapidly growing state bureaucracy: in the second half of the sixteenth century they began to use words such as *nation, state*, and *people* in their modern senses.[6] Through the combined action of these two elites, the nationalist idea began to diffuse throughout the rest of the population. One crucial factor was the state's dissemination of vernacular Bibles and prayerbooks. Writers and theatrical companies also played an important role. The emergence of the nationalist idea required the rejection of two older forms of authority and the idea of community they entailed. First, the English had to detach themselves from the universalist claims of the Catholic church. Second, in a subtler process, they had to transfer their allegiance from the person of the monarch to the concept of the nation. Though almost invisible during the reign of Elizabeth, this transfer had been glaringly obvious earlier, during the reign of her older sister, Mary, and would become so again during the reign of Charles I. Over the course of the sixteenth century the English developed a powerful sense of their political agency as a people.

Discussions of nationalism are complicated by the fact that some inhabitants of a nation may not be fully enfranchised citizens. A further complication is that even a citizen has an identity composed of multiple narratives and affiliations with multiple communities – religious, familial, and professional as well as territorial and political.[7] While political scientists usually describe identifications with nations as gradually displacing identifications with transnational religious communities, both narratives nevertheless might simultaneously exert strong claims on a single person. In Shakespeare's *Richard II*, for example, Mowbray experiences a curious regression of social identities: deprived by exile of his Englishness, he reimagines himself as a member of a broader Christian community and, we later learn (IV.i), dies fighting the Turks on behalf of the Venetians. Mowbray abandons his distinctively early modern national identity for a feudal role as a Christian knight. This vignette can serve to remind us that nations and other imagined communities answer a strong human need. Without them, we cannot define our values and interests – our tongues become unstrung instruments. Self-narration always requires at least the fantasy of a 'common space' within which one can be understood.[8]

Because creation of a collective identity requires a reinvention of the past, the English nationalists of the sixteenth century set about constructing a national literature, a national language, a shared historical memory, and common ancestors. In early modern England many of the fictional genealogies invented to give the infant nation an appearance of antiquity centred on the fall of Troy. The English began to elaborate a fantasy of the translation of empire, the *translatio imperii*, in the late Middle Ages. In the thirteenth century Geoffrey of Monmouth told the story of the colonisation of England by a Trojan named Brut, a grandson of Aeneas. In Geoffrey's narrative King Arthur was descended from Brut. The myths concerning Brut and his posterity served to legitimate a variety of institutions and group identities. Among their other functions, they helped to solidify the Tudor monarchy's shaky claim to the throne. Spenser used the story as part of his project of dynastic legitimation (and dynastic speculation) in *The Faerie Queene*. Use of the myth became particularly intense toward the end of Elizabeth's reign, when it became apparent that James might inherit the crown of England.

James could claim descent from Brut on both sides of his family – both Tudors and Stuarts had Welsh kings among their ancestors. Similarly, the fantasy of a *translatio studii* occupied a central location in English letters. The first printed book published in England was William Caxton's 1478 translation of Raoul Lefebvre's *The Recuyell of the Historyes of Troy*. Extending Virgil's westward translation of empire, Caxton's translation quietly suggested that England had inherited the cultural energies passed from Troy to Rome. The Brut myth helped to defend vernacular literature against accusations of rudeness and belatedness. When the Italian humanist Polydore Virgil suggested that Geoffrey had fabricated the Brut story, he aroused a storm of protest. The Protestant polemicist John Bale furiously denounced Polydore in his 1548 catalogue of English men of letters, *Illustrium Maioris Britanniae Scriptorum Summarium*. Bale needed the myth in order to assert the antiquity and continuity of English literature.[9] At the end of the sixteenth century Thomas Heywood used the Brut myth to glorify not only the English but also his own artistic venue, public theatre. In the dedicatory letter to his Trojan history play, *The Iron Age*, Heywood linked the history play with other, more prestigious literary forms such as the epic: 'For what Pen of note, in one page or other hath not remembered *Troy*, and bewayl'd the sacke, and subuersion of so illustrious a Citty: Which, although it were scituate in *Asia*, yet out of her ashes hath risen, two the rarest Phoenixes in *Europe*, namely *London* and *Rome*.'[10] Later, when Dryden revised Shakespeare's *Troilus and Cressida* in 1679, the prefatory poem by R. Duke concluded with the optimistic thought that 'our great Charles being sung by you, / Old Troy shall grow less famous than the new'.[11]

Toward the end of Elizabeth's reign Troy began to serve with increasing frequency as a point of origin for the English nation, not just for the English monarchy or English letters. George Peele, for instance, claimed that he wrote his pamphlet history of Troy in order that 'my Countrymen famed through the worlde for resolution and fortitude, may marche in equipage of honour and Armes, wyth theyr glorious and renowned predecessors the Troyans'.[12] Similarly, Edward Coke used the myth to reinforce the authority of the common law, claiming that its unbroken descent made it older and more coherent than Roman law. The law, Coke argued, was therefore superior to the monarch. When Sir John Hayward responded to Coke with a defence of monarchical prerogative, he found himself attacking the Brut myth, despite its importance in the iconography of his patron, James I:

> From these [critics] I expect two principall obiections. The first is, that the lawes of *England* were neuer changed since the time of *Brutus*; not onely in the peaceable state of the realme, but not by any of the seueral conquerors thereof: not by the Normanes, Danes, Saxones; no not by the Romanes, who vsually changed the laws of all other countries which they brought vnder the sway of their sword: but that in all other changes, whether of inhabitants, or of state, the lawes doe still remaine the same, which *Brutus* compiled out of the Troian lawes; and therefore it is not fit they should in any point be altered. I will not now spend time vpon this opinion; partly because it is not commonly receiued, but especially for that I haue in a particular treatise examined at large, the parts and proofes of this assertion. Not as derogating any thing from the true dignitie of the common law; but as esteeming hyperbolicall praises now out of season; as neuer suitable but with artlesse times.[13]

Hayward was writing in favour of the union of England and Scotland, and he proposed a merger of the legal systems, rituals, and customs of the two nations. In arguing for this new, hybrid political entity, Hayward reminded his readers of the mixed ethnic heritage of the English people and their institutions. He brought back into view the successive invasions of Britain which Coke's vision of the uncontaminated purity of English institutions had occluded. An attack on the Troy myth generally functioned as an attack on the legitimacy of an institution, an attempt to undo a customary arrangement and to open up a space for change. In his *Hypercritica*, Edmund Bolton expressed a cautious scepticism about Geoffrey of Monmouth's history but warned of the danger of discarding it entirely: 'Nevertheless out of that very Story (let it be what it will) have Titles been framed in open Parliament, both in England, and Ireland, for the Rights of the Crown of England, even to entire Kingdoms. ... If that Work be quite abolished there is a vast Blanck upon the Times of our Country, from the Creation of the World till the coming of Julius Caesar.'[14] One might say that *Troilus and Cressida* works to expand Bolton's 'vast Blanck'. Unlike Heywood's *Iron Age, Troilus and Cressida* completely ignores the Brut story. And unlike Spenser, Shakespeare displays no interest in creating a genealogy of English literature centred on Chaucer. Neither the play nor its prefatory material alludes specifically to Chaucer's *Troilus and Criseyde*.[15] While the works of Shakespeare's contemporaries (and many of his own plays) set out to bolster the prestige of an emergent nation and its literature, *Troilus and Cressida* undercuts the genealogical narratives of literary history and nationalism. The play shows the Troy myth being produced through a series of falsifications.[16] At every stage of the process, a dishonourable deed becomes heroic or a crime is blamed on an innocent victim. The play is not a history but a sceptical analysis of history-making, an emptying out or undoing of the work of the chronicles.

Satire and national belonging

An imagined community presupposes a particular kind of agent, one who is capable of freely choosing to join in such an association and who can meaningfully assent to the reciprocal obligations that constitute it.[17] The politically enfranchised citizen whose agency is seen as defective, incapable of meeting these requirements, poses a severe challenge to this notion of collective sovereignty. If the defective citizen's actions are compulsive and involuntary, then he or she is an animal, a machine, a bundle of appetites, and not a person. The possibility of such a citizen continues to haunt policy debates and liberal theory in our own time, and it cast its shadow even over the origins of nationalism in England.[18] Whether they were literary thinkers such as Ben Jonson and George Puttenham, theologians such as Richard Hooker, or jurists such as Edward Coke, theorists of the imagined community had to develop theories of how the defective citizen was produced and how he might be rehabilitated. They had to imagine the community as resilient and powerful enough to absorb and neutralise aberrant behaviour. In the political theory of Jonson's comical satires, the satirist collaborates with the state in order to discipline dysfunctional citizens, purging them of their humours by showing them how they are perceived by others and by resituating them within the community's web of reciprocal relations. Shakespeare's *Troilus and Cressida* examines the same questions of social control, but it finds no workable solution for the maintenance of a stable imagined community. In *Troilus and Cressida* Ulysses and Nestor form a plan modelled on the conspiracies of Jonson's satirist figures: they stage a pageant in which each Greek leader in turn feigns disdain for Achilles. Ajax in his jealousy of Achilles also uses the language of the satirist: 'I'll let his humour's blood' (II.iii.205).[19] Achilles and Patroclus, though, have a satirical project of their own, one antithetical to that of Nestor and Ulysses. Patroclus mimics the behaviour of the Greek camp's leaders: 'And with ridiculous and awkward action, / Which, slanderer, he "imitation" calls, / He pageants us .... like a strutting player' (I.iii.148–52). In addition to amusing Achilles, this performance has the function of asserting a set of values, a vision of how the community should be organised. Achilles and Patroclus both value the achievements of the warrior over those of the leader or the orator: 'The still and mental parts / That do contrive how many hands shall strike, / When fitness calls them on, and know by measure / Of their observant toil the enemy's weight, / Why this has not a finger's dignity. / They call this bed-work, mapp'ry, closet-war' (I.iii.198–204). Each group uses a theatrical technique derived from comical satire to attack the value system of the other. This symmetrical opposition of satirical projects reveals both systems as local and contingent, lacking the authority of true social norms. Neither plot leads to a satirical purgation.

If Ulysses attempts to employ satire as an instrument of military discipline, the figure of Thersites conducts a sustained critique of nationalism and the war effort. Thersites invents a particularly interesting alternative to national identity in his brief encounter with Margarelon:

Margarelon	Turn, slave, and fight.
Thersites	What art thou?
Margarelon	A bastard son of Priam's.
Thersites	I am a bastard too; I love bastards. I am bastard begot, bastard instructed, bastard in mind, bastard in valour, in everything illegitimate. One bear will not bite another, and wherefore should one bastard? Take heed; the quarrel's most ominous to us; if the son of a whore fight for a whore, he tempts judgement. Farewell, bastard.

(V.vii.13–22)

Although there are conceptions of citizenship that do not involve biological consanguinity, even these conceptions are usually expressed in tropes that involve a genealogy. To belong to a national community is to be a legitimate heir to its history.[20] Thersites inverts the trope, imagining a community defined by illegitimacy and dispossession. He attempts to persuade Margarelon that their national affiliations are not the most important facts about them. Although Thersites advances this theory out of a desire for self-preservation, his contempt for the idea of national difference sounds genuine. In his view his own nationality is an arbitrary label rather than an essential component of his identity. He regards the aristocratic honour culture that motivates the warriors as a dangerous delusion and treats the war as a spectator sport. On the battlefield he cheers alternately for both sides: 'Hold thy whore, Grecian! Now for thy whore, Trojan!' he says to Diomedes and Troilus; and to Paris and Menelaus, 'The cuckold and the cuckold-maker are at it. Now, bull! Now, dog! 'Loo, Paris! 'Loo now, my double-horned Spartan!' (V.iv.22–3; V.vii.9–11). Thersites also attempts to reason his fellow Greeks out of their ideological commitment to the war: 'There's Ulysses and old Nestor, whose wit was mouldy ere your grandsires had nails on their toes, yoke you like draught-oxen, and make you plough up the wars' (II.i.101–4). Where Jonson's satirist figures work to preserve the community and to enforce its norms, Thersites attempts to demonstrate to Ajax and Achilles that their interests diverge from those of their leaders. Thersites adopts what one might call a cosmopolitan point of view, a resistance to simple citizenship that sometimes has the force of an ethical commitment – although at other times Thersites seems more mad than principled.[21]

Thersites occupies a position at once dramatically central and socially marginal. As a social critic, he proves impotent: like the rest of Shakespeare's fools, he has a deep understanding of events but cannot communicate this understanding to the other characters successfully.[22] He uses the verse satirist's language of medical cure and of judicial whipping, but his curses and insults fail to effect lasting changes in his victims' behaviour.[23] His actual function within the community is that of entertainer. Although Ajax and Achilles threaten and even beat Thersites for his insults, they compete for his services: 'Why, my cheese, my digestion, why hast thou not served thyself in to my table so many meals?' Achilles asks (II.iii.38–40). Thersites's impotence within the play's frame is, however, balanced by his power to step outside that frame. Thersites has the Elizabethan fool's privileged relationship to the audience. Like the Vice figure of the morality play, Thersites claims as his own the stage territory closest to the audience, the zone between dramatic fiction and critical reflection on that fiction.[24] Thersites frequently serves as an interpreter of the play's action, like the metatheatrical commentators in Jonson's *Every Man Out of His Humour* and *Cynthia's Revels*. In the scene where Cressida surrenders Troilus's sleeve, Thersites observes Ulysses and Troilus as they observe Cressida and Diomedes. Thersites's perspective brackets those of the other characters. As Robert Weimann points out, Thersites frequently has the last word, offering his bitter assessment of events after the other characters have exited.[25] On the battlefield, offering his commentary on the fighting, he occupies a vantage point that is both metatheatrical and extranational. The clowns and fools played by Will Kemp and Robert Armin generally possessed a similar independence from the social and dramatic conventions that governed the behaviour of the other characters.[26] This independence mirrored the clown's actual position within the theatre company. Armin, who played Thersites, worked simultaneously for the Chamberlain's Men at the Globe and the boys' company at Whitefriars, and also gave solo performances at the Curtain and published his own pamphlets and plays. Armin, like Kemp before him, developed a set of routines that he transported from play to play, and both actors thus functioned as Shakespeare's collaborators in the writing of scripts. The fool worked, in effect, as a free agent.

It is instructive to compare the Thersitean critique of communal identity with the narratives of an emergent English nationalism. In 1579 the Protestant extremist John Stubbes wrote a pamphlet imploring Queen Elizabeth not to marry the Duc d'Alençon. In the pamphlet Stubbes developed a strange and memorable image of the relations among Englishmen:

> It is naturall to all men to abhor forreigne rule as a burden of Egypt, and to vs of England if to any other nation vnder the son. First, it agreeth not vvith thys state or frame of gouernment, to deliuer any trust of vnder gouernment to an alien, but is a poyson to it, when we receiue any such for a gouernour. And that is euident by our lavves and auncient customes of the lande disabling any alien to inherite the highest gouernment of vs. vpon this reason, no doubt because a senceles and careles forreiner, cannot haue the naturall and brotherlike bowells of tender loue towards this people which is required in a gouernor, & which is by birth bredd & drawen out from the teates of a mans own mother country.[27]

Stubbes suggests that all Englishmen share a familial lineage. Their nationality is not an accidental or contingent fact about them but part of the core of their identities, coded into their characters and even perhaps into the chemistry of their bodies. In order to essentialise English national identity in this way, Stubbes has to repress the memory of the ethnic hybridity of the English. Even though much of the English nobility could claim French ancestry, Stubbes represents the French as dangerously alien. English nationalism, in other words, requires the forgetting of ordinary consanguinity: the nation becomes one's true family and the central context for the development of one's identity. The difficulty of the imaginative effort required by nationalism is visible in the strange and even monstrous trope of the mother country as a single body with hundreds of thousands of breasts. This image is uncannily close to the grotesque exaggerations and distortions of satire but is intended to have the opposite effect: Stubbes wants to produce fellow-feeling rather than subject it to scrutiny. *Troilus and Cressida*, as I have argued, mounts a sustained attack on the genealogical trope at the heart of nationalism. With its procession of bastards, cuckolds, exiles, traitors, and racial hybrids, the play persistently undermines the idea that national identity is an unambiguous aspect of self-definition.

Fragments of citizenship

The bad citizens who people *Troilus and Cressida* frequently imagine each other as microcosmic versions of their dysfunctional communities. Thersites, for example, makes Agamemnon's body an image of the Greek army: 'Agamemnon – how if he had boils, full, all over, generally? ... And those boils did run? Say so, did not the general run then? Were not that a botchy core?' (II.i.2–6). The 'general' here is both the leader and his army.[28] Similarly, Ulysses suggests that the choice of a Greek champion will 'boil, / As 'twere, from forth us all, a man distilled / Out of our virtues' (I.iii.345–7). The designated champion, Ajax, proves to be a suitable emblem of his army: like the Greek camp, Ajax seems to be paralysed by internal dissension. In the playful description of Cressida's manservant, Ajax is 'a man into whom nature hath so crowded humours that his valour is crushed into folly, his folly sauced with discretion ... he hath the joints of everything, but everything so out of joint that he is a gouty Briareus, many hands and no use, or a purblind Argus, all eyes and no sight' (I.ii.21–9). And Achilles imagines the bleeding body of Hector as the city of Troy: 'Come, Troy, sink down! / Here lies thy heart, thy sinews, and thy bone' (V.viii.11–12). Individuals and communities in *Troilus and Cressida* are linked by a species of sympathetic magic.

Most of the characters in *Troilus and Cressida* embody in microcosm not one but both communities and the war between them: they are suspended between the moral and emotional claims of Troy and Greece.[29] In some cases these conflicting claims result not just in divided loyalty but in a multiple-personality disorder, with each community trying to produce a particular kind of person: a character manifests two different identities, depending on location or situation. Shakespeare's Achilles, for example, has two distinct personalities. The Iliadic Achilles is the lover of Patroclus, his 'masculine whore', in the words of Thersites (V.i.17). The other Achilles, who comes from Caxton and medieval romance, loves Prima's daughter Polyxena: 'Of this my privacy', Achilles says, 'I have strong reasons'. Ulysses answers: 'But 'gainst your privacy / The reasons are more potent and heroical. / 'Tis known, Achilles, that you are in love / With one of Priam's daughters' (III.iii.190–4).[30] Whereas the first Achilles abstains from battle out of pride, in order to highlight his pre-eminence among the Greeks, the second honours an oath to his lover and her mother, attempting to protect a space within which intimacy can unfold, a space sealed off from the public struggle for reputation. Each nation works to produce its own version of Achilles. Hecuba and her daughter want an Achilles committed to the pleasures and obligations of private relations, while Ulysses wants a warrior who values above all else his reputation and duty to the community. These antithetical claims turn Achilles himself into a war zone: at one point Ulysses suggests to the other Greek leaders that 'Kingdomed Achilles in commotion rages / And batters down himself' (II.iii.169–70). The conflict has at best an ambiguous resolution: Achilles goes into battle to perform his public duty but only out of grief for the loss of his male lover.

The fragmentation of national identity in *Troilus and Cressida* proceeds by a sort of contagion. When characters are pulled away from their communities, they also destabilise the national identities of their friends, relatives, and lovers. The sequence of transformations begins in the play's prehistory with the abduction of Priam's sister, Hesione, by the Greeks. Her child, Ajax, is a hybrid, half Trojan and half Greek. The Trojans in turn seduce Helen away from her husband, leaving her no longer Greek but not fully Trojan: she lives under the shadow of the possibility that she will be returned to her husband. When the Greeks lay siege to Troy, they precipitate the undoing of more national identities. Achilles falls in love with Polyxena, and the Trojan seer Calchas defects to the Greeks. This act of opportunism forces Calchas to abandon not only his city but the identity defined in relation to that city:

> ... Appear it to your mind
> That, through the sight I bear in things to come,
> I have abandoned Troy, left my possessions,

Incurred a traitor's name, exposed myself
From certain and possessed conveniences,
To doubtful fortunes; sequest'ring from me all
That time, acquaintance, custom and condition
Made tame and most familiar to my nature;
And here, to do you service, am become
As new into the world, strange, unacquainted.
(III.iii.3–12)

Despite its hilarious hypocrisy, Calchas's speech has a certain pathos. He has eloquently described the division of identity that the war eventually effects in almost all of the play's characters. Moving from one side to the other involves not only a change of political allegiance but an impoverishment of the self.

Calchas precipitates a similar crisis in his daughter, splitting her into a Trojan self, Troilus's lover, and a Greek self, which Troilus calls 'Diomed's Cressida' (V.ii.135). Her roles develop in relation to the communities in which she resides and, more particularly, to the men who claim her as their property: Troilus and her uncle Pandarus on one side, Diomedes and her father Calchas on the other. Cressida's self-division begins with a conflict between her prudence and her desire for Troilus: 'I have a kind of self resides with you, / But an unkind self that itself will leave / To be another's fool' (III.ii.138–40). One might describe this as a split between Cressida as proprietor of herself and Cressida as erotic commodity, Troilus's property. Cressida develops a new self-conception centred on her connection to Troilus: 'I have forgot my father; / I know no touch of consanguinity; / No kin, no love, no blood, no soul so near me / As the sweet Troilus' (IV.ii.94–7). When Troilus fails to protest the trade, the result is an unmaking of Cressida's identity.[31] By asking the Greeks to exchange their prisoner Antenor for her, Calchas erases her identity as a Trojan, recreating her as 'Diomed's Cressida'. Traces of Troilus's Cressida remain, and the result is a sort of schizophrenia: 'Troilus, farewell! One eye yet looks on thee, / But with my heart the other eye doth see' (V.ii.105–6). Torn between two versions of her identity, Cressida keeps cancelling her own actions: she gives Troilus's sleeve to Diomedes and then takes it back; she makes an appointment with Diomedes, announces that she will not keep it, and then coaxes him back. Her schizophrenia, her loss of agency, reflects her position between the two communities. Cressida's splitting creates in turn a civil war within Troilus: 'Within my soul there doth conduce a fight / Of this strange nature, that a thing inseparate / Divides more wider than the sky and earth' (V.ii.145–7). Troilus finds his powers of reason and decision to be momentarily paralysed.

Ajax has a similar destabilising effect on Hector. The two enemies are cousins – Ajax's mother, Hesione, is Hector's aunt – and this relationship produces conflicting attitudes in Hector: 'This Ajax is half made of Hector's blood; / In love whereof half Hector stays at home; / Half heart, half hand, half Hector comes to seek / This blended knight, half Trojan and half Greek' (IV.v.83–6). Unmoved by this consanguinity, Ajax appears willing and even eager to kill his cousin. Hector, though, is less self-contained, more open to sympathetic identification, more aware of his obligations to others, and imagines a bizarre solution to the problem posed by Ajax's hybrid origins:

> Were thy commixtion Greek and Troyan so,
> That thou couldst say 'This hand is Grecian all,
> And this is Trojan; the sinews of this leg
> All Greek, and this all Troy; my mother's blood
> Runs on the dexter cheek, and this sinister
> Bounds in my father's': by Jove multipotent,
> Thou shouldst not bear from me a Greekish member
> Wherein my sword had not impressure made
> Of our rank feud; but the just gods gainsay
> That any drop thou borrow'dst from thy mother,
> My sacred aunt, should by my mortal sword
> Be drained!
>
> (IV.v.124–35)

In Hector's fantasy Ajax's mixed bloods are separated and his dual nationalities untangled.[32] With firm boundaries drawn around national allegiances, Hector could act freely, guided in an unambiguous way by his sense of the values and interests of Troy. But the Ajax he imagines is an impossible creature, spiritually as well as physically bifurcated, one who would be obliged to battle himself, his left arm against his right. This hybrid monster mirrors Hector's own divided mental state. Without the ethical framework provided by an affiliation to a single community, action becomes impossible. In the space between nations Hector is suspended between systems of values.

Although the encounter with Ajax has only a momentarily paralysing effect on Hector, the claims of the opposing communities cause a more permanent dissociation, splitting him into three different persons. Whereas Cressida becomes a sort of palimpsest, with a second character scribbled over the first in a way that leaves both visible, Hector's selves seem to have no memory of each other. Cressida experiences an agonising self-division, but each of Hector's selves has a sharp, clear outline. If Cressida's character seems shaped by her circumstances, Hector's seems flatter and less human, more like a series of cartoon outlines than a person.

The first version of Hector has a well-developed theory of moral decision-making. During a debate in the Trojan council over whether to return Helen to the Greeks, he displays a knowledge of Aristotle's thinking on self-discipline and the relation between the will and the passions:

> The reasons you allege do more conduce
> To the hot passion of distempered blood
> Than to make up a free determination
> 'Twixt right and wrong; for pleasure and revenge
> Have ears more deaf than adders to the voice
> Of any true decision. Nature craves
> All dues be rendered to their owners. Now
> What nearer debt in all humanity
> Than wife is to the husband? If this law
> Of nature be corrupted through affection,
> And that great minds, of partial indulgence
> To their benumbèd wills, resist the same,
> There is a law in each well-ordered nation
> To curb those raging appetites that are
> Most disobedient and refractory.
> If Helen then be wife to Sparta's king,
> As it is known she is, these moral laws
> Of nature and of nations speak aloud
> To have her back returned. Thus to persist
> In doing wrong extenuates not wrong,
> But makes it much more heavy. Hector's opinion
> Is this in way of truth ....
>
> (II.ii.167–88)

The speech concerns 'true decisions' and 'free determinations', but the nature of Hector's own decision-making remains opaque. In Hector's theory of human agency a true decision requires a reasoned analysis based on law and moral principle. Hector works through such an analysis, reducing the question of whether to return Helen to a series of syllogisms. He sounds genuinely exasperated by the intemperate suggestions of Troilus and Paris. Then, almost as an afterthought, Hector reverses himself, announces that he agrees with his impulsive younger brothers, and subscribes wholeheartedly to the chivalric ethos.

... Yet ne'ertheless,
My sprightly brethren, I propend to you
In resolution to keep Helen still;
For 'tis a cause that hath no mean dependence
Upon our joint and several dignities.
(II.ii.188–92)

His irritation evaporates instantly. Hector goes on to say that before the meeting began he had already decided to announce a challenge to the Greeks. Even during the moment when he argued passionately that the Trojans should surrender Helen, Hector had already committed himself to continuing the conflict. The second Hector advocates a blind nationalism, while the first Hector takes a more cosmopolitan perspective: the 'laws / Of nature and of nations' adjudicate between individual nations.

The phrase 'law of nations', or *ius gentium*, was itself a foreign import. In the Roman Republic the *ius gentium* developed to regulate both the affairs of foreigners living in Rome and Rome's relations with neighbouring states. Subsequent Christian political theories linked the *ius gentium* to natural law, the *ius naturale*, which was apparent to all rational men. In the dedicatory epistle to *The Pandectes of the Law of Nations*, William Fulbecke promises to compare the 'judgments', 'censures', 'advises', and 'practices' of '*the renowmed* Assyrians, *the valiant* Persians, *the spirit-guided* Hebrewes, *the prudent* Grecians, *the admirable* Romanes, *the noble harted* Carthaginians, *the victorious* Macedonians, *the deliberatiue* Turkes, *the politike* Italians, *the chiualrous* French [and] *the most puissant* & inuictis Romano Marte Brittanis.'[33] In his evenhanded attribution of a separate virtue to each nation, Fulbecke demonstrates the peculiar self-estrangement inherent in any serious reflection on the *ius gentium*: the concept requires seeing the similarities between oneself and the Turks and recognising the contingency of every nation's customs and values, even one's own. The first section of Hector's speech displays an objectivity similar to Fulbecke's, but the second lapses into chauvinism. The first Hector has an identity defined in relation to a transnational community of rational men, while the second Hector identifies himself as a Trojan. The gap between sentences before the word 'Yet' is the gap between two emotions, two value systems, and perhaps even two different persons: suddenly, an impetuous knight replaces the prudent moral philosopher, a Trojan replaces a citizen of the world.

In the fifth act of the play Hector mutates again, and a third identity displaces both the moral philosopher and the knight.

The metamorphosis occurs just after Hector has graciously and fool-ishly afforded Achilles a chance to catch his breath. When Achilles departs, Hector notices a Greek in unusually beautiful armour. Hector hunts down this anonymous Greek, kills him, and strips him of his armour.[34] The third version of Hector, unlike the first two, has at least a passing interest in material possessions, and in pursuing them, he exhibits a ruthlessness quite alien to the chivalric Hector. Earlier in the fifth act Hector had spared not only Achilles but also Thersites, while before the day even began Troilus had reproached him for his 'vice of mercy': 'When many times the captive Grecian falls, / Even in the fan and wind of your fair sword, / You let them rise and live' (V.iii.37, 40–2). In both Caxton's *Recuyell* and Lydgate's *Troy-Book*, Hector kills Greeks for their armour. In Shakespeare's version of the story, though, this act of covetousness requires an audience to revise its understanding of Hector.[35] The chivalric Hector views the accumulation of honour in economic terms, but the honour he covets entails a disdain for actual material wealth – and even for the military imperative of reducing the enemy's numbers. The third Hector, on the other hand, operates as a privateer, a John Hawkins or a Francis Drake rather than a Philip Sidney. While the first Hector, the moral philosopher, inhabits a transnational community, and the second Hector has a strong Trojan patriotism, the third Hector does not appear to frame his conduct in relation to any particular community.

One of the most disturbing features of Hector's death is, of necessity, that both the courteous Hector and the acquisitive one die together, one punished for his generosity and the other for his greed. Achilles and his Myrmidons come upon Hector sitting beside the corpse he has just stripped. 'I am unarmed', says Hector; 'forgo this vantage, Greek' (V.viii.9). Achilles nevertheless orders his men to butcher Hector. Achilles's savagery, cowardice, and hypocrisy would be enough to make this incident shocking, but what makes it so resis-tant to placement within a moral framework is the death's double causation. A few minutes before his death the acquisitive Hector killed a weaker man out of paltry self-interest. A few minutes before that the chivalric Hector allowed a winded Achilles to withdraw from combat. One Hector dies unjustly, while the other has forfeited his right to mercy.

When playwrights who subscribed to a nationalist ideology told the story of Troy, they needed to make Hector more unambigu-ously heroic. This, in turn, demanded a Hector with a coherent and continuous personal identity. The comparison between Heywood's version and Shakespeare's underlines the political ambiguities produced by the breakdown of identities in *Troilus and Cressida*. In Heywood's version of the fall of Troy in *The Iron Age*, Hector reverses his position in a less disjunctive fashion, one consistent with the continuity of his personal identity. Like the Hectors of Shakespeare and Caxton, Heywood's Hector begins the scene as an advocate of prudence:

> Hector   ... my reuerent King and father,
> If you pursue this expedition,
> By the vntaunted honor of these armes
> That liue imblazon'd on my burnish't shield,
> It is without good cause, and I deuine
> Of all your flourishing line, by which the Gods
> Haue rectified your fame aboue all Kings,
> Not one shall liue to meate your Sepulchre,
> Or trace your funeral Heralds to the Tombes
> Of your great Ancestours: oh for your honour
> Take not vp vniust Armes.
> Æneas   Prince *Hectors* words
> Will draw on him the imputation
> Of feare and cowardesie.
> Troilus   Fie brother *Hector*,
> If our Aunts rape, and *Troyes* destruction
> Bee not reueng'd, their seuerall blemishes
> The aged hand of Time can neuer wipe
> From our succession.
> Paris   'Twill be registred
> That all King *Priams* sonnes saue one were willing
> And forward to reuenge them on the *Greekes*,
> Onely that *Hector* durst not.
>   (I.i.50–69)

Heywood supplies a motive for Hector's change of heart: resenting the accusation of cowardice, Hector loses his temper.

> Hector   Ha, durst not didst thou say? effeminate boy,
> Go get you to your Sheepe-hooke and your Scrip,
> Thou look'st not like a Souldier, there's no fire
> Within thine eyes, nor quills vpon thy chinne,
> Tell me I dare not? go, rise, get you gone:
> Th'art fitter for young *Oenons* company
> Than for a bench of souldiers ....
>   (I.i.70–6)

This inverts the sequence of Shakespeare's version, in which Hector begins his speech irritated with his brothers and ends by agreeing with them enthusiastically.

An examination of Dryden's post-Restoration revision of *Troilus and Cressida* throws the critical properties of Shakespeare's play into even sharper relief. After programmatically eliminating all of the discontinuities and fragmentations of character in Shakespeare's play, Dryden justified his extensive modifications with an essay on the rules governing the representation of character in tragedy. The essay implicitly chastises Shakespeare for failing to respect the unity of character:

> The last property of manners is, that they be constant, and equal, that is, maintain'd the same through the whole design: thus when Virgil had once given the name of Pious to Æneas, he was bound to show him such, in all his words and actions through the whole Poem ... unless be [a poet] help himself by an acquir'd knowledge of the Passions, what they are in their own nature, and by what springs they are to be mov'd, he will be subject either to raise them where they ought not to be rais'd, or not to raise them by the just degrees of Nature, or to amplify them beyond the natural bounds, or not to observe the crisis and turns of them, in their cooling and decay: all which Errors proceed from want of Judgment in the Poet, and from being unskill'd in the Principles of Moral Philosophy.[36]

Dryden altered the council scene to fit this theory of character: in his version Hector decides to send a challenge to the Greeks only after his little son, Astyanax, offers to send his own challenge. Dryden also pruned much of the lecture on moral philosophy, diminishing the impact of Hector's self-contradiction. Dryden regarded Shakespeare's council scene as flawed by its failure to represent Hector as a character whose identity is continuous; the later playwright attempted to supply the links and explanations lacking in Shakespeare's version.[37] In Dryden's account the gaps and fissures of Shakespeare's play reflect a primitive theory of the passions. Dryden discreetly suggests that his predecessor had an inadequate knowledge of moral philosophy – the same charge Shakespeare's Hector levels at his brothers. But the discontinuities of character in Shakespeare's play force his audiences to examine their beliefs about personal and national identity. While Dryden's play works to bolster the affective claims of the nation, Shakespeare's represents the nation as monstrous, diseased, impossible.

The preceding argument suggests that Shakespeare's *Troilus and Cressida* should be added to the mini-canon of early modern English (and British) nationalism. As we are beginning to recognise, Shakespeare's examinations of national sentiment differ significantly from one play to the next. Shakespeare is always sceptical about the possibility of the nation, but we need to develop better accounts of the variety of his scepticisms.

From Matthew Greenfield, 'Fragments of Nationalism in *Troilus and Cressida*', *Shakespeare Quarterly*, 15 (2) (Winter 2000), 181–200.

Notes

[As the most recent essay in the volume, Matthew Greenfield's contribution both reflects the work of earlier scholars on *Troilus and* Cressida and opens up new areas of investigation. The essay is concerned with the way that Shakespeare's play interrogates ideas of national identity. The historical research, and, in particular, the way that he reads the play against early-modern documents and tracts, makes Greenfield's work both exciting and fresh. Ed.]

This article has been greatly improved by the suggestions of John Hollander, David Quint, Annabel Patterson, David Baker, Jeff Dolven, Mary Floyd-Wilson, Linda Gregerson, Jennifer Lewin, Lawrence Manley, Carla Mazzio, Shannon Miller, Steven Monte, Gail Kern Paster, Tanya Pollard, Kristen Poole, David Southward, and the anonymous readers at *Shakespeare Quarterly*. An earlier version was distributed to a seminar chaired by Claire McEachern at the 1994 annual meeting of the Shakespeare Association of America.

1. See David J. Baker, *Between Nations: Shakespeare, Spenser, Marvell, and the Question of Britain* (Stanford, CA, 1997); Jean Howard and Phyllis Rackin, *Engendering a Nation: A Feminist Account of Shakespeare's English Histories* (London and New York, 1997); Phyllis Rackin, *Stages of History: Shakespeare's English Chronicles* (Ithaca, NY, 1990); Peter Womack, 'Imagining Communities: Theatres and the English Nation in the Sixteenth Century' in *Culture and History 1350–1600: Essays on English Communities, Identities and Writing*, ed. David Aers (Detroit, 1992), 91–145; Richard Helgersen, *Forms of Nationhood: the Elizabethan Writing of England* (Chicago and London, 1992); Michael Neill, 'Broken English and Broken Irish: Nation, Language and the Optic of Power in Shakespeare's Histories', *Shakespeare Quarterly*, 45 (1994), 1–32; Claire McEachern, *The Poetics of English Nationhood, 1590–1612* (Cambridge and New York, 1996), pp. 83–137; and Jonathan Baldo, 'Wars of Memory in Henry V', *Shakespeare Quarterly*, 47 (1996), 132–59.

2. Critics have examined from several different angles the play's fragmentation of character. Linda Charnes suggests that the play's characters

become alienated from their posthumous reputations but remain trapped by them. See *Notorious Identity: Materializing the Subject in Shakespeare* (Cambridge and London, 1993), pp. 70–102. René Girard suggests that desire in the plays passes from character to character, undermining the boundaries of individual subjectivities; see 'The politics of desire in *Troilus and Cressida*', in *Shakespeare and the Question of Theory*, ed. Patricia Parker and Geoffrey Hartman (New York, 1985), pp. 188–209. Valerie Traub focuses on the flow of sexual disease as well as desire *Desire and Anxiety: Circulations of Sexuality in the Shakespearean Drama* (London and New York, 1992) [reprinted in this volume. Ed.]. Carol Cook argues that the play's characters experience a sort of schizo-phrenia resulting from their awareness of the conflicting literary versions of their stories ('Unbodied Figures of Desire', *Theater Journal*, 38 (1986), 34–52. The most influential account of the way that patriarchy splinters gendered subjects is Gayle Greene's 'Shakespeare's Cressida: "A Kind of Self" in *The Woman's Part: Feminist Criticism of Shakespeare*, ed. Carolyn Ruth Swift Lenz, Gayle Greene and Carol Neely (Urbana, Chicago and London, 1980), pp. 133–49. For recent discussions of the fragmentation of the subject in *Troilus and Cressida*, see Douglas Bruster, *Drama and the Market in the Age of Shakespeare* (Cambridge and New York, 1992), pp. 97–117; Eric Mallin, *Inscribing the Time: Shakespeare and the End of Elizabathan England* (Berkeley and Los Angeles, 1995), pp. 25–61; and Heather James, *Shakespeare's Troy: Drama, Politics and the Translations of Empire* (Cambridge and New York, 1997), pp. 85–118 [reprinted in this volume. Ed.].

3. See Benedict Anderson, *Imagined Communities: Reflection on the Origin and Spread of Nationalism* (London, 1994).

4. Along with Anderson, the most important theoretical works on national-ism include Ernest Gellner, *Nations and Nationalism* (Ithaca, NY, and London, 1983); E. J. Hobsbawm, *Nations and Nationalism since 1780: Programme, Myth, Reality* (Cambridge, 1990); and Liah Greenfield, *Nationalism: Five Roads to Modernity* (Cambridge, MA, 1992).

5. Greenfield, *Nationalism*, pp. 1–88. The major theoreticians of nationalism before Greenfield describe nationalism as an Enlightenment phenomenon stemming from the French Revolution. Greenfield argues that nationalism developed much earlier in England. See also Anthony Fletcher, 'The Origins of English Protestantism and the Growth of National Identity' in *Religion and National Identity*, ed. Stuart Mews (Oxford, 1982), pp. 309–18; Christopher Hill, 'the Protestant Nation' in *The Collected Essays of Christopher Hill*, 3 vols (Amherst, MA, 1986), 2: 21–36; and Patrick Collinson, 'The Protestant Nation' in *The Birthpangs of Protestant England: Religious and Cultural Change in the Sixteenth and Seventeenth Centuries* (New York, 1988), pp. 1–27. The seminal work of literary criticism on this topic is Richard Helgerson's *Forms of Nationhood: the Elizabethan Writing of England* (Chicago and London, 1992).

Helgerson scrupulously describes an emergent rather than a dominant idea. The disagreement among these theorists may have to do with the uneven development and diffusion of the national idea and with the oddness of its uneasy coexistence with the monarchy.

6. Greenfield describes the evolution of all three terms (*Nationalism*, pp. 1–26 and 31–43). And Wallace T. MacCaffrey describes the evolution of the modern use of the word 'state' in diplomatic correspondence of the second half of the sixteenth century (*Elizabeth I: War and Politics, 1588–1603* (Princeton, NJ, 1992), pp. 467–8). Quentin Skinner constructs a similar chronology in the *Foundations of Modern Political Thought*, 2 vols (Cambridge, London, New York, and Melbourne, 1978), 2: 349–58.

7. See Hobsbawm, *Nations and Nationalism*, pp. 11–12.

8. I take the phrase 'common space' from Charles Taylor, *Sources of the Self: the Making of the Modern Identity* (Cambridge, MA, 1989), p. 19.

9. For Bales's version of the Brut story, see sigs, B4v–C1r. My history of the myth of Brut is indebted to Hugh A. MacDougall, *Racial Myth in English History: Trojans, Teutons, and Anglo-Saxons* (Hanover, NH, 1982), pp. 7–27.

10. Thomas Heywood, *Thomas Heywood's 'The Iron Age'*, ed. Arlene W. Weiner (New York and London, 1979), ll.17–23.

11. R. Duke, prefatory poem to *Troilus and Cressida*, ed. John Dryden (London, 1679), p. 31. The date of the composition of Heywood's play remains uncertain, and it is not clear which play influenced the other. For a discussion of the relation between the two plays, see the Variorum edition of *Troilus and Cressida*, ed. Harold N. Hillebrand and T. W. Baldwin (Philadelphia and London, 1953), pp. 462–63. Both play-wrights drew heavily on Caxton's *Recuyell*.

12. George Peele, *A Farewell To the most famous Generalles of our English forces by land and sea, Sir John Norris and Sir Frauncis Drakes Knightes* in *The Life and works of George Peele*, Charles Tyler Proputy, gen. ed., 3 vols (New Haven, CT, 1952), 1:220. Elsewhere in his work Peele sometimes construed the Trojans more narrowly as the founders of the city of London or the ancestors of Queen Elizabeth and King James; see 1:211, 214, and 218.

13. John Hayward, *A Treatise of Union of the Two Realmes of [England and Scotland]* (London, 1604), sig. C2r. For Coke's assertion of the antiquity of the common law, see the first volume of his reports, *Les Reportes de Edvvard Coke* (London, 1600), sig, A3r–v. The exchange is briefly discussed in Helgersen, *Forms of Nationhood*, pp. 81–2.

14. Edmund Bolton, *Hypercrtica: or a rule of Judgement, for Writing or Reading out History* (1722), pp. 205–6; quoted here from MacDougall, *Racial Myth*, p. 23.

15. No one has located an unambiguous allusion. Whether Shakespeare borrowed material from Chaucer is a different question, but even this is unclear; see M. C. Bradbrook, 'What Shakespeare did to Chaucer's Troilus and Criseyde' in *The Artist and Society in Shakespeare's England: the Collected Papers of Muriel Bradbrook*, 2 vols (Sussex and Totowa, NJ, 1982), 1:133–43.

16. Douglas Cole is particularly cogent on this point: '[the play] seeks to move its audience through a series of shocks of recognition toward a scepticism about the process of myth-making itself'. See 'Myth and Anti-Myth: the Case of *Troilus and Cressida*', *Shakespeare Quarterly*, 31 (1980), 76–84, esp. p. 78.

17. See Greenfield, *Nationalism*, pp. 1–26.

18. Criminals who do possess a capacity for moral choice, such as Bardolph in *Henry V*, pose a much smaller challenge to the imagined community: they can be held responsible for their misdeeds, punished, and deprived of the privileges of citizens.

19. Quotations from *Troilus and Cressida* follow Kenneth Muir's edition of the play for the Oxford Shakespeare (Oxford, 1982).

20. In *Henry V* the French characterise the English as half-Norman bastards and speculate as to whether this involves a dilution or weakening of their blood or whether hybridity gives them a special vigour. Neither of these possibilities is ever discussed by the English, and even the latter, more positive hypothesis would be damaging to English nationalism in any of its variants. Henry does imagine producing a hybrid child with Katherine that would combine the strengths of both nations, but this hybridity involves an assimilation of France by England – the inverse of the Norman invasion of England.

21. Steven Marx maps some of the humanist traditions behind this ethical commitment in 'Shakespeare's Pacifism', *Renaissance Quarterly*, 45 (1992), 49–95. Marx sees *Troilus and Cressida* as a turning point in Shakespeare's attitude toward militarism and suggests that Shakespeare's transition to irenic values reflects a change in state policy.

22. Literary critics have also generally failed to listen to Thersites carefully, to hear the political philosophy embedded in his railing. One honourable exception to this is Peter Hyland in 'Legitimacy in Interpretation: the Bastard Voice in *Troilus and Cressida*', *Mosiac*, 26 (1993), 1–13. Emphasising Thersites's illegitimacy, Hyland describes him as a spokesman for the disposed and the marginalised.

23. For the satirist's medical metaphor of tenting or lancing a wound, see V.i.10–11; for disease imagery, V.i.17–23.

24. In the terms outlined by Robert Weimann, Thersites has the ability to step out onto the *platea*. For Weimann's discussions of Thersites, see

Shakespeare and the Popular Tradition in the Theater: Studies in the Social Dimension of Dramatic Form and Function, ed. Robert Schwartz (Baltimore and London, 1978), pp. 227–32.

25. See Weimann, ibid., p. 235.

26. I take this account of the fool's independence from convention from David Wiles, *Shakespeare's Clown: Actor and Text in the Elizabethan Playhouse* (Cambridge, 1987), pp. 99 and 143.

27. John Stubbes, *The Discoverie of a Gaping Gulf Whereinto England is Like to be Swallvved by an other French marriage, if the Lord forbid not the banes, by letting her Maiestie see the sin and the punishment thereof* (London, 1579), sig. B8v.

28. For a discussion of the play's puns on *general*, see William Empson, *Some Versions of Pastoral* (London, 1950), pp. 39–42; and for a discussion of the figure of the diseased national community see Jonathan Gil Harries, *Foreign Bodies and the Body Politic: Discourses of Social Pathology in Early Modern England* (Cambridge, 1998).

29. Mihoko Suzuki devotes a paragraph to this question, suggesting that 'the many crossings between the Trojan and Greek camps make the distinction between them increasingly difficult to maintain', see *Metamorphoses of Helen: Authority, Difference, and the Epic* (Ithaca, NY, 1989), p. 252.

30. Heather James argues that in this scene Achilles becomes aware of the multiple literary versions of his character (*Shakespeare's Troy*, pp. 101–6). Gregory W. Bredbeck suggests that it is only our modern belief in the existence of fixed sexual orientations which makes this scene surprising, and that for early modern audiences Shakespeare's Achilles would register as sensually indulgent rather than as a man with two distinct identities; see *Sodomy and Interpretation: Marlowe to Milton* (Ithaca, NY, and London, 1991), pp. 33–48. Achilles, though, seems to have two different value systems as well as two different lovers.

31. Again, I here follow Gayle Greene's account of the conversion of Cressida into an erotic commodity.

32. The editors of the *Variorum Troilus and Cressida* find a source for this image in John Marston's *Antonio's Revenge* (III.i.161–5); see Hillebrand and Baldwin's note to IV.v.142.

33. William Fulbecke, comp. *THE PANDECTES of the law of Nations: CONTAYNING seuerall discourses of the questions, points, and matters of Law, wherein the Nations of the world doe consent and accord. Giuing great light to the vnderstanding and opening of the principall obiects, questions, rules, and cases of the Ciuill Law, and Common law of this Realme of England* (London, 1602), sig. A2r. For a helpful discussion of the doctrine of the law of nations and Shakespeare's use of

it, see George W. Keeton, *Shakespeare's Legal and Political Background* (London, 1967), pp. 67–93. Keeton focuses on Shakespeare's use in *Hamlet* and the history plays of the law of nations. Shakespeare's Henry V, in an ironic misapplication of the concept, makes his claim to France 'by law of nature and of nations' *Henry V*, ed. Gary Taylor (Oxford, 1982), II.iv.80.

34. In 'Virgil's Camilla and the Death of Hector', *Shakespeare Quarterly*, 43 (1992), 219–21, Michael Cameron Andrews discusses the episode's Virgilian source, in which the killer is Camilla rather than Hector. Andrews suggests that in *Troilus and Cressida*, Hector's attraction to the armour implies a dangerous feminisation of his values.

35. For Caxton this behaviour appears to be morally neutral, but Lydgate describes it as 'false coverise' (III.v.354). Kenneth Muir cites Lydgate in his notes and adds, 'It is doubtful whether Shakespeare meant to imply the same moral' (186–7n). Muir resists seeing the ambiguities in Shakespeare's presentation of Hector; see also his introduction, p. 34.

36. John Dryden, 'The Grounds of Criticism in Tragedy' in *Troilus and Cressida, or Truth Found Too Late, A Tragedy*, in *Dryden: the Dramatic Works*, ed. Montague Summers, 6 vols (London, 1932), 5:19 and 22.

37. Another of Dryden's additions to the play is a scene in which Troilus and Hector argue violently over whether to send Cressida to the Greeks. Dryden found it implausible or unacceptable that Troilus should surrender Cressida with so little protest. Unlike Hector's *volte-face*, though, Troilus's willingness to let Cressida go can easily be fitted into a consistent, and consistently negative, idea of his character.

Further Reading

The following list includes books, chapters in books and journal articles about Shakespeare's problem plays. Some refer to just one of the three plays but many include discussions of all three, or provide useful introductions to the concept of the problem play itself or theoretical issues to do with early modern drama.

Janet Adelman, *Suffocating Mothers: Fantasies of Maternal Origin in Shakespeare's Plays, Hamlet to The Tempest* (London and New York: Routledge, 1992).

Anne Barton, *Shakespeare and the Idea of the Play* (London: Chatto & Windus, 1962, pub. under the name of Anne Righter).

John Bayley, 'Time and the Trojans', *Essays in Criticism*, 25 (1975), 55–73.

Catherine Belsey, *Critical Practice* (London and New York: Routledge, 1980).

Emile Benveniste, *Problems in General Linguistics* (Miami: University of Miami Press, 1971).

F. S. Boas, *Shakespeare and his Predecessors* (London: Murry, 1896).

Barbara E. Bowen, *Gender in the Theater of War: Shakespeare's Troilus and Cressida* (New York and London: Garland, 1993).

M. M. Burns, '*Troilus and Cressida*: The Worst of Both Worlds', *Shakespeare Studies*, 13 (1980), 105–30.

Howard Cole, *The 'All's Well' Story From Boccaccio to Shakespeare* (Urbana, IL: University of Illinois Press, 1981).

Anthony B. Dawson, in '*Measure for Measure*, New Historicism, and Theatrical Power', *Shakespeare Quarterly*, 39 (1988), 328–4.

Alan C. Dessen, *Shakespeare and the Later Moral Plays* (Lincoln: University of Nebraska Press, 1986).

Edward Dowden, *Shakspere: A Critical Study of his Mind and Art*, 3rd edn (London: Kegan Paul, 1877).

Juliet Dusinberre, *Shakespeare and the Nature of Women* (London: Macmillan, 1975).

Terry Eagleton, *Literary Theory: An Introduction*, 2nd edn (Oxford: Blackwell, 1996).

William R. Elton, *Shakespeare's Troilus and Cressida and the Inns of Court Revels* (Aldershot: Ashgate, 2000).

Jeanne Addison French, *The Shakespearean Wild: Geography, Genus, Gender* (Nebraska: University of Nebraska Press, 1991).

Marilyn French, *Shakespeare's Division of Experience* (London: Cape, 1982).

Northrop Frye, *The Myth of Deliverance: Reflections on Shakespeare's Problem Plays* (Brighton: Harvester, 1983).

Marjorie Garber, *Coming of Age in Shakespeare* (London: Methuen, 1981).

Jonathan Goldberg, *James I and the Politics of Literature: Jonson, Shakespeare, Donne and their Contemporaries* (Baltimore, MD: Johns Hopkins University Press, 1983).

Stephen Greenblatt (ed.), *The Power of Forms in the English Renaissance* (Norman, OK: Pilgrim Books, 1982).

Richard Hillman, *William Shakespeare: The Problem Plays* (New York: Maxwell Macmillan, 1993).

Lisa Jardine, 'Cultural Confusion and Shakespeare's Learned Heroines: "These are old paradoxes" ', *Shakespeare Quarterly*, 38 (1987), 1–18.

Arnold Kettle (ed.), *Shakespeare in a Changing World* (London: Lawrence & Wishart, 1964).

Alexander Kirsch, *Shakespeare and the Experience of Love* (Cambridge: Cambridge University Press, 1981).

W. W. Lawrence's *Shakespeare's Problem Comedies* (New York: Macmillan, 1931).

Alexander Leggat, 'Substitution in *Measure for Measure*', *Shakespeare Quarterly*, 39 (1988), 342–4.

Carolyn Ruth Swift Lenz, Galyle Greene and Carol Thomas Neely (eds), *The Woman's Part: Feminist Criticism of Shakespeare* (Urbana: University of Illinois Press, 1980).

Richard A. Levin, '*All's Well that Ends Well* and "All Seems Well" ', *Shakespeare Studies*, 13 (1980), 139–42.

Richard A. Levin, *The Multiple Plot in English Renaissance Drama* (Chicago: University of Chicago Press, 1982).

Charles R. Lyons, *Shakespeare and the Ambiguity of Love's Triumph* (The Hague: Mouton, 1971).

David McCandless, *Gender and Performance in Shakespeare's Problem Comedies* (Bloomington: Indiana University Press, 1997).

Kathleen McLuskie, 'The Patriarchal Bard: Feminist Criticism and Shakespeare: *King Lear* and *Measure for Measure*' in Jonathan Dollimore and Alan Sinfield (eds), *Political Shakespeare: Essays in Cultural Materialism*, 2nd edn (Manchester: Manchester University Press, 1994), pp. 88–108.

Laurie E. Maguire, *Studying Shakespeare: A Guide to the Plays* (Oxford: Blackwell, 2004).

Nicholas Marsh, *Three Problem Plays* (Basingstoke: Palgrave Macmillan, 2003).

Carol Thomas Neely, *Broken Nuptials in Shakespeare's Plays* (New Haven, CT: Yale University Press, 1985).

Marianne Novy, *Love's Argument: Gender Relations in Shakespeare* (Chapel Hill: University of North Carolina Press, 1984).

Patricia Parker and Geoffrey Hartman, (eds), *Shakespeare and the Question of Theory* (London: Methuen, 1985).

P. Rossiter, *Angel with Horns* (London: Longmans, 1961).

Emil Roy, 'War and Manliness in Shakespeare's *Troilus and Cressida*', *Comparative Drama*, 7 (1977), 107–20.

James E. Ruoff, *Handbook of Elizabethan & Stuart Literature* (London: Macmillan, 1975).

Ernest Schanzer, *The Problem Plays of Shakespeare: A Study of 'Julius Caesar', 'Measure for Measure', 'Antony and Cleopatra'* (London: Routledge and Kegan Paul, 1963).

George Bernard Shaw, *Plays Pleasant and Unpleasant*, revised edn (London: Constable, 1906).

Meredith Anne Shura, *The Literary Use of the Psychoanalytical* (New Haven, CT: Yale University Press, 1981).

Susan Snyder, '*All's Well That Ends Well* and Shakespeare's Helens: Text and Subtext, Subject and Object', *English Literary Renaissance*, 18 (1988), 66–77.

Kay Stockholder, *Dream Works: Lovers and Families in Shakespeare's Plays* (Toronto: University of Toronto Press, 1987).

David Sundelson, 'Misogyny and Rule in *Measure for Measure*', *Women's Studies*, 9 (1981), 83–91.

Mihoko Suzuki, *Metamorphoses of Helen: Authority, Difference, and the Epic* (Ithaca, NY: Cornell University Press, 1989).

Charles Swann, 'Lucio: Benefactor or Malefactor?', *Critical Quarterly*, 29 (1987), 55–70.

Leonard Tennenhouse, *Power on Display: the Politics of Shakespeare's Genres* (New York and London: Methuen, 1986).

E. M. W. Tillyard, *Shakespeare's Problem Plays* (London: Chatto & Windus, 1950).

Peter Ure, *Shakespeare: the Problem Plays: Troilus and Cressida, All's Well that Ends Well, Measure for Measure, Timon of Athens* (London: Longmans, 1961).

Grant L. Voth and Oliver H. Evans, 'Cressida and the World of the Play', *Shakespeare Studies*, 8 (1975), 231–9.

R. Warren, 'Why Does it End Well? Helena, Bertram and the Sonnets' in Kenneth and Stanley Wells (eds), *Aspects of Shakespeare's Problem Plays* (Cambridge: Cambridge University Press, 1982).

Thomas G. West, 'The Two Truths of *Troilus and Cressida*', in John E. Alvis and Thomas G. West (eds), *Shakespeare as Political Thinker*, 2nd edn (Wilmington, MA: ISI Books, 2000).

Richard Wheeler, 'Marriage and Manhood in *All's Well*', *Bucknell Review*, 21 (1973), 103–24.

Richard Wheeler, *Shakespeare's Development and the Problem Comedies* (Berkeley and Los Angeles: University of California Press, 1981).

Marilyn L. Williamson, *The Patriarchy of Shakespeare's Comedies* (Detroit: Wayne State University Press, 1986).

Linda Woodbridge, *Women and the English Renaissance: Literature and the Nature of Womankind, 1540–1620* (Brighton, Harvester, 1984).

R. A. Yoder, ' "Sons and Daughters of the Game": An Essay on Shakespeare's *Troilus and Cressida*', *Shakespeare Survey*, 25 (1972), 15–16.

Notes on Contributors

Carolyn Asp is Associate Professor in the English Department at Marquette University, Milwaukee, Wisconsin, where her specialties are Renaissance literature, Shakespeare, early modern women writers and drama. She has published in journals such as *Shakespeare Quarterly*, *Modern Philology*, *Papers in Language and Literature* and *Psychology and Literature*. She has written *A Study of Thomas Middleton's Tragicomedies* (Salzburg, 1974), and has translated Jacques Lacan's *The Family Complexes,* which appeared as a monograph in *Textual Studies*.

Jonathan Dollimore was formerly Professor of English at the University of York and a Professor in the Humanities Research Centre at the University of Sussex. His books include, with Alan Sinfield, *Political Shakespeare: Essays in Cultural Materialism* (Manchester and New York, 1985, second edition 1994), *Sexual Dissidence* (Oxford, 1991), *Death, Desire and Loss in Western Culture* (London, 1998) and *Sex Literature and Censorship* (Oxford, 2001). A third edition of his first book, *Radical Tragedy* (Brighton), which has been continuously in print since its first publication in 1984, appeared in 2003. He is now a full-time writer based at his home in the south of England.

Peter Erickson is a research librarian at Clark Art Institute, Williamstown, Massachusetts, and author of *Patriarchal Structures in Shakespeare's Drama* (Berkeley, 1985) and *Rewriting Shakespeare, Rewriting Ourselves* (Berkeley, 1991), and co-editor, with Coppélia Kahn, of *Shakespeare's 'Rough Magic': Renaissance Essays in Honor of C. L. Barber* (Newark and London, 1985) and, with Clark Hulse, of *Early Modern Visual Culture: Representation, Race, and Empire in Renaissance England* (Philadelphia, 2000). He is currently co-editing *Approaches to Teaching Shakespeare's Othello* for the Modern Language Association.

Matthew Greenfield is Assistant Professor of English at the College of Staten Island of the City University of New York. He is co-editor, with Jennifer Klein Morrison, of *Edmund Spenser: Essays on Culture and Allegory* (Aldershot, 2000) and is completing a book project called *Satire and Social Memory in Early Modern England*. He has essays published or

226

forthcoming in *PMLA*, *Shakespeare Quarterly*, *Raritan*, *English Literary Renaissance*, and several anthologies, including *British Identities and English Renaissance Literature* (Cambridge, 2002), ed. David Baker and Willy Maley. His poems have appeared in journals including the *Paris Review*, the *Western Humanities Review*, the *Southwest Review*, and *Tikkun*.

Richard Hillman is Professor of English Renaissance literature at the Université François-Rabelais (Tours) and a member of that institution's Centre d'Études Supérieures de la Renaissance. His books include *Shakespearean Subversions: The Trickster and the Play-text* (London and New York, 1992), *Intertextuality and Romance in Renaissance Drama* (London, 1992), *William Shakespeare: The Problem Plays* (New York, 1993), *Self-Speaking in Medieval and Early Modern English Drama* (Basingstoke, 1997) and *Shakespeare, Marlowe and the Politics of France* (Basingstoke, 2002). He has undertaken a number of translations; two volumes of the work of Marie de Gournay have appeared (translated with the collaboration of Colette Quesnel): *Preface to the Essays of Michel de Montaigne by His Adoptive Daughter, Marie le Jars de Gournay* (Tempe, 1998) and *Apology for the Woman Writing and Other Works* (Chicago, 2002). He is editor of *Renaissance and Reformation / Renaissance et Réforme*.

Heather James is Associate Professor of English and Comparative Literature at the University of Southern California. Her publications include *Shakespeare's Troy: Drama, Politics, and the Translation of Empire* (Cambridge, 1997), and numerous essays on Shakespeare, Sandys, Milton, Marguerite de Navarre, and Castiglione. Her current work focuses on Ovid and the question of politics in early modern England. She is also co-editor of the *Norton Anthology of World Literature*.

Leah S. Marcus is Edwin Mims Professor of English at Vanderbilt University. Her books include *Childhood and Cultural Despair* (Pittsburgh, 1978), *The Politics of Mirth* (Chicago, 1986), *Puzzling Shakespeare* (Berkeley, 1988), and *Unediting the Renaissance* (London and New York, 1996). More recently, she has edited (with Janet Mueller and Mary Beth Rose) two volumes of the *Collected Works of Queen Elizabeth I* (Chicago, 2000, 2003).

Leah Scragg is a Senior Lecturer in the Department of English and American Studies at Manchester University where she has taught since 1965. Her many publications include *Discovering Shakespeare's Meaning* (London, 1988), *Shakespeare's Mouldy Tales* (London, 1992), *Shakespeare's Alternative Tales* (London, 1996), and a modern-spelling edition of the two parts of Lyly's *Euphues* (Manchester, 2003).

Vivian Thomas was formerly lecturer in English Literature at the University of Birmingham. His publications include *Julius Caesar* (London, 1992), *Shakespeare's Roman Worlds* (London and New York, 1989) and *The Moral Universe of Shakespeare's Problem Plays* (London, 1987, second edition London and New York 1991). He is currently preparing a volume on *Shakespeare's Political and Economic Language*. Resident in Stratford-upon-Avon for over twenty years, he has been a frequent reviewer of the Royal Shakespeare Company's productions and is a part-time lecturer at the University of Warwick.

Valerie Traub is Professor of English and Women's Studies at the University of Michigan. She is the author of *The Renaissance of Lesbianism in Early Modern England* (Cambridge, 2002), *Desire and Anxiety: Circulations of Sexuality in Shakespearean Drama* (London and New York, 1992), and co-editor of *Feminist Readings of Early Modern Culture: Emerging Subjects* (Cambridge, 1996).

Index